DOOMSDAY DENIED

A Survivor's Guide to the 21st Century

Stephanie Ocko

Fulcrum Publishing
Golden, Colorado

To Susan Urstadt
1943–1997

Copyright © 1997 Stephanie Ocko
Cover image of the Earth from outer space courtesy NASA (digitally manipulated.)
Book design by Bill Spahr

All rights reserved. No part of this book may be reproduced, stored in a retrieval system, or transmitted in any form or by any means, electronic, mechanical, photocopying, recording, or otherwise, without the prior written permission of the publisher.

The chapters in this book address some of the concerns, both global and domestic, for the twenty-first century, providing pertinent information and lists of organizations the reader can use. This information is provided for reference purposes only. The author and the publisher assume no responsibility for potential loss or injury sustained by persons using this book.

Library of Congress Cataloging-in-Publication Data

Ocko, Stephanie.
    Doomsday denied : a survivor's guide to the 21st century / Stephanie Ocko.
       p. cm.
    Includes bibliographical references and index.
    ISBN 1-55591-289-3
      1. Twenty-first century—Forecasts.   I. Title.
CB161.O2   1997
303.49'09'05—dc21   96-45317
                                                                              CIP

Printed in the United States of America
0 9 8 7 6 5 4 3 2 1

Fulcrum Publishing
350 Indiana Street, Suite 350
Golden, Colorado 80401-5093
(800) 992-2908 • (303) 277-1623

DOOMSDAY DENIED

Contents

Preface	VII
Introduction	IX

1 Ozone Depletion   1
A Year-Round Tan

2 Global Warming   9
Latitudes with an Attitude

3 Insects   19
Good Bugs/Bad Bugs

4 Deadly Viruses   31
The Armies of Armageddon

5 Electromagnetic Fields   45
No Place to Picnic

6 Natural Disasters   55
Acts of God and Man

7 Asteroids and Comets   65
Heads Up!

8 Cars   75
Our 3,000-Pound Gorillas

9 The Homeless   83
Invisible People

10 Deteriorating Infrastructure   93
If It Ain't Broke ...

11 Population   105
Adam, Eve, and the Condom

12 Cloning — 115
Downloading the Monster

13 Plutonium — 123
A Clear and Present Nightmare

14 Soil Degradation — 133
Ciao, Garden of Eden

15 Terrorism — 143
Say It Isn't So

16 Guns — 153
Wild America

17 The Economy — 163
Deconstructing the American Dream

18 Privacy — 175
Strangers in the Closet

19 Alien Abductions — 181
No Postcards from the Edge

20 Chemicals — 191
Unmixing the Elixirs

21 Psychics — 201
Psi-Zing Up the Unknown

For Further Reading — 209
Glossary — 215
Index — 219
About the Author — 227

Preface

Whether a "doomsday" mentality exists or not is debatable; many people believe a new century and a new millennium are ho-hum items. They are arguably right. We might also be on the verge of even bigger changes: another ice age that cycles every 10,000 years; a new Earth–Moon axis tilt that comes every 40,000 years; a switch from a circular to an elliptical orbit around the sun that comes every 100,000 years. Will worrying help?

A thousand years ago "doomsday" was do-or-die. Today we live in a volatile sea of data where concerns shift like ocean currents and pop like bubbles on the surface. This book grew out of conversations after dinner with people from all walks of life from around the world, when talk turned to things to worry about at century's end. The chapters in this book address some of those concerns—lack of privacy, ozone depletion, being hit by an asteroid or a stray bullet, or having to go to work by boat when sea levels rise dramatically. Some people worried about the sad state of education, drugs, and the consequences of national computer failure, each of which warrants a book in itself. Others worried about the dulling of human communication from too much TV and the casual jargon on the internet.

In the subjects covered in this book I have included a brief history and the current state of affairs, concluding each chapter with references to organizations that can give the reader a handle on the topic and access to more information or involvement. The fact remains—whether you worry or not—the concerns are real. And like all tough things, the only way out of them is through them.

Thanks to all who shared their thoughts and ideas; to my agent, Susan Urstadt; to readers and helpers Jeanne Fredericks, Steve Ocko, Peter and Elizabeth; and to Roger Archibald, realist and optimist.

Introduction

A thousand years ago, when the millennium was at an end, monks were the archivists, and the news was bad. Evil was gathering its vile army, and the Antichrist was due. With breathtaking detail they described the end: raging fires and whooshing floods, violent wars, tumultuous earthquakes, and the general loosing of great horned beasts across the land. No one had calendars, but the word spread, and people prepared for the end by repenting or by giving up and giving in to all or most of the seven deadly sins. Those who repented counted on being saved in heaven, far away from the general rearrangement of things on Earth.

This millennium the apocalypse is everywhere. Global communications tune us in equally to neighborhood crimes and remote disasters. More than ever before, we are aware of an astounding number of events, any of which could qualify as an unhealthy apocalypse, from the decline of habitats and the creation of ozone holes to deadly chemicals in subway trains and the sinister path of Lyme disease in the central nervous system.

Throughout history, people have predicted dramatic ends to civilization, and not always at the end of a century or a millennium. Aztecs expected the end every 52 years, based on the transit of the Pleiades, and sacrificed humans to allay the possibility. Often, the end was thought to be the result of a triumph of evil, or a fulfilling of a religious script, or a carefully wrought arithmetical design that could pinpoint the exact moment when the end would come. A capacity for imagining a collective apocalyptic end, usually preceded by anxiously interpreted signs, seems to be written into our psyches.

The end of the last century is comfortable by comparison. Fictional imagination moved easily to trips to the bottom of the ocean with Jules Verne to Martian invasions with H.G. Wells. Science was a mixture of mystery and experiment: Dr. Jekyll developed a potion that turned him into Mr. Hyde; newspapers reported stories of individuals who blew up, leaving behind only traces of their spontaneous immolations; a blue man's body, thought to have been a well-preserved remnant of the Stone Age, was exhibited in a glass coffin throughout Europe; hustlers put together collections of large bones and called them dinosaurs.

Otherwise, scientists argued over the existence of Paleolithic sea monsters and believed that the Earth, once a sun whose planet was the moon, would gradually freeze, and Eskimos would move to the equator (a safe 70,000 years from now). Then, after humans had devolved back to fish in a hundred million years, the frozen Earth would crack like a glass, and its pieces float silently into space.

Today, we have neither the luxury of time nor a good grip on the problems. If all goes well, the Earth (a hundred million years from now) will come to an end in the darkness that will prevail when the sun dies. But before then! We could fry without ozone, be blown to smithereens by a nuclear bomb, suffer a decade of winter caused by a collision with a comet, be ruled by madmen who manage to take over wealth, or be weakened or annihilated by new or old viruses that have mutated beyond our immunity.

Potential sudden ends surround us. On the subway and in the wilderness it looks as if the end is near. But those of us who are fortunate enough to witness the end, not only of a century but of a millennium, are witnesses to extreme global change. It's as if we are inside the whirlwind. In response, like those before us who have consciously confronted the end, we have the choice to pray or to play. But, thanks to information technology, we have another option: We can stay awake and become aware. Then, like all the other humans throughout history who thought they faced the end, we can avoid or confront it head-on and, the drama notwithstanding, survive.

1 Ozone Depletion

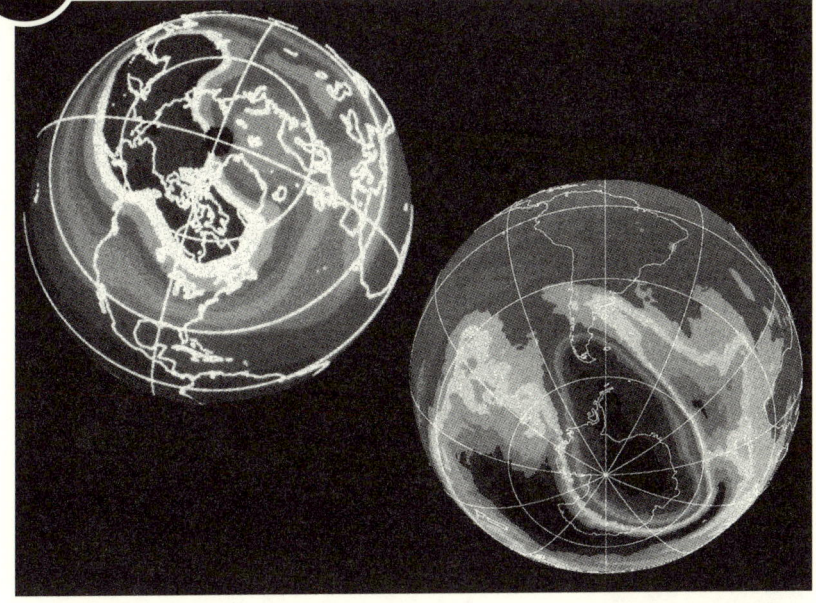

A Year-Round Tan

WE'RE BALD. The protective ozone layer is thinning all around the globe, but the trouble is real at the poles. The hole above the Antarctic is about the size of the United States and not getting any smaller. Photo credit: NASA.

A famous editor once said that he couldn't see how one person using underarm spray deodorant in a basement apartment in New York City could possibly cause a hole in the ozone layer over the Antarctic.

Well, that person caused not only the hole over the Antarctic, but thinned the ozone layer around the entire Earth. But that person wasn't alone: at least 2.3 billion others were also using underarm spray deodorant. And they were joined by countless others who were taking orange juice out of their refrigerators cooled by Freon, or spraying pesticide on ants, or sterilizing surgical instruments, or zipping through the air in a supersonic jet, or drinking out of Styrofoam cups, or putting out fires with a fire extinguisher.

The offending element here is something called chlorofluorocarbons (CFCs), used at least since the 1930s as a refrigerant; as the soft foam rubber in mattresses and the stiff foam in refrigerator walls; as a metal solvent; and as a propellant in spray cans. When it was first discovered, it seemed to be the ideal chemical: it didn't react with anything and it was nontoxic to humans and animals. The trouble is, it drifts around in the air after it's released, then slowly rises into the stratosphere, where its chlorine destroys ozone. It does this again and again, because one chlorine atom can zap 100,000 ozone molecules. The worst news is that it takes about a hundred years for CFCs to decay. (Aerosol spray cans were banned in 1978: present-day spray cans use nonozone depleting propellants.)

We meant well. While we figured out efficient ways to keep food from spoiling, we inadvertently dissolved the invisible envelope around the Earth that protects us from burning. Exactly how much of an effect unfiltered ultraviolet (UV) rays will have not only on our skins, from deepest black to lily white, but on our immune systems as well as on plants, animals, forests, and even marine life, we don't really know. Some things have already happened; studies of a possible nuclear winter outline for us the worst effects of ozone depletion.

The Effects of UVB

"Severe, persistent declines in stratospheric ozone could seriously damage life on Earth," say Arjun Makhijani and Kevin R. Gurney, ozone physicists at the Massachusetts Institute of Technology. The scariest thing about intense ultraviolet B and C rays is that they appear to alter DNA processes by interfering with photosynthesis in plants. They also affect the cell structure of marine life exposed to UVB rays 30 meters down in tropical waters. In some people, they destroy the human immune system by attacking T-cells in the skin. Some marine life is showing signs of new adaptations by avoiding midday sunlight or by living in deeper waters or changing their pigmentation. Frogs are mysteriously declining in huge numbers around the entire globe. Phytoplankton in Antarctica declined by 6 percent in 1993.

In humans the number of skin cancers, especially basal cell and squamous, has risen dramatically. Malignant melanoma has had a 4 to 5 percent increase in the United States in the last 10 years. UVB also increases the incidence of herpes—not just cold sores, but genital herpes, which might be present as a latent virus activated by UV light. Eyes suffer from numerous reactions to UVB rays: from temporary gritty snow blindness to conjunctival tumors and cataracts. Total permanent blindness has affected people who must remain outdoors for long periods without sunglasses. Most appalling, wild animals might also be subject to blindness, according to Makhijani and Gurney, and unfiltered sunlight will also change some animals' skin pigmentation, thus exposing them to their enemies.

Worst-Case Scenario

In 1975 the National Academy of Sciences released a report on the effects of a world nuclear war in which the ozone layer would be destroyed. A 70 percent depletion of the ozone layer in midlatitudes would cause human skin to blister after 10 minutes in the sun. Crops would be difficult to grow, and cattle would have to graze at dusk, compromising their milk production. Mass starvation and major epidemics including decreased immune systems throughout the world could result from lack of ozone.

What Ozone Is

Ozone is a gas in the atmosphere, named from the Greek word *ozein*, which means to smell. Faintly blue, ozone is recognizable by its pungent odor, which can be smelled in the air during a lightning storm. There are two kinds of ozone. Surface ozone is the product of nitrogen oxides and hydrocarbons from automobile exhaust, which creates city smogs and can irritate the lungs and the mucous membranes of the nose and mouth. Ten percent of Earth's ozone is this type of ozone, which finds its way into the troposphere along with all the other greenhouse gases that contribute to global warming.

The other 90 percent of Earth's ozone resides above the greenhouse gases, in the stratosphere—that part of the atmosphere where supersonic planes fly in the deepening blue of the darkness of space that pilots see when they push the envelope. This stratospheric ozone is the good ozone, and it's disappearing.

Here, between 11 and 30 miles above the Earth, penetrating sunlight changes oxygen molecules into a three-atomed variety, referred to as O_3, or ozone. Ozone molecules band together to absorb the savage UV rays from the sun that, if allowed to reach the Earth, would kill life as we know it. The ozone production in the stratosphere is kept in check by rising gases—nitrogen, chlorine, and hydrogen—from natural biological processes constantly going on in the soil and in the ocean. This interchange maintains the right balance: ozone screens out some of the harmful UVB rays and all of the extremely harmful UVC rays, but still lets in enough light from the sun for living things to grow. Nontoxic UVA rays actually help in our bodies' absorption of vitamin D.

If it could be compressed around the Earth, this protective gas would be less than one-eighth of an inch thick. But in the stratosphere, it swirls around the Earth in waves, concentrating more in some places during certain seasons affected by temperatures, solar activity, and other atmospheric changes. That's why scientists talk about the seasonal hole in the ozone over the Antarctic, where the poles create a vortex for the gas that is stronger in cold temperatures.

The Holes at the Poles

The hole over the Antarctic did not exist before the mid-1970s. Since then, it has been increasing in size and decreasing in ozone. Ozone is measured in Dobson Units—1 DU=1 millimeter—detected in a column of air from the surface of the Earth to the stratosphere. In December 1960 there were 350 DU; in December 1990, only 150. NASA/NOAA satellites have measured a hole the size of the continental United States, and getting bigger. Current ozone loss is estimated at 60 percent—enough to damage photosynthesis in whole crops of wheat, sorghum, and peas in Australia.

In 1996 satellite data recorded not a hole but a "deficiency" over the North Pole, stretching from western Siberia to Greenland, or about a third of the northern hemisphere. Long periods of intense cold (-108°F) caused clouds to form in the stratosphere. Here ice crystals created platforms that accelerated the reaction of chlorine and bromine atoms to attack ozone.

But the loss is not just at the poles. Thinning over the midlatitudes, where most people live, has been estimated at 7.5 percent.

Science and Policy

Unlike global warming, in which the science has been hampered by the difficulty of precise input parameters in computer models and compromised by fossil fuel industrial giants, the ozone story is a

Chapter 1: Ozone Depletion

marriage of science and policy—with some problems. In 1970 British genius James Lovelock, author of the Gaia theory, was the first to measure CFCs in the atmosphere and found them everywhere. Three years later Sherwood Rowland and Mario Molina, chemists at the University of California–Irvine, collaborated on the theory that chlorine from CFCs was probably annihilating ozone in the stratosphere. Confirmation of their theory came from lots of follow-up international research in balloons, satellites, aircraft, and from ground measurements that detected the villains chlorine and bromine and identified the household chemicals CFCs and halocarbons as the main perpetrators. In October 1995 Rowland, Molina, and atmospheric chemist Paul J. Crutzen, who codeveloped the theory of the nuclear winter, received the Nobel Prize in chemistry for their work with ozone.

Montreal Protocol

In 1987, 150 developed and developing countries adopted the Montreal Protocol on Substances that Deplete the Ozone Layer. The Protocol set deadlines for the reduction and elimination of a list of ozone-depleting chemicals, including carbon tetrachloride, which is used in dry cleaning, and nitrous oxides produced by high-altitude aircraft. To developing nations the Protocol gave an extra 10 years to phase out the chemicals, and a promise to pay $149 million to help them find alternatives to CFCs. If everybody conformed and reduced, normal levels of ozone were expected to return in 50 years.

The good news is that only 360,000 tons of CFCs were released into the atmosphere in 1995, compared with 1 million tons in 1985. Major chemical manufacturers like ICI in the United Kingdom and DuPont in the United States have stopped production of CFCs altogether, and CFCs are banned in industrialized countries. The bad news is, the pledges of the $149 million have not been fulfilled for third world countries, whose representatives are using it as leverage to ask for more time to phase out their ozone-depleting chemicals. A case in point is the quick and dirty pesticide methyl bromide, used around the world from tobacco fields in Zimbabwe to citrus groves in Florida. It's as violent with ozone as it is with insects. But it facilitates bringing crops to market, and farmers are reluctant to give up a good thing. The United States put off talking about it until 1997; developing countries plan to use it voraciously so they can freeze it at current levels in 2002.

Smugglers

Nor is that all. CFCs have become a hot ticket on the black market. Customs officers in Miami say the traffic in smuggled CFCs beat out illegal drugs in 1995. The biggest offenders, India and China, are illegally selling them not just to other third world countries, but to car salesmen in the United States who need them to service air conditioning units in automobiles. Stockpiled old refrigerators are another item being unloaded on the third world by salesmen in the so-called developed nations.

Ozone physicist James Anderson observed, "We've learned often enough that everytime we've thought things were reasonably predictable, that's when we get our next shock." It's not bad enough that prediction of the time when ozone can return to healthy levels is compromised by shaky conformity to international agreements and shady traffic in offending chemicals. A real threat is volcanoes. Every eruption creates billions of aerosols, tiny dust particles, whose molecules increase chlorine and bromine destruction of the ozone layer. No one can control volcanoes.

What nuclear physicist David Fisher has called "a planetary time bomb," the ozone layer is riddled with long-lived destructive chemicals, some of which haven't even drifted up yet. Most scientists predict that any balance is a half-century to a century away; and at least 6 percent of CFCs now there will live beyond 2300. For most of us alive today, UVB should be a concern for the rest of our lives.

❓ What You Can Do

Refrigerators
40 percent of CFCs in the United States came from domestic refrigerators. Be aware that not all refrigerators sold today are CFC-free. Those that are are labeled. The American Council for an Energy-Efficient Economy (ACEEE) publishes Consumer Guide to Home Energy Savings for under $10. Request a catalog from ACEEE, 2140 Shattuck Avenue, Suite 202, Berkeley, CA 94704; (510) 949-9914; website: http://crest.org.aceee.

Air Conditioning

Alternatives to Freon for coolants in building and car air-conditioning systems exist. Call the Stratospheric Ozone Hotline (800) 296-1996.

Skin

No matter what the color of your skin, you need protection of at least 15 SPF, and more if you plan to be in the sun for long periods. Apply it a half hour before going out and reapply it often. Some new sun protections claim to shield the skin from UVB and UVC rays. Hats not only shade your eyes but protect the skin on your scalp.

The American Cancer Society provides free facts on sun damage and protection: (800) ACS-2345. Request a brochure on skin cancers from the American Academy of Dermatology, P.O. Box 4114, Schaumburg, IL 60168-4014. The National Weather Service and the Environmental Protection Agency (EPA) have developed a UV index with recommendations for exposure precautions; website: http://www.epa.gov; or request a copy from the Stratospheric Ozone Hotline (800) 296-1996.

Eyes

All sunglasses are better than none; the best carry a label that says they block out 100 percent of the sun's harmful rays. If you will be on the open water, on snow, or sand, wear glasses that cover the sides of your eyes.

Ozone ACTION is a nonprofit activist, educational group dedicated to providing information on UV damage from stratospheric ozone depletion. It also tracks the black market in CFCs. Ozone ACTION, 1621 Connecticut Avenue NW, Washington, D.C. 20009; (202) 265-6738; e-mail: ozone_action@ ozone.org.; or visit their home page website: http://www.ozone.org/.

Global Warming

Latitudes with an Attitude

COOLING OFF. Pockets of windmills around the world translate wind into energy and trade it for fossil-based fuels, like this group that whirs across the hills in Altamont Pass, California. Solar power and wind power, which the Department of Energy estimated in 1992 could provide 15 times the energy that the world currently consumes, are clean and quiet and ready to roll. Photo credit: American Wind Energy Association.

It's hot, it's cold, we laugh, we cry. It's 100° for 10 days straight in Chicago—blame it on global warming; it's 40° below zero in Minneapolis—blame it on global warming. The fact is, global warming might be the cause, but the effects that actually touch us are global climate change. Those who live in the northern midlatitudes—where most of the world's population is—will feel it most: it will rain and snow more in some places and not at all elsewhere. Some places will fry; others will freeze. The name of the game is *extremes*.

"Whatever happened to Al Gore's theory of global warming?" asked a call-in listener on a talk show in Boston during a heavy snowstorm. "What *did* happen to the theory of global warming?" asked the host.

Well, this is it.

The statistics may not be overwhelming, but latest reports indicate global temperature is up by 1°F. Hardly a fever. But mysterious things are happening. Sea levels are rising. Rogue icebergs are breaking off the Antarctic ice shelf. Tornadoes won't quit. Precipitation is 5 percent higher than all previous records. Fish are disappearing. Infectious diseases and insects are everywhere.

Climatologists have become the psychics of the 1990s. They know the Earth is warming and why, but developing computer models that predict how much it will warm, by when, and what effects it will have on land and sea are difficult. The problem is that we're talking about the whole planet and trying to understand in one cram course all of its millions of delicately balanced systems.

Worst-Case Scenario

Worst case, the Southwest will be a desert; the Midwest will be a dust bowl; millions in hot polluted cities will line up for handouts of rice flown in from somewhere else on Earth. Sea levels will rise, the Great Lakes will become one large body of water, south Florida will be an undersea adventure, and the buildings of Manhattan will be the new Atlantic archipelago.

The realistic scenario is almost as stupefying as the worst-case: According to global warming expert Thomas Karl of the National Climate Data Center in Asheville, North Carolina, you can confidently expect hotter summer nights, heat waves, violent coastal storms, increased tornadoes and thunderstorms, sudden bursts of rain, blizzards, droughts, warmer, wetter winters, and fierce cold spells. You can also expect lots of insects and emerging viruses.

How Did All This Happen?

The place where we live, this planet, the only place we call home, is a delicate and sensitive collection of systems. Like our bodies, it regulates its own temperature to the optimum level and is exquisitely tuned to give us the best temperature. We may sweat or shiver or adapt our lifestyles to extreme cold and heat, but life survives.

Surrounding the Earth is a protective atmosphere, the lower part of which, the troposphere, where jets fly and weather forms, collects all the gases given off by every living thing on Earth, which naturally decay over time. Nitrogen, oxygen, and water vapor make

Chapter 2: Global Warming

up more than 90 percent of the chemicals in the troposphere, which is also a collection point for trace chemicals. These are chiefly carbon dioxide, given off in breath and released in burning wood and fuel; methane, from rotting things, swamp gas, rice fields, and landfills; nitrous oxide (dentists' laughing gas) from fertilizers; chlorofluorocarbons (CFCs), from refrigerants and Styrofoam; and ozone, from smog.

Add heat. Each day the sun heats the Earth. Some heat is reflected directly back into space from sea ice, deserts, and cloud tops. Other heat is stored in the Earth and ocean as infrared heat and goes back into space at night. Some goes off into outer space, but a critical amount is stored in the troposphere, and this determines the temperature on Earth: too little infrared, and we could freeze like Mars; too much infrared, and we could fry like Venus.

Venus, here we come.

What's happening is that the infrared that's going back into the troposphere is staying there because it is trapped by too much gas. It works in the same way that heat is stored in a greenhouse, hence the greenhouse effect and global warming.

Although all trace chemicals are measurably higher, the main gas that has been collecting out of control is carbon dioxide (CO_2). Slow to decay, it's been heaping up over the last 200 years, according to analysis of air bubbles trapped in Antarctic and Greenland ice, a time frame that correlates suspiciously with the beginning of the Industrial Revolution, when coal-burning factories fired up to produce mass goods.

In 1988 NASA scientist James Hansen and the National Center for Atmospheric Research climatologist Stephen Schneider announced, along with others, that the Earth was heating up and that a lot of the cause was humans burning oil and coal to heat and cool homes, factories, and office buildings and to power cars, trains, jets, tractors, and more cars. Denial set in. Cautious scientists questioned the data: how could we really know the cause was human-made and not natural? The Earth is subject to many cosmic influences, including cycles that come around every several thousand years, evidenced in things like ice cores and ancient tree rings. But the message was muddied further by reaction from alarmed oil giants and whole countries, like Kuwait and Saudi Arabia, with big stakes in fossil fuels.

While the Earth warmed, scientists argued among themselves and developed computer models to gauge the warming's impact (which big fuel corporations made fun of). Then in 1990 an international coalition of 178 countries created the Intergovernmental Panel on Climate Change (IPCC), to study the causes of global warming and the economic impact of reversing it. Released in 1995, their final report indicated that humans indeed were the main cause of the super collection of gases in the troposphere. The rise has been exponential since 1980, and 1995 was the hottest year on record. The IPCC recommended that each government had to promise to reduce or eliminate emissions of CO_2, and to keep them at or below levels recorded in 1990.

Easier said than done. The principal sources of CO_2 are burning or clearing forests (trees breathe in CO_2 and give off oxygen) and burning the fossil fuels, oil, coal, and, to a lesser extent, natural gas. (They're called "fossil" because they are the result of decaying plants and animals that have turned into deposits of oil and coal after being stored in rocks and the ocean for about 450 million years.)

More people equals more CO_2; and the release of CO_2 is not equal around the world. The United States, for example, releases 5 tons per capita per year compared with the average of slightly more than 1 ton per capita per year in the rest of the world. Many less-developed countries have no government controls on fuel use and industrial pollution, because they are in a race to establish viable economies. China, for example, diverts rivers to power industries with smokestacks pointed straight at the greenhouse band; Russia's breadbasket is threatened by soil overuse; acid rain rots railroad tracks in East Europe.

For small island nations, those in the middle of the rapidly rising oceans, like Palau and Bermuda, the threat is real. With sea levels having risen in 1996 by 1 to 3 millimeters, they signed an agreement to reduce their CO_2 emissions in half by the year 2000. In hurricane-prone Bermuda, no fewer than 12 insurance companies are working with scientists from the Bermuda Biological Research Station to study risk predictions of violent storms.

The insurance industry gives global warming the legitimacy that fossil-fuel giants deny it. Greenpeace International Solar Initiative Director Jeremy Leggatt has persuaded several insurance companies in the United Kingdom, Europe, and Asia to examine losses incurred by global climate change, from failed farms due to drought, to towns damaged by severe coastal storms. Investing several billion dollars each year, insurance companies are now focusing on supporting solar energy development.

Chapter 2: Global Warming

Opening the Greenhouse Door

Turnaround timing is tricky. Short-term turnaround—reducing present emissions radically—is impossible because it would involve not only megabuck industries folding up overnight, but lifestyle changes in every citizen. Most scientists agree that long-term reversal of global warming is currently in the economic, sociological, and political ballparks. It will be costly to change energy sources, whether it's in the United States or Burkina Faso. Finding and developing alternative energy sources on a national scale involves big-time retrofitting, not to mention education. Some behavior changes will be forced: some coastal dwellers will have to move; many farmers will rethink their crops. Politically, governments will legislate whatever the traffic will bear, always persuaded by lobbyists operating not always for the good of humankind. Some countries will enforce a carbon tax.

There are no fast fixes. Some cowboy experiments to balance the U.S. emission rate are messing-with-nature techniques (with unknown consequences). One geoengineering idea would ship a hundred 60-square-mile mirrors into orbit to reflect the sun back into space. Another would capture some CO_2 and put it back into the Earth or oceans, or bury it in gypsum walls. One scientist would shoot lasers at CO_2, sending it into space. And at the Moss Landing Marine Labs in California, marine biologist Kenneth Coale has been shipping out into the South Pacific to scatter a half ton of iron over 60 square miles of ocean. The so-called Geritol Solution stimulates the growth of ocean plants called phytoplankton, which absorb greatly increased amounts of CO_2 from the ocean.

More realistic are new renewable energy technologies such as solar thermal panels (used to heat water), photovoltaic cells (used to power electricity), wind power plants, geothermal power (from Earth's natural supply of hot water, including water heated by hot rocks a mile down, which is used successfully in parts of California), even a perfected cold fusion, or refurbished nuclear plants. Some communities and companies already rely on solar and wind technologies for their power; to make a real difference, these technologies will have to be national in scope. Although greenhouse gases accumulate as you read this, a measured scientific view advises going along with the increase until new technologies are in place, which is thought to be very soon.

Expect little change except extremes until 2000. After that it could get hotter and wilder. With changes in the use of fossil fuels, most predictions see warming dropping off by the middle of the next century and returning to a kind of normal by 2100. If we do absolutely nothing to stop burning fossil fuels, by 2100 the global temperature will be 3.6° hotter. It doesn't seem like much, but the last Ice Age was only 5° colder.

Bear in mind that effects of global warming are not equal around the globe and vary from day to day. Global warming is also affected by seasonal variations, night and day, and the temperature of the ocean. But until 2100, you or your friends might experience some differences: you might pay more for some foods, like citrus fruits or beef, and less for grains, like wheat.

If you are a farmer, you might move the farm north or grow different crops, including drought- and pest-resistant varieties of vegetables. Lack of water and expensive feed will force you to give up cattle. Less nitrogen in the soil will demand more fertilizer. Changed ecosystems will allow insects to move in from elsewhere. Without any natural enemies, they will breed unhindered. Lessened nitrogen in the leaves they eat will force them to eat more.

Water will become a tradable commodity. While some countries in the Middle East will go to war over water, you might pay more for it. Or if you live in an area whose reservoirs are suddenly inundated, your community might sell it to one afflicted with drought.

Droughts and floods will happen quickly and often.

Rising sea levels will diminish islands, bury beaches, and produce ever higher tides that dig away the foundations of coastal homes and flood salt marshes where young fish grow. Salt water will seep into freshwater aquifers, making the water undrinkable and causing droughts.

More violent storms will eat away coasts, engorging deltas, like the Mississippi, and destroying mangrove swamps that anchor land. Warmer oceans will permit toxins to breed in larger populations of phytoplankton near the coast.

Some fish will not be able to tolerate warmer rivers. Salmon in Wyoming, for example, according to a recent study, will probably move to more northern rivers.

If global warming happens fast, whole forests will die. Otherwise, spruce and fir trees will gradually move north. Other forest plants, including shrubs and mosses, will respond to soil warming at different rates. Forest animals and birds will change, and according to a Harvard forest study, species' richness will decline.

Cities, already urban-heat islands, will experience severe heat waves (in which night temperatures cool only slightly). Heat-related deaths, from heat stroke to hyperthermia, especially of the elderly, the ill, and those without access to cooling, will rise by the hundreds.

More insects and rodents will carry viruses once thought to be conquered, like plague; or new to the midlatitudes, like malaria.

How Much and When?

Scientists cannot predict for sure. More recent predictions have been modified by some surprising cooling elements: more clouds forming over land and sea, caused by greater precipitation, which is caused by global warming. In some regions sulfate aerosols (sulfur particles from industry and marine organisms bonded with dust) have lowered the local temperatures.

The Mysteries

Most enigmatic is the ocean. Its reaction time is slow. Oceans are governed not only by surface temperatures but by deep ocean currents, with different intensities of salt, which loop around the marine globe, rising and falling. They take time to warm up, time to cool down. The ocean is a major carbon sink—carbon is absorbed there and turned into oxygen by phytoplankton. Sea levels will rise with the melting of polar and glacial ice, but it's not known what the effects are of a lot of freshwater running into salt water. Oceans will continue to rise long after CO_2 emissions are stopped.

It is known that surface temperatures of the ocean greatly affect our weather. The El Niño, the warming of the surface waters in the eastern tropical Pacific, causes changes in air pressure, which increase thunderstorms in Hawaii, cause floods in California, and speed up jet stream winds that stop Atlantic hurricanes from hitting the coast. But when the deep cold Humbolt Current rises up on the Pacific Coast of South America, an event known as the La Niña, pressure changes bring droughts to the Midwest (as in 1988) and encourage hurricanes to come ashore (as Hurricane Hugo in 1989).

And natural warming might be taking place as well. The sun might be getting hotter. Ancient ice cores illustrate that the Earth has warmed and cooled over the years in different areas for different lengths of time. Temperature is affected by the tilt of the Earth on its axis, by sun spots, solar flares, and a hundred other things. Significantly, just before the last Ice Age a little more than 10,000 years ago, the Earth underwent a kind of global warming and increased precipitation. In the northern latitudes, this fell as snow on glaciers, which gradually increased their mass, which in turn cooled the atmosphere, causing the Ice Age. And, according to accepted theory, ice ages happen every 10,000 or so years, so we're due for another one. We forget that human life as we know it—hunting, farming, fishing, pot making, fighting, exploring, city building, trading, banking, and sending probes into space—has all taken place in what scientists call "an interglacial." This chilling term means that we as humans grew up after the last ice sheet melted, and here we are on the verge of another one. But this time, the pre–Ice Age warming has a little help from the 6 billion people on Earth.

Should We Worry about Ice Now?

When all of this is over, when global warming peaks sometime in the middle of the next century and temperatures come back to current norms in nobody knows exactly how many millennia, our latitudes will gradually freeze: tundra, ice, quiet, cold. And Manhattan, Washington, Disneyland, and Vegas will be buried under layers yet to come, lost cities for future archaeologists.

Until then, change is inevitable. No magic alchemy can recall the excess gases from the troposphere, and even it if did, the Earth would take some time to rebound. If we learn nothing else from global warming, it is that we are not alone on the planet and that we need to take a more ruthless responsibility for our behavior as global citizens. It's all we have.

What You Can Do

Small Fixes
Reduce your energy use: use low-voltage lightbulbs; heat the body, not the space; and turn off air-conditioning and heating units when no one is there. Insulate and ventilate.

Chapter 2: Global Warming

Carpool: use fuel-efficient cars and public transportation; bike, walk, move closer to work. The average airplane drinks 300,000 gallons of fuel to cross the Atlantic, but, according to the World Travel and Tourism Environment Research Centre in Oxford, United Kingdom, airlines are using a more efficient fuel that will reduce fuel use in half by 2005.

End urban sprawl: move to neighborhoods where you can walk to stores, schools, libraries, churches; investigate energy self-sufficient communities springing up around the country.

Home Energy Briefs on appliances, windows, lighting, and other topics are available for $2 each from Rocky Mountain Institute, 1739 Snowmass Creek Road, Snowmass, CO 81654-9199; (970) 927-3851.

Plant trees, as many as you can afford, wherever trees will grow. To give you an idea, a forest the size of Alaska would absorb all the current extra CO_2 in 40 years. National Arbor Day Foundation, (402) 474-5655.

Wind

Traverse City, Michigan, built a windmill that is a vision of the future, although it currently services only 3 percent of its customers.

To find out more about installing a windmill, investing in community windmills, or how wind harnessing technology works, ask for a catalog and fact sheets for individual windmills from The American Wind Energy Association, 122 C Street NW, Washington, D.C. 20001; (800) 634-4299; (202) 383-2500; e-mail: 7395895@mcimail.com.

Solar

For information, contact American Solar Energy Society, 2400 Central Avenue, Boulder, CO 30301; (303) 443-3130.

Energy Efficiency & Renewable Energy Clearinghouse, P.O. Box 3048, Merrifield, VA 22116; (800) 363-3732; website: http//www.eren.doe.gov.

National Climatic Data Center, 151 Patton Avenue, Rm. 120, Asheville, NC 28801-2733; (704) 271-4800; e-mail: orders@ncdc.noaa.gov.

Electric Power Research Institute, P.O. Box 10412, Palo Alto, CA 94303; (415) 855-2000.

3 Insects

Good Bugs/Bad Bugs

THE POSTER CHILD OF INSECTS. A mosquito fills its belly with human blood, an event that takes tact and skill. Its saliva teems with viruses; it's resistant to most pesticides; and if humans move up the mountains, it will not be far behind. Photo credit: Roger Archibald.

At the close of the last century, insects fell into two categories: household pests, of which bedbugs were a major player, and interesting creatures encountered on walks in the woods. Butterflies were big, and many were skewered on pins and placed in natural history museums; universities sponsored treks to the tropics to bag more exotic insects. Housewives, meanwhile, swatted flies and mosquitoes and placed the legs of the bed in little pots of water to discourage intrusion by bedbugs.

At the close of this century, while entomologists declare insects to be the most highly adapted life forms on Earth, the average citizen can only wonder if the mosquito in the bedroom will merely bite or deliver some exotic fever.

Is it any wonder we feel schizophrenic about insects? Throughout the 1990s—

- Tens of thousands of unusual orange and black beetles swarmed on the warm sides of public buildings and private homes from Maine to Virginia, indifferent to people, seeking only warmth and each other to breed. In the same places, more wasps than ever before simply appeared.
- A hundred poisonous Australian redback spiders arrived in Osaka, Japan, by freighter.
- Deadly black widow spiders began appearing in Great Britain.
- Killer bees from Brazil swarmed in New Mexico, Texas, and California, sometimes stinging their victims to death.
- Lyme ticks left the woods and moved to people's backyards in New England.
- The super-hungry Asian tiger mosquito stung people in broad daylight in Georgia.
- Decayed body parts of cockroaches, accumulated from decades of slum housing in the South Bronx in New York City and inhaled by residents, caused asthma to be endemic.

Is climate change causing the number of insects to balloon? Are they moving around the world more on trains, planes, ships, and in tourists' suitcases? Are all insects naturally poisonous or potential carriers of disease? Can we afford to just swat pests and ignore the rest?

The answer to all these questions is yes—and no.

Traveling insects are nothing new: Insects go where people go. Viking ships hosted cockroach passengers; and Gypsy moths and Japanese beetles hitched rides to settle in North America. But with increases in global population, global trade, and global tourism, more and more insects from other countries will take world tours carried in shipping vessels, tucked away on planes, and hidden in suitcases among the suntan lotion and snorkeling masks. Inspecting every freighter's cargo or tourist's luggage is impossible, despite the World Health Organization's call for extra vigilance when it became alarmed at the increased incidents of malaria among airport workers.

Chapter 3: Insects

Black widows and other arthropods are naturally poisonous and have always been. But some insects carry pathogens, tiny microbial viruses that cause malaria, dengue fever, yellow fever, encephalitis, and other diseases. Because these viruses develop inside the insect carrier within a couple of weeks, a virulent mosquito leaving Rio by plane, for example, could infect a half dozen people in Chicago in a matter of days. New diseases have always threatened the American population, especially in major ports, but quarantines and vaccination programs regularly stamp them out. Now changes in insect habitats around the world plus increased conditions favoring the development of viruses challenge public health programs.

We will see more of species we've barely noticed before, like the orange and black nine-spotted Asian "Halloween bugs" mentioned above. They have been in this country since 1916, but never in such huge numbers. Global climate change, with its extremes in cold and hot temperatures and changed rain and snow patterns, throws insects off their usual instincts. Many insects' habits and habitats will change. And not all insects will survive. While some species will have population booms, others will vanish. Millions of Monarch butterflies died in 1995, for example, killed by a freak snow storm at their winter weathering spot in Mexico, to which they annually migrate. The Monarchs will survive, but insects account for 38 percent of all the species on the Endangered Species Act List. Entomologists point out that in addition to destroyed habitats, weather changes will cause the plants that sustain insects to die or to mature at different times. Plus, insects will be faced with new enemies, or none at all, which will cause population problems and subsequent feeding problems.

What this all means is that we share our planet with a whole other universe of complex sophisticates that, like it or not, we will have to become familiar with. Listen to them on a summer night, or any night in the tropics, and you will hear a pulse of life that is immediate, deafening, overwhelming. Be thankful that they are smaller than we are; if they were our size, we would be history.

Their numbers are amazing:

- Eighty percent of all species on Earth are insects.
- Eighty-four percent of the insect families alive during the Cretaceous Period (100 million years ago) have direct descendants alive today.

- Scientists know of about 900,000 species of insects. But they expect to record between 10 million and 100 million more.

The Nature of the Beast

A main fact about insects is that they breed fast, rolling over generations almost as fast as you can read this page. In the process, they not only replicate their species, but mutate, trying on new adaptations to new environments, throwing out the ones that don't work, keeping the ones that promote life. As a result, they quickly develop resistance to insecticides: fifty mosquito species have been resistant to most insecticides since 1947; houseflies have tossed off DDT since 1947; Drosophilia fruitflies have developed a resistance to metals in their diet; and German cockroaches the world over are able to resist all pesticides.

Another fact about insects is that each stage (larval, pupa, and adult) has its own developmental time frame, food needs, and defenses. Insects work in harmony with plants; in fact, many species of plants and insects develop in unison: insects pollinate the plants, which provide food to insects; birds and bats eat insects; birds of prey and small animals eat birds and bats, and so on. A well-tuned ecosystem, timed for sychronicity, is like a good symphony.

Insects are incredibly varied and sophisticated. They range from butterflies with 8-inch wingspans to fairyflies (wasps of the Mymaridae family) that are 1/1,000th of an inch long, flying dots smaller than the periods on this page.

Insects can communicate through smell and ultrasound. They defend themselves by changing color and size, by growing small and invisible or big and obvious to resemble dried leaves or bird droppings. They release chemicals that can stun their enemies and give humans blinding headaches or attract friends and mates. The bombardier beetle shoots a nasty substance that is just short of boiling temperature out of the combustion chamber in the tip of its abdomen. Monarch caterpillars eat milkweed, which creates a toxin that makes birds sick.

Insects have some bad habits: mantises eat their mates after sex. Some insects use each other: ants, for example, enslave other smaller ants, but they protect some small flies in return for rewards of food. (In fact, a whole new genus of wingless legless fly was discovered living symbiotically among ants.) The ichneumon wasp deposits its eggs into a living grasshopper or katydid. In a short time, the eggs eat the organs of the innocent host, until the wasp larvae emerge to form cocoons on top of the ravaged carcass. The Tumbu fly in parts of Africa deposits its larvae in human tissue under the skin.

And we use insects. In medical research, physicians look for antiviral elements in some species, watch drugged spiders spin webs, and study insects' reactions in weightless Shuttle trips. In the Tropics, many people who live near the rainforest use the soldier leafcutter ant, which has large pincers, to close wounds. Angered at being disturbed, the ant, placed on top of the wound, snaps its pincers shut. It stays that way for a week until it drops off, dead of starvation, after the wound has healed.

Add Change

Global climate change can interrupt any stage of an insect's development. A study in the United Kingdom, for example, found that increases in air pollution caused aphids to develop faster than the plants they eat, which caused them to fly farther in search of food. This meant that areas formerly free of aphids were suddenly beset with lots of aphids.

Increased warming in air temperatures has also reduced the size of the eggs of the mosquito *Aedes aegypti* that carries dengue and yellow fever. Smaller eggs mean smaller adults, and smaller adults have to eat more blood to develop their eggs. The result—more mosquito bites of the dangerous kind.

But that's not all. Scientists predict that increases in carbon dioxide in the atmosphere, as a part of global warming, will cause the reduction of nitrogen in leaves and plants—the principal nutrient that insects depend on. This means that insects will have to eat more to get what they need, and might develop more slowly, which means that more larvae and adolescents, like caterpillars, will be around longer in the season stripping plants of leaves. Global warming, incidentally, is expected to influence plants to produce larger leaves.

Because insects respond so quickly, they are important *bioindicators*—they reflect the health of the whole place. During the 1930s drought in the Midwest, thousands of spiders, unable to find food or water, migrated inside homes. Unusual mutations, usually the theme of insect sci-fi films, do happen, but so far no insect has grown to the size of a small car. Nevertheless, bees at the Chernobyl nuclear accident site, for example, have signaled trouble with some strange deformities—uneven antennae, extra eyes. And larvae of small gnats near polluted Lake Erie have mutated asymmetrical body parts.

Killer Bees

Our main challenge of insects is trying to understand them. Take killer bees, for example. Officially called Africanized honeybees because they were imported from West Africa in 1954 to Brazil to augment a new commercial honey production, they were dubbed killer bees, or the "Bad Boys from Brazil" by *Time* magazine in 1968. Stars of a bad movie called *The Swarm*, the bees have behaved like the wild child in captivity: frightened, obtuse, and vicious when cornered. Smaller than European honeybees, they are ten times faster. They are born, breed, and die faster, collect more pollen in a day, have trigger-sensitive tempers, and pack up and take off at a moment's notice (*absconding*). Over the past three decades, they have flown and hitched rides on northbound trains and ships like pioneering immigrants. Africanized honeybees have been found in spools of electrical wire shipped to California, on oil drilling gear, in a private residence and a junkyard in New Mexico, in manholes, air conditioning ducts, rock clefts, on branches overhanging hikers' trails, and in the hold of a ship docked in Cleveland, Ohio, which had come through the St. Lawrence Seaway.

Entomologists emphasize that the bees really do prefer to live calmly, but they are easily provoked. Small dead animals are often found near their nests, there are anecdotes of a horse and a mule having been stung to death by the same swarm, and attacks on humans in Latin America and the United States number in the hundreds, some of them having resulted in death. The deaths were caused not from a lethal reaction to an unusual toxicity in the bee venom, but from the sheer number of bee stings (in the thousands), which the human system cannot sustain.

Attempts are being made to interbreed them with European honeybees to increase the yield of honey, and some have succeeded; but hybrids have been found swarming in the wild, having absconded.

How to Spot Them
The first warning signs are more than the usual number of bees flying around. If you can, leave then, before they swarm. Never poke

or throw something at a nest. Entomologists warn that if you expect to be in an area where they are, carry epinephrine with you. If you are stung a lot, get to a medical center as soon as possible. If you keep Africanized honeybees, always wear a beesuit and make sure the hives are well away from human populations.

Despite all of this, the risk of death from killer bees is, according to entomologist Mark L. Winston, who lived among them in French Guiana and who wrote the book *Killer Bees*, about the same as being hit by lightning.

Ticks

Ticks suck blood, not with a quick getaway like mosquitoes, or even Dracula, but like a leech. They burrow their heads into human flesh and draw in blood until their small insect bodies swell into round polyps, and they become part of the anatomy. Ticks like human midsections, armpits, groins, and scalps; and have fouled up many a walk in the woods. Long known to be a carrier of Rocky Mountain spotted fever, in the last few years, ticks have become carriers of far more dangerous diseases, most recently human granulocytic erhlichiosis (HGE), which can be fatal.

The Lyme tick, so-called after Lyme, Connecticut, where it was first identified, is now spread across the United States. The spirochete of Lyme disease, left untreated, affects the central nervous system. This tick's biting nymph is particularly dangerous because of its size—smaller than the dot of an "i"—and has been around for who knows how long, but researchers believe it was responsible for many unrecognized problems in joints and even personality a hundred years ago. The problem is its huge population.

The best defense against any tick is to stay out of the woods. Ticks like thick ground cover, so stay on paths, if you do go out. Check and be checked (especially in the hair) every hour or so. Ticks like warmth and will work their way to the warmest parts of your body. Cover your body with clothes, and cover your clothes with a repellent. Deet® is the best. If you find a tick, remove it with tweezers as soon as possible; don't touch it; and keep it in a sealed plastic bag or jar for later identification.

The Usual Suspects

Far more prevalent are cockroaches, mosquitoes, and fleas. They like us more than we like them. Cockroaches eat garbage and excrement and, as such, carry bacteria, but they are not as dangerous as mosquitoes, which are hosts to malaria, dengue fever, and other viruses often fatal to humans, or as fleas and lice, which transport organisms that cause typhus and bubonic and pneumonic plague. These small, insecticide-resistant, highly prevalent insects coupled with human population increases and crowded conditions in cities are expected to cause new epidemics.

Among the most insecticide-resistant insects are mosquitoes. Female mosquitoes need blood from which they derive protein to develop their eggs which they will then deposit in water. Most buzz and warn victims of their approach. The *Anopheles* mosquito, however, which carries the malaria protozoa, is subtly different. It does not buzz; and its rear end sticks up when it rests on a wall. Mosquitoes puncture the skin and insert a tube into the flesh of the victim, which then searches for a capillary or vein from which to draw blood. Protozoa, like malaria, develop in the gut of the mosquito then move to the saliva. If the mosquito saliva is infected, the protozoa can be transmitted during the process of drawing the blood.

Global climate change has already influenced the spread of bugs and bacteria. Evidence indicates that warming and wind shifts have carried yellow-fever mosquitoes up mountains in Rwanda, which before supported too cool a climate for them.

Entomologists know of 3,500 species of cockroaches. From the small busy ones, to the huge sluggish ones, to the airborne ones, they have been around for 250 million years, more or less unchanged, waving their antennas, scurrying about in a ceaseless search for food. Where humans are, cockroaches are. A century ago, the U.S. Department of Agriculture published a list of household pests. Mosquitoes, fleas, bedbugs, and houseflies were the four most prevalent pests. Cockroaches were all the way down the list after book lice, and the text mentioned that cockroaches were the natural enemies of bedbugs.

In the Great Age of Sail, when imports and exports winged around the world on small ships with glorious billowing sails and small dim sleeping compartments, cockroaches were so abundant that sailors were given extra shore leave for capturing 300 of them.

One captain recorded waking up to see the waving feelers of a large cockroach beneath his eyes as the insect fed on the mucous inside his nose. Closer to home, in 1995 a graduate student at an eastern university awoke to find a 1-inch cockroach trapped in her ear. Cockroaches do have natural enemies, but not the kind you want to import: wasps, spiders, and snakes. One of the reasons cockroaches have survived so long is their uncanny sensitivity to vibrations: They are able to perceive (and run from) a movement as slight as one-millionth of a millimeter.

Good Vs. Bad

"Good" bugs are still used to fight "bad" bugs. The problems here are ones of ecological balance. Many environmentally aware householders discovered that after their imported preying mantises ate unwanted garden pests, nothing kept the mantises' population in check. To get around good-bug overpopulation, for example, aerial spraying planes over California's cotton fields release thousands of sterile moths, natural enemies of the pink boll weevils, which are anathema to cotton crops. The moths eat the weevils but do not reproduce themselves.

Based on the belief that pests cannot be controlled, only managed, the U.S. Department of Agriculture is developing an ecologically based pest management (EBPM) system, which will set up guidelines for organizing the intricate balancing act necessary to maximize crop yield and optimize the insect troops.

Our Love-Hate Relationship

How we react to insects in the near future is critical. We have a weird bug-human history. A hundred years ago in Mexico, nuns made clothes for fleas, which they then sold, presumably to other magnifying-glass hobbyists. In Europe and the United States throughout this century, flea circuses for the credulous were a regular feature of the traveling circus. On the other end of the scale, psychiatrists have identified a whole complex called *delusionary parasitosis*, which afflicts an unfortunate few by making them believe that insects are permanent residents in parts of the body, buzzing in the ear, burrowing in the small intestine. Many more suffer from insect-dread, that cold feeling that comes from knowing your sleeping quarters are being shared with something that prefers darkness. Exposure to pictures is the best cure, therapists say; a virtual computer program has been developed to counteract phobias.

Coping with Pests

Entomologists advise identifying the space where you would least welcome an insect visitor. Then draw a line around it. To protect it, keep your space clean and try some natural insect repellents, such as boric acid (useful against cockroaches), herbs, such as mint, eucalyptus, and basil, garlic, and other safe insect repellents. Some say B-vitamins taken a few weeks before encounter will turn away biting black flies. Ultrasound machines that can be plugged in or clipped on a belt emit a high frequency that repels most insects.

If you come back from a tropical country, shake out your clothes to get eggs off of them. Termites lay eggs inside many wooden artifacts from tropical countries; they should be sprayed. In the wild, make your own value judgments: the insect repellent Deet®, for example, is not perfect, but in the short haul, it's better than dengue fever or Lyme disease. Keep it off your face, and use it sparingly.

Entomologists apologize that their subjects are not big and fuzzy enough to evoke affection, but ask people to respect insects' admirable adaptation to life on the planet we share. Although known pathogen carriers are better eradicated, public health officials, after several futile years of trying, have given up on malaria mosquitoes. It's best to learn to recognize them and avoid them. And have a heart: many insect species, like other species on Earth, will not respond to global climate change, and the weak will die.

❓ What You Can Do

Insect-Interest Groups
The Entomological Society of America: For $85 a year (or $10 if you are in the 5th to the 12th grade), you can join 8,500 other members who keep up on insect issues with publications and an annual conference. The Entomological Society of America, 9301 Annapolis Road, Lanham, MD 20706; (301) 731-4535; e-mail: info@entsoc.org.

Chapter 3: Insects

The funkiest sci-fi bug films—*Black Scorpion*, *Wasp Woman*, and *Giant Spider Invasion*, for example—are shown each year on the last Saturday in February at the Insect Fear Film Festival at the University of Illinois–Champaign-Urbana. Call (217) 333-2910 for information.

To vent your bug woes, or identify an insect, call the Entomological Society (see address and phone number on page 28); or, on the West Coast, the Insect Hotline at the Department of Insect Biology at the University of California–Berkeley, (510) 642-5565.

4 Deadly Viruses

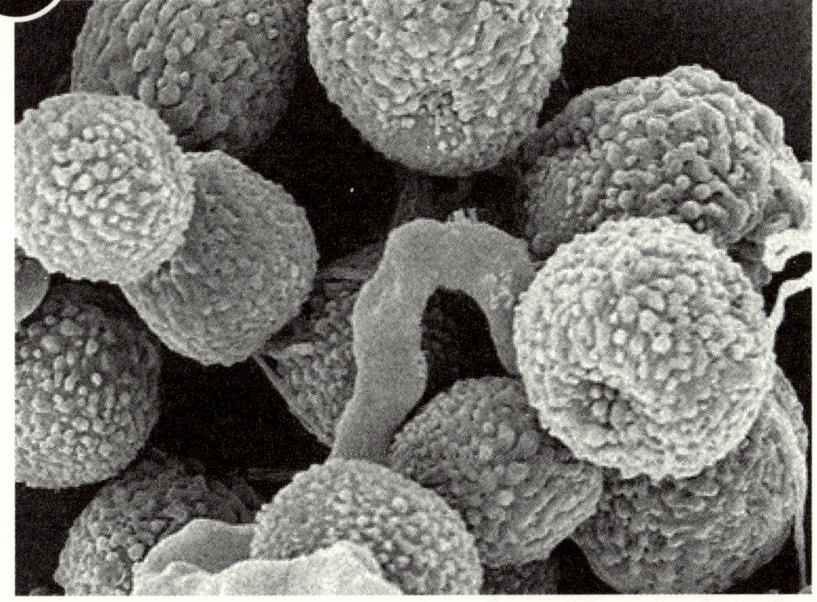

The Armies of Armageddon

MICROBES: THE TOP OF THE FOOD CHAIN. Like all microbes, these slime mold spores, 45 microns wide (shown here magnified in an electron microscope), are so small that they can eat and breed wherever they want. And they do. Photo credit: Shirley Owens, Center for Electron Optics, Michigan State University.

VIRUS FROM HELL EATS MAN ALIVE!
Wife Watches in Horror as Husband's Arm Disappears!

Microbes have made it to the tabloids. Nothing personifies the Apocalypse better than the microscopic armies of pathogenic protozoa, viruses, bacteria, and fungi eating away at our bodies in ways that amaze the family doctor. At least six books on the subject, three of which made it to *The New York Times* bestseller list, helped spread the horrific details. And anxious public health officials, legitimately seeking expanded funding, have helped fuel the imagination.

Could we wake up one night bleeding uncontrollably from all orifices? Will we stumble on something that will eat us from the inside out (like the necrotizing fascitis of the tabloids, actually a rare and controllable strep infection)? How much should we really worry about microbes?

The Threat Is Real

Climate change, huge increases in human population, cutting down whole forests or exhausting the soil, plus a lot of to and fro in trains, planes, and ships have opened what Dr. Stephen Morse, a virologist at Rockefeller University in New York City, has called the "microbial superhighway." He adds, "We cannot call any disease truly exotic today." Physicians call them "emerging" viruses, which means simply that they appear suddenly. But they have been around a long time. They just haven't dramatically and rapidly killed a lot of people in one place at one time before, like the Ebola virus; or appeared in the middle of northern latitude cities, like the malaria that turned up in the New York borough of Queens.

Our present-day black death, Human Immunodeficiency Virus (HIV), came out of nowhere and woke us up. At first, it rode specific populations like homosexuals or intravenous drug users, but now it also infects nondrug-using heterosexual women and children, and in many countries in Asia and Africa, it is transmitted primarily through heterosexual intercourse. Between 1985 and 1995, the World Health Organization estimated that the virus had attacked 18 million adults and 1.5 million children. In the United States alone, it is estimated that between 630,000 and 900,000 men, women, and children, most of whom are young men and minorities, are infected with HIV. In 1995, of the 500,000 reported cases of AIDS, more than half the people died. Because it is transmitted into the blood by sexual contact, HIV challenges our concepts of sex and death. A truly savage virus, it takes a slow 8 to 10 years to kill its victims, exposing patients to every other opportunistic pathogenic microbes that come along. It also mutates daily to avoid extinction and leaves lab technicians weary in trying to design a possible vaccine.

Microbes live in the world of the electron microscope. They are incredibly small: an arenavirus, for example, which causes a hemorraghic fever, is a sphere 300 nanometers in diameter. (A nanometer is one-billionth of a meter.) Single-celled with a ferocious will to live, microbes are, as microbiologist and Nobel Laureate Joshua Lederberg has said, "at the top of the food chain." They have been

Chapter 4: Deadly Viruses

around for 3,500 million years and are very good at what they do, which is invade other living cells in plants, insects, animals, and humans, use them to reproduce, then leave the devastated cell to move with the family to other living cells. We can only admire their multifaceted adaptability: they live with us symbiotically in the intestinal tract, they know how to age the finest wines and cheeses and brew the best beer, and they can clean up oil spills like Captain Midnight. As with insects, we barely know them. Microbiologists have identified more than 15 whole kingdoms of bacteria and 4,000 species of microbes, a mere 2 percent of the estimated three million around. In fact, the American Academy of Microbiologists is seeking a substantial grant to make a microbe inventory.

It's their dark side that concerns us. They mutate with the speed of lightning, develop resistances to antibiotics, and suddenly change hosts. They hide in the saliva of fleas, in the feces of lice. We breathe them in the air, drink them in water, eat them in our food. Uncannily, they seem at times to be able to predict our moves to defend ourselves.

Ironically, our greatest potential epidemics come not from exotic viruses, but from old friends that have been around a long time. Influenza, for example, with a remarkable ability to mutate rapidly, is a perpetual threat. Our response depends on how quickly we can develop, manufacture, and deliver vaccines. The almost forgotten flu epidemic of 1918 killed an astounding 20 million people, leaving 500,000 dead in this country alone.

An even greater threat are food-borne diseases—salmonella, e-coli, staphylococcus auras, listeria, and campylobacter—from which several thousand deaths occur each year. These microbes now can travel from the central commissary of a fast-food chain, survive intense heat and cold, and infect who knows how many people.

Water-borne diseases, like cholera, could become a real worry with climate change and increased sewage from coastal overpopulation. The cryptosporidium bacteria that freak rainstorms flushed into the public water supply in Milwaukee in 1993 infected 400,000 people. Grown in cattle feces, the bacteria were so small they squeezed through the treatment plant filtration system. Since then, embarrassed city water departments across the United States are re-examining their filtration capability, or lack thereof.

But it is the glimmer of truly exotic epidemics that keep virologists, microbiologists, and public health epidemiologists on their toes. Diseases have always been exported and imported: Could Ebola work its way across the ocean? In 1994, for example, 37 cases of tropical, mosquito-borne dengue fever (which, untreated, causes internal and external bleeding, and against which there is no vaccine) appeared in the United States, twice the number of cases in the six preceding years. The virus could have come from mosquitoes hitching rides on airplanes or ships.

The famous bubonic plague leapt from country to country on trade ships and slipped into Europe from Asia in the 1300s as the famous Black Death. Carried by fleas that rode infected rats and hid in trade goods, like rugs and hides, it also periodically troubled crowded sections of San Francisco in the early 1900s.

When people move around, pathogens go with them. Whole Native American tribes were wiped out by infections imported with European explorers. The diseases might have been chicken pox, measles, or even rhinoviruses—the common cold; but Indians had neither immunity nor medicines to be used against them. Europeans suffered too: half of explorer Hernando De Soto's men died in Florida in 1539 from swamp-related diseases.

For the better part of a century, vaccines have given us excellent health. Our current leading causes of death—cancer and heart disease—are not infectious. But at the turn of the last century, infections were real threats. Measles, diphtheria, tetanus, typhus, scarlet fever, polio, and smallpox sent many an anxious parent or spouse racing on foot or by horse and carriage in search of the doctor. Tuberculosis was endemic. Before antibiotics, like penicillin, the drug menu was limited, and the diseases filled graveyards. Nobelist Joshua Lederberg cries for more public awareness of new threats. "We are in the eye of the storm," he said. "The world is more vulnerable than ever before."

Stephen Morse agrees. "Infectious diseases are the leading cause of death worldwide," he says. From 1980 to 1992 deaths in the United States from infectious diseases rose 58 percent. Although most of these were attributed to AIDS, 22 percent were not. Widespread public health programs with childhood vaccination, quarantines, and control of vectors help keep epidemics to a minimum. But these are times of subtle changes.

Our defenses can only do so much. Over the years, the body develops immunity to a number of diseases—the vague "flus" that keep us down for a day. And vaccines introduce a weakened pathogenic microbe that causes our white blood cells to set up a defense against that infection. That's why, in the face of something we have

Chapter 4: Deadly Viruses

never encountered before, we are very vulnerable. And we have every reason to worry when microbes go bad, as in HIV, for example, when the virus disables our natural immune system by taking over our white blood and T-cells.

The Reasons for New Concern

Climate Change and Ozone Layer Depletion

Global warming affects the population of vectors—the insects and small animals that carry the pathogens for disease. The right rains and warmth, for example, gave the Southwest a bumper crop of piñon nuts a couple of years ago. These are the favored food of the deer mice, which are the main vectors of the hantaviruses that have reappeared. More deer mice mean more infected deer mice, which increase the risk of humans inhaling dried rodent urine and feces and contracting the virus. To date, more than 119 cases have been reported in 23 states, more than half of them fatal.

A gradual increase in global temperatures causes what meteorologists call "extreme convective events." This means that in some places it will rain more than it has ever rained before. It also means that some vectors will benefit greatly: mosquitoes, for example, which like it warm and wet, will thrive as never before. Getting rid of them is not too easy: more than 50 mosquito species are insecticide-resistant, including the malaria mosquito, *Anopheles*. Moreover, they mutate and adapt to new living conditions: the mosquito responsible for yellow and dengue fevers, the *Aedes aegypti*, has begun to move up into the Rwandan mountains, formerly where humans used to go to get away from disease (see chapter 3).

U.S. public health officials point out that malaria is as much a potential threat in the United States as it is in Africa. Mosquitoes that carry *Plasmodium vivans*, a malaria protozoa, turned up in Houston, Texas, and New York City in 1994, causing a few cases of malaria. Public health sleuths decided that the malaria was not brought back by travelers, but was resident. In the United States, malaria is not as rare as most people think—until after World War II, it was endemic in parts of the country, and not only in the South. In 1991 several cases turned up in rural New Jersey. The difference now is that it is appearing in cities. The culex mosquito, which carries equine encephalitis, is also making a robust appearance.

35

On the coasts, global warming will cause a rise in the surface and deep ocean temperatures, which will create ideal conditions for toxins to thrive in the expanded population of algae. The result—trouble. A cholera outbreak in 1991 in Chile, which infected 300 and killed 11 people, was a classic food chain disaster: People ate the raw shellfish that had eaten the tiny plankton that had eaten the algae that was contaminated. Cholera induces a devastating diarrhea, especially in the marginally healthy. Red tides, another name for algae bloom, occur periodically off the East Coast, where sewage systems are inadequate to handle the number of people who have rushed to live there. Shellfish that eat the contaminated algae become the vector of pathogens that cause paralytic shellfish poisoning, amnesiac shellfish poisoning, and diarrheic shellfish poisoning, nerve toxins that can be fatal to humans.

Finally, the depletion of the ozone layer will cause increased ultraviolet rays. In people often exposed to the sun, the rays affect the immune system by destroying the white blood and Langerhans cells that exist in the epidermis.

Viral Behavior

HIV is the premier mutator, but the malaria protozoa are not far behind. *Plasmodium falciparum* develops in the gut of the mosquito, then moves to its saliva (without a microscope, imagine a tinier pinpoint on top of a tiny pinpoint). Within the last two decades, the pathogen developed a resistance to quinine products, the usual antimalarial drug. More than that, the *Plasmodium falciparum* predicts its most beneficial path in its hosts' cells and mutates, avoiding cells changed by a drug, such as quinine. The result is that more than 350 million people suffer from malaria, of whom one to two million die annually.

Hantavirus is an example of a zoonose, which is a virus that is transmitted from an animal to a human. In the case of the hantavirus, the rodent vectors—deer mice, cotton rats, chipmunks, and other small animals—do not get ill: they drop the virus in urine and feces, which dry, become airborne, and can be inhaled by humans.

Then there are those that are transported by fleas. The bacterium *Yersinia pestis* that causes plague lives in the saliva of fleas that live on infected mice and rats. The plague-carrying fleas undergo their own torment: the bacteria close the throat of the flea, making it impossible for the flea to have a blood meal. This increases the hunger of the flea, which causes it to go on a desperate search for food, biting everything along the way. When it feeds, say on a human victim, the blood that is blocked from going down the throat of the flea mixes with some of the deadly bacteria, which is then reinjected into the victim's bite wound.

Nor is bubonic plague eliminated in the United States. Statistics for the 1980s (the latest records according to the Centers for Disease Control [CDC]) indicate that an average of 18 cases occur annually, particularly in the West, from California to Oklahoma and in northern New Mexico, Arizona, southern Colorado, western Nevada, and southern Oregon.

Ticks are a nightmare. Bacteria (which cause Lyme disease), viruses (which cause Colorado tick fever), rickettsia (which cause Rocky Mountain spotted fever and human granulocytic ehrlichiosis), and protozoa (which cause babesiosis) all prefer to live on ticks, the most prevalent vector for disease in the United States. Because it takes two years for a tick to develop into an adult, larvae and nymphs also require blood to grow. They bite a lot, and some of them are too small to see. Adult Lyme deer ticks are less than a quarter of an inch long, and the nymphs are the size of George Washington's eye on a quarter. (Don't rush to shoot the deer: only a small population of adult ticks live on deer. Many more tick larvae and nymphs live on mice and other rodents.)

Lyme disease, which is identifiable by the red bullseye rash that develops after a bite, resembles syphilis, also caused by a spirochete that invades the bloodstream. If left untreated, the disease causes arthritis and invades the nervous system as well, causing emotional, mental, or behavioral disorders.

Ticks, like fleas and flies, are pool feeders: the sucked blood mixes with their saliva, which is the place where the pathogen lives; saliva and blood mix in the wound of the victim.

The good news is that ticks in general, and the rickettsia that causes Rocky Mountain spotted fever, don't like high temperatures (except for warm body parts), which means that a significant rise in global temperatures might subdue them. And fortunately, a vaccine against Lyme disease is moments away.

Human-Made Changes
Major land-changing projects, such as cutting down huge sections of forests, release viruses and bacteria long latent in the soil. Many

of them, like a bleeding fever that ravaged a Nicaraguan village, lack names until they are analyzed in a lab (in this case, leptospirosis, a rat-borne virus). Dam-building projects uproot acres and acres of insect and animal habitats then create pools that are perfect for breeding insects. Two hundred thousand people languished with Rift Valley fever that took hold of the mosquitoes that bred like wildfire after the Aswan Dam was built in Egypt in 1970.

The rise in the number of ticks that carry the spirochete that causes Lyme disease is due not only to population explosions among ticks, but to more people playing outdoors. Suburban living is also to blame. New homes built on the edge of woods court ticks by invading territories formerly reserved for deer and rodents.

War does its part in producing pathogens. Soldiers and bombs alter the landscape, and researchers under defense contracts investigate and experiment with biological weapons. Simple mistakes release new pathogens into a population; laboratory accidents infect workers.

Overpopulation

More people around the world are being born, and more people are moving. In Africa, some are moving from dried-up farms to cities to look for work; others are moving from a war-torn country to a more peaceful country. According to United Nations statistics, 80 percent of all people on the planet will live in cities by the year 2010. The parts of cities where people are compromised by poor sanitation and poor nutrition are epidemic time bombs.

In 1992 healthcare workers in New York City realized that cases of tuberculosis had tripled since 1978, mostly among the homeless and people in nursing homes. Worse, the mycobacterium tuberculosis (TB) in 20 percent of those infected had mutated to become drug-resistant. TB, an airborne virus spread by sneezing, coughing, singing, even talking, is highly contagious. One man, for example, a regular in a Minneapolis bar, is thought to have infected 45 other regulars over several months. In the early 1990s public health officials reported three cases of TB transmitted among passengers on a long airplane trip.

As many as three million people die of TB every year, mostly in poorer countries, where it is endemic. Because TB can lay dormant (without symptoms) for several years, immigrants unknowingly carry the disease with them. In New York and in Los Angeles, where a similar epidemic was threatening, healthcare workers screened and treated members of at-risk groups: homeless people, nursing home residents, prisoners, and others, and by 1995 the numbers of infected people dropped in New York and in Los Angeles. It looked as if the crisis was passed. But treatment requires long-term doses of several antibiotics, and breaks in the treatment can create drug-resistant strains of the bacterium.

A lot of garbage collects in cities, and garbage attracts animals that used to live in the wilderness, like raccoons, skunks, opossums, bats, foxes, and coyotes. Some of these carry rabies. According to the CDC, cases of human rabies, contracted in the saliva during a bite, have doubled in the last ten years in cities. Rats are already endemic in large cities, and future warmer temperatures will increase their numbers. In Baltimore's inner city, Johns Hopkins microbiologist Gregory Glass estimates that 20 percent of the rats are infected with rotavirus, transmittable in their dried feces and urine, which causes severe diarrhea.

Food-Borne Diseases

Food-borne bacteria level millions each year, and many cases go unreported. Diarrhea that raged through passengers on a cruise ship in 1994 was caused by the bacterium *Shigella flexneri* on inadequately washed fruits and vegetables. But shigella can reach farther than one dining table when salads are infected at a central commissary of a restaurant chain, as happened in 1992 in Michigan.

New strains of Escheria-coli, E-coli O157:H7, have been found in undercooked hamburger. Two strains, including E-coli 0104, often called travelers' diarrhea, turned up in Missoula, Montana, in 1994, on lettuce and in milk. Using contaminated water on farm crops can start a chain of bacteria that goes all the way to a restaurant. Unclean conditions in slaughterhouses allow microbes to embed themselves secretly in meat that winds up in sanitary wrappers in supermarkets. In food supply plants and restaurants, poor management of food-handlers, who are not encouraged to wash their hands or to stay home when they are sick, spreads disease. Too much volume, poor restaurant management, plus overbreeding insects and rapidly mutating microbes all go into a dangerous stew.

Early Warning Systems

One of the problems with emerging viruses is that the initial symptoms of many infections are more or less alike: aches and pains, fever, headache, sometimes nausea. The average clinic doctor is not prepared to deal with exotic diseases. But early recognition in some cases is imperative: in Baltimore's inner city, for example, Gregory Glass discovered that the long-term kidney and liver damage caused by several rat-borne diseases was missed by clinicians who treated the symptoms superficially as simple flus. Because only a few died, the diseases, leptosporosis and lymphocytic chomomeningitis (LCM) were not reported to the CDC. "Rates will only go up," said Glass. "Even minor changes in vectors and human populations have dramatic impacts. And a body count is not an appropriate measure."

Humans are not as fast at adapting and mutating as microbes, but we do adapt and mutate. Several international surveillance systems have been set up with the help of the United Nations. Stephen Morse, of Rockefeller University, who generated one of them, ProMED (Program for Monitoring Emerging Diseases), a network that collects data to avoid potential outbreaks of virulent disease, said, "Some of us have been paralyzed by complacency—thinking wrongly that the threat of infectious diseases is past." ProMED, an international e-mail network, is a nongovernmental organization composed of 80 countries that collects data on reported diseases and their treatment and reports on vector behavior.

With an electronic communications network, early recognition of disease will be easier. With a databank, the small-town doctor in northern New Hampshire, for example, who sees a patient in the advanced bleeding stages of Ebola, will know that he is dealing with an exotic disease.

In the 1980s NASA began its Global Monitoring and Human Health Program in which remote sensing systems work with computer-based geographical systems and observers stationed on land to plot vector-borne diseases. In part of what is called "landscape epidemiology," satellites are able to detect and identify areas ripe for an epidemic. Swamps near tropical cities or unmanaged pasture lands, for example, are breeding places for disease-bearing mosquitoes. Early warning alerts local public health officials.

Ready response follows surveillance. From places like the CDC Epidemic Intelligence Service, international teams of physicians and field epidemiologists like forensic detectives travel to epidemic hotspots and bag mosquitoes, fleas, spiders, small animals, rats, and bats to sort for clues back at the lab. They take blood samples from victims and study the prevailing social system in which the disease has taken hold. Biotechnologists in the lab use efficient and quick diagnostic techniques to isolate viruses. DNA fingerprinting, such as polymerase chain reaction (PCR), identifies viruses by synthesizing DNA from a molecule, and enzyme-linked immunosorbent assay (ELISA) checks the level of antibodies that the body has called on to fight invading microbes. Researchers can then work on creating appropriate antibiotics and vaccines.

The risk of a major epidemic of an emerging virus in this country is low, researchers believe, because of public health measures that counteract any sweeping microbial army. But in the marginal areas in cities in less-developed countries where, for example, environmental or political refugees gather, the risk rises dramatically. Individually, the risk of contracting a newly emerging virus depends on the state of a person's health, good nutrition, up-to-date immunizations, and, in a very simple way, personal hygiene. Ask any doctor for a bottom-line resistance tactic, and he or she is likely to say, "Wash your hands."

What are the odds of contracting necrotizing fascitis, which begins with all of the usual symptoms, plus a severe pain over a bruise, develops rapidly into gangrene, and, untreated, ends in sudden death? It's a streptococcus group-A infection; it's been around at least since 1799, when a British naval officer came down with it, and, for unknown reasons, its annual numbers are sharply up. Those most at risk are infants, the elderly, and the immune-deficient, but it is treatable with antibiotics, and a vaccine exists against it.

In H.G. Wells's *War of the Worlds*, it is Earth's native microbes that stop the invading Martians. Wells did not speculate what we might catch from the Martians. But our battle against Earth's microbes is not stranger: we fight against shape-changing aliens that take over our bodies to get what they want. If nothing else, as we learn more about microbes, we become aware of the fact that the push to life on Earth is highly competitive—and not all species will survive.

Some Emerging Viruses

DISEASE	VECTOR	TRANSMISSION
malaria	mosquitoes	bite infects blood
hantavirus	deer mice	inhaled contaminated dried feces
Lyme disease	deer ticks	bite infects blood
cryptosporidium	water	bacteria infect intestines
E-coli	undercooked meat, poultry	bacteria infect intestines
cholera	toxic seafood	bacteria infect intestines
tuberculosis	infected people	inhaled virus
dengue fever	mosquitoes	bite infects blood
yellow fever	mosquitoes	bite infects blood
Ebola virus	infected people and possibly wild animals	infects blood
AIDS	infected people	sexual or blood content
plague	fleas on rodents	bite infects blood
schistosomiasis	snails/worm larvae	penetrate skin, infects blood
sleeping sickness	flies	bite infects blood
river blindness	flies	worm eats eyes
rabies virus	infected animals	saliva in bite wound
equine encephalitis	infected humans	inhaled from droplets
"mad cow" disease	infected cattle	eating contaminated beef (Creutzfeldt-Jakob disease)
meningitis	infected people	inhaled bacteria

What You Can Do

The Centers for Disease Control in Atlanta will fax information on a variety of diseases. Follow the prompts after dialing (404) 332-4565.

ProMED identifies worldwide outbreaks. To subscribe, contact them through e-mail: majordomo@usa.healthnet.org. To report an outbreak, contact e-mail: promed@usa.healthnet.org.

International Association for Medical Assistance to Travelers (IAMAT) produces information on countries around the world, needed immunizations, the state of drinking water and food, etc. IAMAT, 417 Center Street, Lewiston, NY 14092; (716) 754-4883.

The U.S. Deptartment of Agriculture maintains a meat and poultry hotline and gives information on safe cooking practices: (800) 535-4555.

The Food and Drug Administration has a Seafood Hotline: (800) 332-4010.

Safe Tables Our Priority (STOP) is a California-based grassroots organization created by victims of food-borne illnesses. They lobby for greater surveillance of food practices, especially cattle handling. For information, call (800) 350-7867.

5 Electromagnetic Fields

No Place to Picnic

THE CLOSER YOU ARE, THE FASTER MY HEART BEATS. High-voltage power lines buzz and hum their way across the country's power grid. Trees and fences shield nearby houses from the jolts of electricity (which can trigger a fluorescent lightbulb), but the magnetic forces go through everything—the trees, the fences, the houses, the people. Photo credit: Roger Archibald.

A thousand years ago, it was, if nothing else, quiet. No radio or television, no telephones, no cars, no industrial machinery, no 18-wheelers barreling down the highway, no trains whining into the night, no jets. People stayed put and gossiped. Life was lived by the rhythms of the seasons, the sun and moon, and the pulses of Earth's natural magnetic vibrations, possibly reflected in Gregorian chants.

A hundred years ago, the artificial electromagnetic noise began. Thomas Edison's electricity lit the Victorian darkness, and Nicola Tesla played with alternating electrical current and harnassed Niagara Falls's power for Buffalo, New York. Guglielmo Marconi miraculously tapped out radio messages across the ocean, and doctors in health spas used "Galvanic batteries" to invigorate the middle aged. While ladies worried that newly discovered X-rays could penetrate their skirts and reveal their undergarments, zealous physicians, fascinated with X-rays, inadvertantly blistered their patients.

Today, electromagnetic fields (EMFs) surround us. In the United States alone, more than seven million microwave transmitters carry messages day and night around the world, and tens of thousands of miles of power lines transmit 765,000 volts of electricity to communities across the country. In each community, substations link up to lines that connect the main source to transformers that send current into streetlights, baseball fields, and public and private buldings. Inside homes, people plug in toasters, TVs, radios, clocks, computer terminals, electric blankets, hair dryers, microwave ovens, copy machines, sewing machines, vacuum cleaners, and electric razors. On the street and in cars, people pull cellular phones out of their pockets for a quick call on the run. On their own radio and microwave frequencies, members of the military communicate with satellites and submarines. And for the past few decades, MTV, *I Love Lucy*, and CNN, among others, have been cruising through space and cosmic gas, tunneling through other galaxies to who knows where. An eavesdropping Martian might wonder why we have the need to say so much to each other.

EMFs are the lowest part of the spectrum of radiation that extends from lethal gamma rays and X-rays to ultraviolet light, visible light, infrared rays, radar waves, microwaves, and radio waves, which range from very high frequency (VHF) to extremely low frequency (ELF). The EMFs that concern us comprise mostly the lowest end of the spectrum: ELF, as well as radar, microwaves, and radio waves.

The Effects

That we are awash in a sea of electromagnetic pollution is obvious. Yet scientists argue over whether or not, how much, and in what way electromagnetism might affect humans. For every study that links a few ill or dead people to EMFs, another criticizes it as poor science, bad data-gathering technique, or media hype, or genuinely finds no linkage at all. More than 400 lawsuits claiming that electromagnetic pollution from high-voltage wires caused cancer have been brought against utility companies, and some plaintiffs have won. At a recent conference of the Risk and Insurance Management Society, Risk Control Services Director David Bricknell called EMF a "nightmare" that could be bigger than the asbestos lawsuit

Chapter 5: Electromagnetic Fields

mania of the 1980s. In 1996 a three-year National Research Council study found no health effects from EMFs near power lines. But although some scientists and public officials recommend "prudent avoidance" of EMFs, at the moment we don't really know what electromagnetism's effects are.

Uncertain science aside, the reasons for the disjunctures in the various EMF-cancer link studies are due in part to the fact that electromagnetism is, above all, invisible: it can't be perceived without instruments. As such, it can be abused, dismissed as a myth, or misread.

Every time you turn on an appliance or an office machine, you trigger an electrical current flow. This in turn creates a magnetic field. If you could see these events as visible colors, your hair dryer, for example, would be infused with bright green (the path of the electricity), and your hair dryer and your head would be surrounded by and imbued with orange (the magnetic field). The magnetic field can penetrate your head.

Another reason studies vary, many scientists believe, is that so many factors are involved: long exposure to EMFs at high levels, long exposure at low levels, short exposure at high levels, and short exposure at low levels might cause different reactions in different people. Utility line workers, for example, or sewing machine operators in sweat shops, or traffic police who handle radar units are more heavily exposed than the person who uses an electric razor each morning or who copies a four-page report. But some studies suggest that it is the short spurts of EMFs, the "flashbulb" effect caused by turning a motor on or off, that are detrimental. Other studies identify weak and continuous EMFs as the villain. Because cancer is slow to develop, numerous other factors, including genetics, might be accountable.

Most studies looking for an EMF-cancer link are done by epidemiologists who try to find out who uses what, how close, how often, and at what levels of intensity. Physicians try to figure out the physiobiology: how does cancer get started if electric currents do not penetrate the body, and magnetic fields, by themselves, are not known to be harmful?

Take high-voltage power lines and child leukemia, for example. A landmark study done in Denver in 1979 found 344 deaths from childhood cancer in houses with a close proximity to a transmitter line. Later studies elsewhere found no provable connection between

47

childhood cancer and EMFs. But a recent British study suggested that the missing link in EMFs and cancer is radon. Radon is a known cancer-causing, naturally occurring radioactive gas that comes from decaying uranium deposits in the ground. The study found that when radon mixed with EMFs from high-voltage power lines, it created tiny vibrating aerosols easy to inhale that were possibly the cause of several cases of childhood leukemia that occurred nearby.

Worst-Case Scenario

What might seem flimsy proof to some scientists should act as a gentle prod to the average EMF-polluted citizen. In studies done on animals in the laboratory, and through analysis of human death records, EMFs have been linked to child and other leukemias, brain cancer, eye cancer, colorectal cancer, high blood pressure, heart arrythmia, bradycardia, impaired immune system, raised core temperature, epilepsy, locomotor problems, forgetfulness, withdrawal, depression, and suicide. A 1978 Russian study on bacteria (anthrax, typhus, pneumonia, and staphyloccocus) discovered that EMF exposure stimulated not only their growth but their resistance to antibiotics. Some studies have linked miscarriages to exposure to pollution from computer terminals and electric blankets.

But that's not all. During the Cold War, the United States and the Soviet Union were rumored to have experimented with microwave beams targeted at the general populations for purposes of fuzzing their minds (to create forgetful or sick enemies). Workers at the severely beamed American Embassy in Moscow in the 1980s reportedly suffered from altered red and white blood cell counts.

"To be sure, these risks have not been conclusively proven," said Louis Slesin, editor of *Microwave News,* when referring to all the studies, "but neither have they been convincingly dismissed. As the NCRP [National Council of Radiation Protection] committee concluded in its draft report [in 1995]: 'Findings are sufficiently consistent and form a sufficiently coherent picture to suggest plausible connections between ELF [extreme low frequency]–EMF exposures and disruption of normal biological processes.'"

What seems to emerge with some degree of stability in health risk–EMF studies is that human cells and cell activity are affected. No direct links between human cancers and EMFs have been found as they have been with cosmic radiation sources, such as X-rays and gamma rays, which destroy cellular bonds. But in several studies, EMF exposure has been found to act on cells in ways that induce "modifications on their structures and/or on their functionality," according to Paolo Bernardi and Guglielmo D'Inzeo in a paper presented at the 1988 International Course on Worldwide Nonionizing Radiation Safety Standards. EMFs have also been found to alter the neurotransmitter acetylcholine and calcium receptors on the cell membrane, and affect the formation of red and white blood cells. A 1994 study at Stanford University confirmed the same finding: EMFs disrupt the cell membranes, so-called gatekeepers, and allow the admission of chemicals normally kept out. Two studies confirm the fact that nightly exposure to high levels of EMFs prevent the production of melatonin in the pineal gland, a power source in fighting tumors like breast cancer. And dogs that spend a lot of time outdoors under power lines were found to have high rates of lymphoma.

Radio waves, like microwaves, heat tissue. In 1986 editors Charles Polk and Elliot Postow wrote in *Handbook of Biological Effects of Electromagnetic Fields* that there was "general agreement" that exposure to high-power density radio frequencies affects human testes and ovaries, and that chronic low-level exposure impairs sperm production and reproductive function.

Conservatively, scientists say that the presence of EMFs can exacerbate the development of a cancer that has already started. But cancer is only one thing that happens at the cellular level. Part of being alive on Earth is that our cells constantly die and renew themselves. Altered, they will affect the health of all other systems. "A change at one level may well trigger secondary changes throughout an organism," said physician Robert O. Becker in his book *The Body Electric*.

The Levels of Electromagnetism

Earth's natural electromagnetism is a beautiful thing. The magnetic field generated by the hot and active iron and nickel core of the Earth meets the electrically charged gas of the ionosphere, the outermost layer of the Earth's atmosphere, 60 miles up, and together, they form what Becker describes as "an electrodynamic, resonating cavity" that surrounds the Earth and produces extreme low frequency (ELF) micropulses. These vary from 25 per second to one every 10 seconds and are influenced by the daily and monthly pull of the moon on the Earth and the 11- and 22-year cycles of solar magnetic activity. It is the Earth's natural magnetism that allows birds, butterflies, and bees to navigate and migrate. When solar winds move ions from the ionosphere into the magnetosphere in the upper atmosphere, the result is the beautiful aurora borealis.

In the human body, electromagnetism is a whole field waiting to be explored. Our systems are electrical—pumping our hearts, contracting muscles, allowing cells to communicate, and producing magnetism visible in Kirlian photographs as auras. Electricity was the key factor of life in the body parts Dr. Frankenstein sewed together. A popular cure to revive the old *élan vital*, some years after Mary Shelley wrote her book, was to hook up to a battery for a little direct current.

Chinese acupuncture points are related to the electromagnetic flow in the body, and electromagnetism is at work in biofeedback, in which the conscious mind controls the autonomic nervous system to lower blood pressure, for example. Magnetism affects neurochemicals like dopamine and seratonin in the brain and, directly applied, can accelerate the mending of broken bones. Robert Becker has been a pioneer in the study of electromagnetism and the regeneration of body parts, and believes that humans, like starfish and salamanders, have the capacity to replace lost tissue and nerves. (See "For Futher Reading" for more information).

The Measurements of Electromagnetism

Electromagnetism is measured in wavelengths, the distance between the peaks on the waves, and in frequency, or the number of peaks or cycles per second. These are referred to as hertz (Hz) (from Heinrich Hertz, the discoverer of electromagnetic radiation). Direct current (DC) is steady and generally thought not to be dangerous: the Earth's magnetic field is DC, as are most battery-operated machines. But alternating current (AC) is a different story: it changes its direction 60 times a second, sustaining itself longer over great transmission distances. This is the frequency of the U.S. electrical power supply, which is a very busy system.

In the United States, EMFs are measured in gauss units, typically milligauss (mG), or 1/1000th of a gauss. Internationally, the code is in microteslas (one microtesla equals 10 mG). Several gaussmeters are currently on the market for about $150: some will

Chapter 5: Electromagnetic Fields

average the readout from several readings in the same area, which is a cause of confusion in using a gaussmeter. Safety? No federal EMF safety standards exist. Some states do have guidelines (call your local public utilities department).

The major sources of EMFs are high-voltage power lines, domestic appliances, and office machines. In any area, rates of exposure differ from moment to moment, according to use and proximity. Prudent avoidance means that you minimize your use of a machine and keep a certain distance from it: EMFs fall off dramatically with distance. Don't let your kids play under power lines.

Houses

The average background magnetic field in a home ranges from 0.5 mG to 4 mG, which is high. Epidemiologists suspect EMF problems when the readings are at 2 mG, although cancer linkages have been made at lower levels. At the point at which outside wires enter the house (the "service drops"), readings can be as high as 5 mG. EMFs can be created when wires are grounded to water pipes (and can extend the field to other houses attached to the same water system) in older houses or in unusual wiring within walls. If you suspect dangerous EMFs in your house, wiring can be corrected by rewiring with bundled pairs of hot wires or by installing current-interrupting insulators.

Bedrooms—Move your bed or your child's bed away from any external sources of electricity and away from an electric clock, which at close range can measure as much as 14.8 mG. Five feet away, the danger is diminished. Remember that magnetism penetrates everything, so find out what your neighbors are doing on the other side of the wall: color TV can create 7 mG (according to *Consumer Reports, May 1994*), and the backside of a computer terminal can generate as much as 60 mG. Before 1989, electric blankets were linked closely with miscarriages; in that year, Sunbeam produced one with safely bundled wires that reduced EMFs by 95 percent.

Kitchens—Every electrical appliance is a source of EMFs, especially operating microwave ovens which, 6 inches away, can register 36.9 mG with a microwave reader. If you stand 4 feet away, that number falls to 2.1 mG. If you microwave something for a long time, step out of the room. Make sure the gasket on the door is not damaged.

Offices
Fluorescent lights give off more than twice as much electromagnetism as incandescent lightbulbs. Six inches away from an operating copy machine the EMF is about 20 mG, a number that falls dramatically the farther away you get. Most computer companies are now producing low-emission monitors, but in the average visual display terminal (VDT) of a modern office, the sides and back can measure as much as 60 mG. Keep at least an arm's length from the screen at which you work, and at least 3 feet from the VDT behind or next to you. (Remember that walls do not block EMFs.) Laptops generate lower levels of EMFs, but users tend to work closer to the screen.

Cellular Phones
The jury is still out on the long-term safety of cellular phones. Never touch the antenna to your head: they operate in the radio frequency of 800 to 900 MHz (megaHertz), and radio and microwaves both heat tissue. Pacemakers can be interrupted by digital cellular phones, according to a U.S. study that corroborates one done in Italy and Switzerland. Anti-theft devices can also temporarily affect heart pacemakers.

Other Sources of Radiation
Radon occurs in soil and water from wells near deposits of uranium. It is the product of the decaying element that passes into the air and through your house. An inexpensive radon tester, available in some hardward stores, will tell you if you should worry. The EPA (see page 53) publishes a list of state radon contacts who can recommend a qualified contractor who will suggest ways in which you block it. The link between radon and human lung cancer is undisputed.

X-rays are now delivered at relatively safe levels. Minimize dental X-rays and wear a lead apron. Cosmic rays are dangerous and are higher at high elevations such as on mountains and in airplanes.

Chapter 5: Electromagnetic Fields

The Future

The players in the EMF game are utility companies and telecommunications corporations, with the biggest investments and the most influence on policy makers. The bottom line is figuring out who should pay for research and installation of the new shielding technology necessary in high-voltage power lines and microwave communications, and for current-interrupting insulators in private and public living and work spaces wherever electrical appliances are used. The insurance industry is devising disclaimers for their clients to offset rewriting workers' compensation and product liability insurance, but new fabrics are being developed to protect utility workers. As scientists continue their health research, some real estate agents are offering property near high-voltage power lines at a discount or with a disclaimer.

Setting safety standards is a delicate issue: in 1995 the National Council on Radiation Protection (NCRP) recommended that exposure be limited to levels from near 0 to 3 kHz, but that limitation could compromise the nation's whole power grid. "There are limits to what one can consider without going back to the Dark Ages," said Thomas Tenforde of the NCRP.

Information is a beginning; sorting out the responsibilities, the capabilities, and the realities of EMF prevention will take some time.

❓ What You Can Do

The EPA EMF Infoline is (800) 363-2382. Call for a free copy of *Questions and Answers about EMF,* an excellent source of information about the subject prepared by the National Institute of Environmental Health Sciences and the U.S. Deptartment of Energy. Also request free copies of two highly informative booklets prepared by the EPA: *Questions and Answers about Electric and Magnetic Fields (EMFs)* and *EMF in Your Environment.*

On the Net, look for EPA on the Web at EMF-Link: http:/infoventures.com.

Microwave News watchdogs EMF issues. For information about subscriptions, their *Resource Directory,* and reprints of articles, contact them at: P.O. Box 1799, Grand Central Station, New York, NY 10163; (212) 517-2800.

Call the customer service rep of your local electric company to have someone read the EMF levels in your home or work space; many do free of charge.

Several New Age companies sell gaussmeters as well as diodes and other items thought to protect the body from dangerous EMFs, such as jewelry, VDT shields, and hats that protect against radiowaves. Try the catalogs of Tools for Exploration, (800) 456-9887; Ener-G-Polari-T, P.O. Box 2449, Prescott, AZ 86302, (520) 778-5039; and Magnetic Specialties from Mid-American Marketing Corp., 1531 E. Main Street, Eaton, OH 45320, (800) 922-1744.

The National Safety Council publishes information on radon and sells a Radon Detection Kit for $9.95; (800) 767-7236.

For information on radon and other contaminants in drinking water, call the EPA Safe Drinking Water Hotline: (800) 426-4791.

The NCRP publishes a folder, *Radiation Protection and You*, and will send a bibliography of their publications: The National Council on Radiation Protection and Measurements, 7910 Woodmont Avenue, Suite 1016, Bethesda, MD 20814; (301) 657-2652.

6 Natural Disasters

Acts of God and Man

WHEN THE EARTH SPEAKS. The hill behind Highway 101 gave way in March 1995 and slid into La Conchita, California. It buried, pushed, shifted, and crumbled houses like toys in this seaside village. Photo credit: R.L. Schuster, U.S. Geological Survey.

A potent natural disaster is not a disaster if humans, their property, or their crops are not affected. The oak tree that falls in the forest with no one to hear it, the tornado that dances across wasteland, or the hurricane that washes away a desolate shore are non-events. But add a few people, and the drama is distinct. When Hurricane Andrew blew across the southern United States in 1992, it destroyed, damaged, dislocated, and disrupted enough people and their possessions to cause more than $15 billion worth of disaster. And no major cities were hit. Insurers grow pale at the thought that similar destruction a few miles away in Miami, for example, would have totaled in the mega-billions.

Natural disasters—tornadoes, hurricanes, landslides, mudslides, avalanches, heat waves, cold spells, forest fires, droughts, earthquakes, volcanoes, blizzards, thunderstorms, floods, and flashfloods—mean big bucks these days, chiefly due to the fact that there are more extreme disasters and more folks living in harm's way. Coastal areas, already crowded with more than 55 million people, continue to stack up houses unable to withstand quixotic ocean winds. According to Federal Emergency Management Agency (FEMA) statistics, more than one-third of the entire U.S. population live near areas prone to floods from rivers, lakes, and streams, as well as the oceans. And overpopulated California is at high earthquake risk both in the north and the south.

Risky Insurance

The headache of the insurance industry, natural disasters devastate the human as well as the natural landscape. Nine insurance companies went bankrupt after Hurricane Andrew, and lawsuits continue in California after the Northridge Earthquake in 1993 (some residents claim their potential damage was underestimated by their insurers). Private insurers have been compromised by the federal government which started selling cheap flood insurance in 1968 to coastal dwellers. Inadvertently, the easy insurance encouraged more daredevil homeowners to build as close to the shore as they could, knowing that rebuilding funds would flow in after storm damage, which often happened. It also gave rise to inspectors who overlooked new building codes. FEMA has tightened the conditions under which it grants insurance, but the memory lingers on. More than a quarter of the number of homes destroyed in Hurricane Andrew had not conformed to new hurricane building codes.

American insurance companies are slow to put their investments in new energy technologies, but global warming has changed the way insurers think about writing policies. Global climate change will encourage more frequent, sudden, and intense storms, with more extreme temperatures, more droughts, more sudden bursts of rain, more heat waves. Computer models indicate that even a slight rise in surface ocean temperature will excite more severe hurricanes.

In exposed Bermuda, twelve reinsurers have invested in research aimed at better hurricane prediction. Allstate and State Farm, south Florida's biggest insurers, have held off writing new policies until the state agrees to pick up some of the cost. Fearing the worst, the destruction of a major city, for example, many private companies are talking with the federal government to develop some sort of combined insurance. Some insurance companies, real estate developers, and private investors, hedging or speculating about seasonal disasters, have begun investing in catastrophe futures offered on the Chicago Board of Trade as a novel way of spreading around the losses from a major ($5 million) catastrophe.

Above all, insurers are asking homeowners to share the risk by paying heftier premiums and higher deductibles, by conforming to stricter building codes, and by not buying properties that teeter on sand bluffs or sit on a fault.

The Building Industry

Meanwhile, construction research goes on. Engineers at the Idaho National Engineering Labs are blasting test buildings with jet-engine winds, and researchers from Clemson University and FEMA are testing materials and house construction, looking for the best wind-resisters.

But old ways of building prevail. Builders benefit, for example, every time a shingle blows off. The Insurance Institute for Property Loss Reduction is trying to get shingle companies to imprint their logo on their product so the failures will be identified when they hit the ground. "The building code for roofing products on coasts is only 60 miles per hour," explains spokesperson Dick Griebel, "so when the wind blows 110 miles per hour, the roof is the first to go." But the 60-mile-per-hour standard was set 30 years ago, not because the winds were gentler, but because the industry test fans couldn't go faster than 60 miles per hour.

Inertia is the problem in the building industry, Griebel says. "The costs of installing new technology is insignificant in a new house, but nobody wants to be first." The result: People pay with their houses, sometimes with their lives.

Geologist Jeffrey R. Keaton, who specializes in natural hazards, says, "The general public attitude toward hazards seems to be that individuals are not responsible for living in a hazard zone. If the federal government will not bail them out, then these individuals will search for some 'responsible party' to sue for damages." Most people involved in the problems agree that changes have to be market-driven: If buyers take responsibility for their risk, they will automatically demand the best and the safest if they care about their families, their property, and themselves.

Weather Predictions

A hundred years ago, observation stations throughout the country relayed local barometric pressure, wind direction, and observed conditions to the Weather Bureau via a telegraph. Tapping out their data twice a day and authorized to interrupt all other communication, weather observers were able to relay emergency information to local officials. But once delivered, the message lost its urgency: Without radios and telephones in every home, citizens relied on rumor.

Today, the National Weather Service receives data from satellites stationed above the equator and orbiting the poles, from 161 Doppler radars at 250-mile intervals, from airplanes and ships at sea, and from automated surface observations systems at airports. All this is fed into supercomputers at warning and forecast centers for instant global forecasts that are promulgated to radio and broadcast and cable television. Tornadoes and flashfloods can be detected in time for ample warning.

In 1996 the movie *Twister*, able to replicate the intensity of the storms by using computer imaging, raised consciousness about wind in the same year that nature produced tornadoes of unprecedented number and strength in the central and south United States.

Thunderstorms

Quick and dramatic, thunderstorms will be predictable with a meteorological forecast tool called Auto-nowcaster. Developed by scientists at the National Center for Atmospheric Research (NCAR) in Boulder, Colorado, for the Federal Aviation Administration, Auto-Nowcaster can predict thunderstorms 30 minutes in advance. Cumulus clouds can develop into a thunderstorm in 10 to 20 minutes. Finding out exactly how and why and what chemistry is involved draws NCAR scientists into the storm-forming clouds in high- and low-altitude planes and in trucks with radar scanners and a variety of other measuring equipment.

Hurricanes

Not all weather events are so predictable. Hurricanes, for example, elude us. Once they have formed around an eye into swirling arms

Chapter 6: Natural Disasters

of clouds, some 50,000 feet tall, it's not clear what maniacal force drives them from within (low pressures zones? the temperature of the ocean?). "Our ability to forecast where a hurricane will go has improved 1 percent a year over the last 20 years," says Frank Lepore, public affairs officer with the National Oceanic and Atmospheric Administration (NOAA) in Miami. "But the coastal population has increased 3 to 4 percent." After satellites pick up the moody and changeable storm, NOAA sends planes to fly through the towering clouds, seeking its aerial height and low pressure center. When the storm is 240 miles off land, Doppler radar tracks it, and officials can give a warning 10 to 24 hours in advance. "Trouble is, many communities take 24 hours to evacuate," says Lepore.

Earthquakes

Earthquakes have the same wildcard aspect. Seismologists agree that the "Big One" will strike southern California with a 25 to 70 percent degree of certainty within the next 20 to 50 years. But no one knows exactly when, where, or how much damage to plan for. Los Angeles is near six major faults and gets a major 7+ earthquake every 140 years, which, many seismologists believe, is near. But 44 other states, especially Alaska, are liable to earthquakes, and underground rumbling might even be slowing down Old Faithful in Yellowstone National Park, which is behaving less than reliably. An earthquake at the New Madrid Fault in southern Missouri, which some scientists say could be worse than southern California, is imminent enough for nurses to do earthquake preparedness exercises. Seismologists have recently registered the strong possibility of a giant earthquake of magnitude 9 in the Pacific Northwest, between British Columbia and northern California.

Volcanoes

Volcanoes are like fairy-tale giants: they sleep and snore and snort, and villagers tiptoe around them until one day they explode. Nothing on Earth is as violent: Mount St. Helens, which threw off its top in 1988, and Mount Pinatubo, which exploded in 1991, both dimmed the sun with their dust for months after. Scientists watch the Pacific Northwest for other volcanic eruptions expected soon, and Popocatepetl Volcano or El Popo (south of Mexico City) rumbles enough to rile scientists (but not the villagers who live around it). The same truce exists between villagers and Sicily's Mount Etna, which is rumbling uncomfortably. In the Pacific Ocean, the volcano goddess Pele is creating a new island with magma from Mount Kilauea volcano, which has been flowing for 10 years.

Droughts

Earthquakes and volcanoes are unpredictable and sudden. But other natural disasters, like drought, are so slow to develop that people aren't sure they are there. Drying out is a day-to-day process: crops fade and wells get low, but a little rain perks things up, including optimism. Many farmers stayed during the worst droughts of the Dust Bowl in the 1930s, certain it would rain tomorrow. When drought is well established, the dry topsoil blows away and is formed into clouds that look like rainclouds. What has been called the worst drought of the century settled into Kansas in 1996, where major wheat losses affected the flour and baking industries. The expanse of dry soil blows across the Great Plains into dunes that, over time, are expected to produce a major desert. Crop insurance gets the farmers started again, often with drought-resistant crops. But livestock and poultry that have no water to drink have to be slaughtered, subsequently creating a glut on the market.

Floods

According to NOAA statistics, flashfloods kill more people each year than any other catastrophe. But major floods are rare. The flooding of the Mississippi and its tributaries in 1994 was not the first, but it was the worst: whole towns were carried away, at least 50 people died, and gruesomely, the dead were freed from their graves, to float or sink in their coffins. But emergency response was quick from FEMA, public health personnel, and hundreds of volunteers who filled sandbags and helped out in shelters.

Heat Waves

Not all crises get such a response. Before confused and embarrassed city leaders realized what was happening in the devastating three-day Chicago heat wave of 1995, more than 500 people had died.

Chapter 6: Natural Disasters

Too late came the frantic call for fans. Overflow from the city morgue was handled in two refrigerated tractor trailers. The final death count remains ambiguous because heat waves kill both by raising the core temperature to 107°F, and by exacerbating respiratory and cardiac disease. The final toll may in fact be 700.

Heat waves are pretty straightforward in their description: a certain number of days with high dewpoints and unrelenting night heat. But no warning system exists for them. Cities, called urban heat islands, become breathless canyons in summer. If cities are forewarned of a heat wave, they will have time to prepare. So believes climatologist Laurence Kalkstein of the University of Delaware who initiated a program with the Philadelphia Commissioner of Health to announce the arrival of a heat wave, issuing watches and warnings. Kalkstein found in studies of city heat waves around the world that after the temperature reaches 100°F, deaths rise exponentially. Prepared city officials can distribute fans to people or take people to air-conditioned shelters.

Social factors, however, complicate heat waves: most of the Chicagoans were elderly and living alone. Many refused to leave their apartments to go to air-conditioned shelters; some were afraid to open their windows because of high crime in their neighborhoods. More than a few had no relatives and were buried without mourners.

In the Event of an Emergency ...

FEMA's Federal Response Plan divides the duties of organizing an emergency situation among 27 government agencies, each with a specialty. Cities living on the brink, like Los Angeles and Miami Beach, have developed emergency disaster plans. During earthquakes, buildings collapse, highways disappear, roads cave in, sidewalks buckle, gas lines break, electric wires fall; then fires start, hydrants crazily spew water, sewage systems ooze. During hurricanes, trees are uprooted, everything that is not bolted down flies off, breaking glass is everywhere, roofs fly off, cars are overturned, roads are impassable. Seawater rushes into city streets and public water supplies, rivers flood, and if the moon is right and the tide is high, a tsunami races toward land.

Public health emergency studies look at the best ways to provide food and clean water; set up waste disposal units and portable toilets; provide medical care for the wounded and for the increased number of heart attack victims; give immunizations to avert epidemics of diseases, like cholera, which come from contaminated water; and dispose of the dead. Mental health relief follows the turmoil period, providing help to adults suffering from post-traumatic depression and to children tormented by insomnia and nightmares three to six months later.

But in a great emergency, will everything run smoothly? San Francisco weathered a brutal earthquake in 1989 largely because its population pitched in and generously helped restore order. Communities hit by common disaster tend to bond together to help. But in overpopulated areas, such as the coasts, survival might not be so smooth.

"In hurricanes, flooding is the killer," says Frank Lepore at NOAA headquarters in Miami. New Orleans, for example, is 20 inches below sea level, and in a storm surge, will instantly flood. The city has an evacuation plan estimated to take 30 hours. "It doesn't take a whole lot to screw up an evacuation route," says Lepore. "Cars catch on fire, have flat tires; plus, evacuation routes can expose people to the storm." The interstate inland from New Orleans is raised above the sides of the road for drainage. Each side, says Lepore, becomes a lake after 12 to 40 inches of hurricane rain. Swift gusts of 130- or 140-mile-per-hour winds can send cars, wheels up, into the lake.

In south Florida, Lepore says, residents marginalize the possibility of a disaster. The only people who turn up for awareness lectures are "dyed-in-the-wool weather groupies," while most people are complacent and content to build "the insurance claim of tomorrow," he says. "Increased storm activity and population, and a population without experience in violent storms is a recipe for disaster."

Catastrophe experts emphasize the absolute necessity of having a disaster plan if you live near a potential disaster area. There is no room for complacency if you live in a high-risk area: Make a plan, practice it, and follow it when you need it. In the final analysis, surviving a disaster is each person's personal responsibility, shaped by compassion for others.

❓ What You Can Do

Natural Disasters Preparedness Information
The Federal Emergency Management Agency can supply you with information on many aspects of dealing with natural disasters. Their website: http://www.fema.gov.

For publications from FEMA, call (800) 480-2520.

For information on the federal flood insurance program, call (800) 427-4661. FEMA's National Flood Insurance Program refuses to underwrite anyone who lives in a high-risk area. Although FEMA provides disaster assistance in major catastrophes, such as the flooding of the Mississippi and its tributaries in 1994, it strongly encourages businesses, homeowners, and renters to buy insurance.

For information on federal emergency training programs, some of which are correspondence courses for nonprofessionals, call (800) 238-3358. Some states give emergency training and preparedness courses: call your local FEMA office.

Weather
The National Weather Service online: http://www.nws.noaa.gov. For excellent preparedness guides for hurricanes, tornadoes, winter storms, and thunderstorms and lightning, contact NWS, 1325 East West Highway, Silver Spring, MD 20910; (301) 713-0622; website: http://www.ncdc.noaaa.gov\. For weather data: http://nic.fb4.noaa.gov.

If you would like to train to be a severe-weather watcher, join SkyWarn, a program in which volunteers across the country keep an eye open for dangerous weather. Contact: Warning and Preparedness Meteorologist, NWS Forecast Office, RD #1, Box 107, Sterling, VA 22170; (703) 260-0209.

Earthquakes
The U.S. Geological Survey's National Earthquake Information Center will supply you with information on being prepared, including *Tremor Tips*, and a catalog: USGS, NEIC, P.O. Box 25046, Denver Federal Center, MS 967, Denver, CO 80225; (303) 273-8500.

Seismo-Watch records earthquakes as they happen, produces a newsletter, and an on-the-spot fax alert bulletin: Advanced Geologic Exploration, P.O. Box 18012, Reno, NV 89511; (800) 852-2960; website: http://www.seismo-watch.com.

Tsunami
For booklets on surviving the giant wave, contact the International Tsunami Information Center, P.O. Box 50027, Honolulu, HI 96850-4993; (808) 541-1657.

Landslides
The National Landslide Information Center offers information on house siting: *Look Before You Build* and *Homeowner's Guide for Flood, Debris, and Erosion Control*; (800) 654-4966; website: http://gldage.cr.usgs.gov.

Volcanoes
To access monthly bulletins on volcanoes, contact The Global Volcanism Network, Museum of Natural History, MRC 129, Smithsonian Institution, Washington, D.C. 20560; (202) 357-4795.

7 Asteroids and Comets

Heads Up!

PEBBLES IN THE SKY. Hundreds of thousands of tons of cosmic debris hit the Earth daily. Most is too small to be noticed. But one day a behemoth like this could come. The NEAR project, conducted for NASA by Johns Hopkins University Physics Laboratory and launched in February 1996, will rendezvous with the near-Earth asteroid Eros in late 1998. Photo credit: Johns Hopkins University Physics Laboratory/NASA.

In 1994, when astronomers watched Comet Shoemaker-Levy 9 plunge into Jupiter, send out debris from the planet's surface, then settle under a long dark cloud from the firestorm, they were finally able to understand the simple physics and sheer magnitude of a large fast-moving space object slamming into a larger stationary object. All hell breaks loose.

Could it happen here? Shortly before Comet Shoemaker-Levy 9 hit Jupiter, scientists found evidence of a 100-million-megaton impact in the ocean off the Yucatan peninsula at Chicxulub. Sixty-five million years ago, this 1-kilometer-wide asteroid sped through the Earth's atmosphere, traveling between 15 and 20 kilometers per second (6 and 12 miles) and plunged into the limestone under the shallow water off present-day Mexico, leaving a crater 180 kilometers (108 miles) wide.

Doomsday Denied: A Survivor's Guide to the 21st Century

From the Jupiter event, NASA research scientists Owen Toon and Kevin Zahnle were able to construct a theory of what happened after the Yucatan event: the atmospheric shockwave was probably heard and felt around the world. On impact, tons of Earth debris, called ejecta, were sent miles into space, before raining down again on the Earth. Heated by friction, the returning debris (the sky was filled with shooting stars) created a firestorm that turned the sky red and set fire to "continent-size" forests and grasslands alike.

The temperature of the ocean rose dramatically, giving birth to so-called hypercanes, hurricanes of more than 600 miles per hour, according to a model developed by atmospheric scientist Kerry Emanuel at MIT. Soot then obscured the sun for a decade or more, during which time cold prevailed, and photosynthesis stopped. The layer of soot found in rocks today is the legacy of that event, called K-T, marking the change from the Cretaceous to the Tertiary eras, or the time when all the dinosaurs died. Fish died in the thousands, as fossils found in Antarctica attest.

Ejecta spread out in a wide area from impact: large rocks pummeled nearby Belize, fragments rained on the North Pacific. Other exploding fragments left their mark in a line of craters running from Iowa (the Manson Crater), to Alaska, to Russia.

But this was not the first: geologists have recently uncovered a 700-kilometer (420-mile) line of craters stretching from Illinois to Kansas that date from 330 to 310 million years ago; and another 100-kilometer (60-mile) string of craters under the Sahara Desert from Chad, one of which is 12.6 kilometers (7.5 miles) in diameter, that date from 360 million years ago.

Most of Earth's scars are covered by forests and oceans or erased by erosion. But the Earth is indeed pockmarked—in fact, some believe the Moon itself is a piece of Earth ejected from the Tonga Trench beneath the Pacific Ocean into space after a collision with an asteroid. For a picture of craters, we have only to look at the Moon. Craters there measure more than 300 kilometers (180 miles) across, ringed by mountains caused by the impacts.

These are the big ones, the 1-kilometer-plus hits, thought to happen once every million years. In fact, 100 metric tons of space debris hit the Earth every day. Defense Department explosion monitors in the outer atmosphere report dozens of explosions from entering bits and pieces of tiny asteroids, called *Arjunas*. Most burn up before they reach the surface of the Earth; what's left is the size of microns, and many of them hit cars.

When a meteor flashes across the sky, its landing point, if there is one, is not always obvious. In a clever piece of detective work involving "thousands of phone calls," astronomer Peter Brown of the University of West Ontario was able to piece together the trajectory of a meteoroid by collecting videos taken by people at football games on an autumn afternoon in 1992. On an "earth-grazing trajectory" after it entered the atmosphere over Kentucky, Brown said, the meteoroid finally broke up over New Jersey and landed as microfragments, one of which hit a car in Peekskill, New York.

Asteroids

Called minor planets, asteroids behave like planets and are in fact parts of a planet that either exploded or never made it into shape. Most orbit in a belt between Mars and Jupiter, and the more they keep records, the more scientists believe asteroids number in the hundreds of thousands. As many as ten thousand of them might be Earth-crossing asteroids (ECAs) or Near-Earth Asteroids (NEAs) that travel in eccentric orbits that cross the orbit of the Earth. Because asteroids occasionally collide in orbit, there is a lot of chaotic debris. But it is these Near-Earth Objects (NEOs) of a kilometer or more that NASA is interested in.

Asteroids range in size from smaller than pebbles to larger than cities. Composed of rock or metals, some may be the eroded nuclei of comets that have lost their icy tails. At least one, 5145 Pholus, appears to have organic matter in it. Asteroid 433 Eros, 35 kilometers (14 miles) wide, will be studied by instruments aboard NASA spacecraft *NEAR* (Near-Earth Asteroid Rendezvous) in 1998 to help scientists understand why this behemoth has such an unstable orbit.

Some asteroids have their own moons. Ida, for example, 55 kilometers (33 miles) long, is accompanied by 1.2-kilometer (1/5-mile) Dactyl. On a close flyby in 1993, the spacecraft *Galileo* recorded craters and building-size boulders on Ida's surface. Twin asteroid Gaspra-Toutatis is expected to be viewable from Earth when it comes within 1 million miles in 2004, 2008, and 2012.

Scientists believe a 15-megaton asteroid hits the Earth about once every 300 years. Mile-wide Meteor Crater in Arizona was created by a chiefly iron asteroid about 30 meters (90 feet) in diameter that hit about 50,000 years ago.

Ten-megaton asteroids, however, come about once every hundred years. One thought to have been about 60 to 80 meters across ripped across the Earth and exploded at about 8 kilometers (4.8 miles) in the atmosphere above Russia in June 1908. It left no crater, only 2,000 square kilometers (1,200 miles) of leveled forest and tiny fragments of rock found in the resin of trees. The explosion over Tunguska had a force equal to 2,000 times that of the Hiroshima bomb (which had a force of 20,000 tons of TNT). Some surviving nomadic reindeer herders were left unconscious for days, whole herds were killed, and tents were set aflame; and for decades after, the charred area was thought to be enchanted by the herders' god, Ogdy, who had shown his anger in a fireball.

According to astronomer Tom Gehrels, principal investigator of Spacewatch, which keeps track of potential planetary visitors, it's the 1-kilometer ones to watch out for. There are thought to be between 1,000 and 2,000 of them that, statistically, hit the Earth once every 300,000 years. "Such a collision can happen at any time," Gehrels points out, "a year from now, in 20 years, or not in a million years." Traveling at a speed of 20 kilometers per second, the impact would be equal to "millions of times the energy released at Hiroshima in 1945." But we can relax. Asteroids 10 kilometers wide hit Earth only once every 100 million years, and the last is thought to have been the one that hit the Yucatan 65 million years ago. (So we're probably good for another 35 million years.)

Comets

If asteroids pose a threat, comets pose a threat and a half. Composed of ice, dirt, and chemicals (they may be propelled by emissions of carbon monoxide), comets orbit the outer solar system from a reservoir called the Kuiper Belt or Disk, beyond Neptune. Scientists believe some 10,000 objects 100 to 300 kilometers in diameter are here. As their orbits draw nearer to the sun and their ice melts, comets develop tails and comas. One comet, Schaumasse, is on a parallel orbit with the Earth. But others travel in long, wide orbits that bring them into flybys with the Earth once every several years. Chiron, the largest known nucleus, about 200 kilometers (120 miles) in diameter (about the size of New Hampshire and Vermont), is 25

Chapter 7: Asteroids and Comets

times bigger than Comet Halley and on an apparently unstable orbit.

Comets are mysterious because they are hard to study. One of the reasons scientists are uncomfortable about comets is that they change their orbits as they decay. Because they are composed partly of melting ice, they are subject to chaotic variability. Another problem with comets, astronomers say, is that we don't have good data on them before 200 years ago, which means that a giant on a long several-hundred year orbit currently could be winging its way into our backyard. The third problem is that they are fast, traveling on an average of 60 kilometers per second (about 130,000 miles an hour). And that can cause damage, as Comet Shoemaker-Levy 9 demonstrated.

"Comet Swift-Tuttle," *Sky & Telescope* magazine recently said, "is the single most dangerous object known to humankind." Comet Swift-Tuttle was first recorded July 15, 1862. Astronomers calculated it would return in 1979 and 1983. But it was inexplicably late; it didn't appear until August 1992, when it lit up the night skies among the Perseids showers of shooting stars. It passed by at a comfortable distance. But it will be back. The trouble is exactly when and how close are subject to the fact that Swift-Tuttle is given to dancing like what is described as a "whirling dervish." Astronomers believe it will return on August 5, 2126, at a distance of 23 million kilometers, or (1.3 million miles). Swift-Tuttle is thought to be about the same size as NEAR's object of study, asteroid 433 Eros, with a nucleus of 25 kilometers (14 miles), and fast (130,000 miles per hour).

Comets are thought to harbor hydrocarbons, the sources of life, which might have been the first life on Earth. Comet Hyakutake, a fuzzy ball over the United States in April 1996, was found to be emitting X-rays in a crescent on the side that faced the sun.

Not all meteoroid are comets or asteroids. Scientists working in Antarctica for the past 20 years have found 15,000 specimens, scattered, according to astronomer Ralph Harvey, like "blueberries over ice pancakes." Much of this matter, most of it no larger than a dime, dates from 4.5 to 6 billion years ago. "It amounts to pristine material from the solar system," says Harvey, of Case Western Reserve. And some rocks have come from Mars, Mercury, and the Moon in what appears to be a regular cosmic exchange, leading Harvey to believe, in a complete paradigm shift, that the Earth may have sent life to other planets in its ejecta from early asteroid impacts.

The Odds

What are your odds of being a statistic in an asteroid hit? Based on the prehistoric record, most astronomers believe that a major asteroid or comet hits the Earth once every millennium at an impact equal to 2,500 Hiroshima bombs, and that once every million years, a major space invader hits at a force of 50 million Hiroshimas. So you could say your odds are one in a million.

David Morrison, space science director of NASA Ames Research Center, points out that statistics are low, but if one big one hits the Earth, it's curtains for everyone. The extent of total destruction defies the imagination: huge tsunamis after the impact, decades of darkness, crop failure, global starvation, disrupted ecosystems on land and sea. Cities would not be able to afford to operate in the global winter, and Earth's entire economic balance would be altered. Even a small impact that devastated one area would have global consequences, as would a hit on any city in the world. Ecological consequences alone, according to Morrison, could "kill a billion people and destabilize civilization. It would end the world as we know it."

Senior physicist Gregory Canavan of Los Alamos National Laboratory figures losses incurred from a 2-kilometer-wide asteroid striking the Earth would be equal to multiplying the world's gross product ($20 trillion) times the two decades it would take to get back to normal, divided by the frequency of a likely impact, and comes up with $400 million a year for a million years. Daniel Seligman, otherwise known as "Mr. Statistics," of *Fortune* magazine bases his risk assessment on the value of the average American life ($3 million) times the number of Americans, adjusting for population increases, divided by one-in-a-million odds, and comes up with $28 billion. (Both figures far outweigh the $1 million start-up costs of a surveillance system.)

Near-Earth Objects Census

In 1990 the U.S. Congress called for a panel to investigate the risk of impact from an asteroid or a comet and authorized NASA to set up an investigative group to find the best way to detect and deter or destroy any unwanted space invaders. NASA proposed Spaceguard Survey, a global system of six computerized telescopes that would track invaders and set up an early-warning system. But funding was

Chapter 7: Asteroids and Comets

not forthcoming. In 1995 NASA's Near-Earth Objects Survey Working Group again solicited Congress, this time for $24 million for 5 years, to do a census of all asteroids and comets that occasionally cross Earth's orbit. To do this, they proposed an international collaboration working with the U.S. Air Force's network of telescopes. NASA astronomers tried to convey the urgency of the problem: Two thousand to three thousand NEAs one kilometer or greater in diameter occasionally cross the orbit of the Earth, and any one of them would mean curtains for life on Earth.

In 1996 Congress funded the project with $1 million, enough for NASA to install a robotic camera in one of the Air Force telescopes on Mount Haleakala, Hawaii, in a project called Near-Earth Asteroid Tracking (NEAT). The camera on Mount Haleakala is expected to produce as many as 10 reports of nearby asteroids and comets a month. Designed to identify fast-moving objects in the night sky by comparing digitized images, the telescope picked up four previously unknown NEOs in the first month.

How Do We Get Rid of Them?

But once the meteors are in the crosshairs, then what do we do? According to Tom Gehrels, we need about 50 years' prior notice in order to deploy a deterring rocket. With an early-warning system from a census, NASA observers could clear out the population from an area of expected impact from a small fast-moving object. Astronomers met with Pentagon officials at the Department of Energy's Lawrence Livermore Lab in California in 1994 and decided that a large object headed toward Earth could be steered out of its orbit or blown up into tiny fragments.

Inventor of the hydrogen bomb Edward Teller suggested testing nuclear weapons on asteroids, an idea that China has seconded as an important peaceful use of nuclear power. If larger asteroids were destroyed with a nuclear device, another device would have to destroy the secondary fragments that resulted from the explosion so they wouldn't fall to Earth and create a firestorm. Because it's not really known how a chunk of rock or metal that has been sailing through space for several million years would behave if it were hit by any device, the Pentagon plans to launch Clementine 2 in 1998 to fly 15 million kilometers (9 million miles) into space to meet three asteroids and fire 20-kilogram nonnuclear projectiles at them.

Other theorists would use neutron bombs to bump an object into another orbit. Some would put up solar sails on the surface of the object to reflect the sun's radiation and change the orbit, or set off a series of electric sparks from guns placed on the surface. The sparks would send chips into space, and the changed shape would alter the orbit away from Earth.

Putting Them to Use

Optimistically, scientists talk of a future when it will be possible not only to deter rogue or expected comets and asteroids, but to catch them in nets, bring them safely to Earth, and mine them of their rare metals. Comets, loaded with hydrocarbons, may carry viruses and bacteria, which could be studied, and some of which might even have been the initial life on Earth. Objection that life in a comet or asteroid would be fried on impact was challenged by the recent find of 5-billion-year-old buckyballs (carbon molecules) that came from outside our solar system. Found by NASA geochemist Jeff Bada in mountains ringing a crater in Sudbury, Ontario, they indicate that amino acids, the stuff of cells, might survive a fiery impact as well. Comet Halley, due back in 2136, has been thought to harbor a thousand "OPEC [Organization of Petroleum Exporting Countries] years" with its minable store of hydrocarbons, or fossil fuels.

Keeping Watch

At Kitt Peak near Tucson, Arizona, since 1984, Tom Gehrels has headed Spacewatch, a computerized telescope, a prototype of what NASA wants, uniquely designed to spot small Earth-crossing asteroids. Using fast computers and electronic light detectors, astronomers in Siding Spring, Australia, and at Mount Palomar Observatory in the Mojave Desert scan the skies with lots of help from amateur astronomers. New electronic cameras are being installed at the Cote d'Azur Observatory in the south of France and the Lowell Observatory in Flagstaff, Arizona.

Should We Worry?

The little ones might be nettlesome because they come often and fast, but the big ones will be noticed with a lot of lead time. "If there

Chapter 7: Asteroids and Comets

is an asteroid out there with our name on it, we should know by about the year 2008," says Gehrels. Between now and then, you take your chances. As writer Patrick Cooke said in *Forbes* (October 1995), if you see a light in the sky that keeps on getting bigger night after night until it's way bigger than the full moon, it's time to retire to the backyard with a carton of Camels and a few bottles of your favorite booze. "You won't be around for the hangover," he wrote.

What You Can Do

Amateur observers are always welcome—they are needed. The main clearinghouse for comet and asteroid sightings is Harvard–Smithsonian Astrophysical Observatory, Planetary Sciences Division, 60 Garden Street, Cambridge, MA 02138; (617) 495-7280; website: http://cfa-www.harvard.edu/cfa/ps/icq.html.

To report a comet, contact the Central Bureau for Astronomical Telegrams; website: http://cfa-www.harvard.edu/cfa/ps/cbat.html.

Comet Observation Homepage, Charles Morris; website: http://encke.jpl.nasa.gov.

International Comet Quarterly, Dan Green, editor, (617) 495-7440.

For information on watching Chiron, contact the Chiron Perihelion Campaign at the e-mail address, cpc@astro.umd.edu.

The American Association of Variable Star Observers (AAVSO) welcomes amateur skywatchers to collect data on stars that change their size or shape. AAVSO, 25 Birch Street, Cambridge MA 02138; (617) 354-0484; e-mail: aavso@aavso.org.; website: http://www.aavso.org.

If you spot any extraterrestrial intelligence, or if you would like to join astronomers who are seriously searching, contact The SETI League, Inc., 433 Liberty Street, P.O. Box 555, Little Ferry, NJ 07643; (800) TAU-SETI; (201) 641-1770.

8 Cars

Our 3,000-Pound Gorillas

SOON TO BE THE SIZE OF A BOOK. The long arm of steel pincers waits to carry another car to the cruncher where it will be condensed and tossed into the car landfill. All the speed, the motors that purred like cougars or jaguars, the ergonomic seats covered in your choice of plush-and-leather or all leather, and your initials in the signal flags on the driver's door will be gone, gone, gone. Photo credit: Roger Archibald.

Only slightly louder than the murmur of the wind in the trees, a hundred years ago cars put-putted along dusty rutted roads at 10 miles per hour, got stuck in mud, tipped over like top hats, and crashed woodenly into each other, splintering their bumpers. At the turn of the century, these cars were much like the cattle-drawn wood carts of 1,000 years before, or, for that matter, the toy wheeled vehicles found in archaeological digs at sites dated to 2,500 B.C. We were born to travel; getting it right takes time.

Of 260 million people in the United States in 1993, there were 196 million registered cars, buses, and trucks. Since 1896 when the Duryea Brothers made and marketed the first handful of gas-powered internal combustion engine motorcars in Springfield, Massachusetts, automobiles have driven our economy, shaped our societies, and met a lot of psychological needs. We bank from our cars, eat in our cars, commute from the country to the city and from the city to the country in our cars. We use them as stereo cubicles for music and as mobile advertisements for our club and university affiliations and our political and philosophical opinions, such as "Save the Whales" or "Bike for Clean Air." Teenagers ride to their proms in Cadillacs the size of ships; retirees prowl the country in motorized houses. Robbers use them for getaways; lunatics use them to shoot from; drunks use them as weapons.

At mid-century, recreational vehicles and off-road vehicles, derivatives of Jeeps used in wars and African game-trackers, and vans like the 18-foot-long Suburban carry young professionals, their kids, and their goods around the suburbs and to the city and back. Many of the rich lust after the Lamborghini Diablo Roadster VT ($249,000), and the not so rich plod to and from work in Ford Escorts or Geo Metros ($10,500). Some drivers hang fuzzy dice and cardboard deodorants in the shape of pinetrees from their rearview mirrors; some stick statues of saints on the dashboard and display the insignia of their ballcaps in a row in the back window next to a box of Kleenex. Professional drivers maneuver racecars at Indianapolis; devotees participate in antique-auto parades or sports-car rallies.

Cars, more than trains, generated tourism as car use created paved roads, freeways, cloverleafs, motels, campsites, and national parks. Touring companies transport hundreds at a time in motorcoaches to national monuments and compete for space on the highways with 18-wheeled, sometimes double-container trucks transporting the nation's imports, exports, and manufactured and grown goods around the country. At Christmas, acres and acres of mall parking lots are filled with a shining sea of cars. In cities, parking competition is fierce: many a driver pushes his car's backside into a metered parking place, only to meet a competitor nosing into the same space from behind. Meter readers roam the streets with steely eyes and trigger fingers, ready to write tickets to insure a steady city revenue, or to recommend a Denver boot, or to call a tow truck to drag a car to a lot miles away. And at night across the land, millions and millions of cars sit silent in garages, at curbs, in parking lots, waiting faithfully to be fired up again in the morning.

It is the sheer bulk of the beast that weighs heavily on the continent. Cars accumulate year after year from the mass production lines of the "Big Three" auto manufacturers in Detroit and the smaller assembly points of imported cars, which produced more than 6.6 million cars in 1994, according to the American Automobile Manufacturers' Association. Each year new cars are introduced with great fanfare, rendering passé the ones that we have. *Blue Book* values plummet, and old cars die. But they do not go to heaven. In less-developed countries, cars abandoned by the side of the road are used to make other things, their metal parts cut to be shaped into household utensils like bowls. In the United States, a car no longer in service is transported on a carrier to an automobile graveyard and ignominiously dumped into a pile of rusting chassis. The best parts are recycled; what's left is squeezed into a small cube and hauled to a landfill to decay. Some parts will never decay.

But it is not just the solid waste that decays toxically in landfills. Lead batteries, millions of gallons of used oil, air-conditioning coolant, radiator coolant, brake fluid, steering fluid, and other lubricants have to go somewhere. Then there are spare parts that are not reusable—fuel pumps, transmission gears, flywheels, old air filters, mufflers, radiators, billions of tires, and old gas station pumps. And gasoline, a fossil fuel transported sloshing in trucks and pumped into underground storage tanks in gas stations, sometimes seeps out of cracks and flows into local water supplies, unknown to neighbors until they notice their tap water smells like gasoline—it may in fact be gasoline.

From Athens to Paris to Rome to Mogadishu to New York, Chicago, Los Angeles, and every city in between, air polluted with easy-to-inhale, microscopic particles of nitrogen oxides, hydrocarbons, ozone, sulfur dioxide, and carbon monoxide (CO or "urban monoxide") from combustion engines is a fact of life. Even the Parthenon is being eaten. The biggest offender is carbon monoxide. The poisonous byproduct of incomplete combustion, CO is given off especially in stop-and-go driving and during idling, which is why it is dangerous to linger in a closed parking garage. The gas is invisible, tasteless, and odorless, but it enters the body and mixes with the blood, and until the victim becomes unconscious the only symptoms are headache, a kind of fatigue, and nausea. The Centers for Disease Control estimates that about 500 people in the United States alone die accidentally each year of CO poisoning.

The federal Clean Air Acts have mandated the use of unleaded gas and catalytic converters and set allowable standards for pollutants, but cities still suffer from smog. According to the Natural Resources

Defense Council, 64,000 deaths a year can be attributed to breathing particles of pollutants smaller than 2.5 microns. Less-developed countries have absolutely no controls, and many black-market workers hawk gasoline, leaded or not, in jerri cans. Our intention may be good, but our numbers are out of control: anyone stuck in a city gridlock dreams of an oxygen mask.

Then there is the problem of safety. In 1994 a motor vehicle–related death happened every 13 minutes; an injury, every 16 seconds, according to the National Safety Council. Airbags provide a lot of protection to the upper body but none to the lower extremities, and they must be used with safety belts to be effective. Numerous studies done on driving with lights on during the day conclude that it adds another dimension of safety: older drivers with less keen vision and bicyclists are more likely to see and respond to daytime headlights.

The United States spends a lot of money on cars. In 1994 total personal cost of all cars, trucks, and RVs, including initial cost, gasoline, tires, repairs, road tolls, and insurance, was computed to be about $495 million. But an analysis by the Congressional Office of Technology Assessment found that this figure reflects only part of the total cost of cars in the nation. It does not include, as Daniel Sperling says in his book *Future Drive*, "traffic congestion, accidents, the cost of buying oil from a cartel ... national security costs associated with oil importation, environmental degradation, and traffic courts."

Time to Say Good-Bye

The gasoline-powered internal combustion engine automobile we all know and love is teetering on the brink of a cliff. The steel-based mass–production-line industry driven by gross amounts of fossil fuel has encountered critical mass. Sociologists don't know how people respond during major economic evolutions such as this one: tolerance of the sheer ambiguity of change varies day to day. But there may be some graceful solutions on the drawing board to the automotive paradigm shift—not only in redesigning the car, but in rethinking lifestyles.

Some Solutions

Urban rapid transit and commuter rails linking suburbs to city centers have been around for almost a century: riding trolleys on Sunday afternoons was a favorite pastime before World War I. But the

Chapter 8: Cars

tension between maintenance costs and rider fees has never been resolved, and most urban mass transit systems are money-losers. Although they transport hundreds of people daily, cars often break down or brakes catch on fire or fail, upkeep is minimal, and connecting bus service can be dicey.

Most urban planners would like to ban cars altogether from downtown sections of cities, a move that makes businesses pale. One solution is short-term hire vehicles. France, for example, with car company Peugeot-Citroen is building TULIP (Transport Urbain Libre Individuel et Public), which will provide electric cars on a daily basis. Between 50,000 and 100,000 two-seater Tulipmobiles will be available at 5,000 pickup points (where they will recharge) throughout Paris, and the cars, renting at about $8 an hour, will be tracked by infrared beacons from the central station.

Another idea on the drawing board is called Intelligent Transport, which uses sophisticated navigation systems to guide cars in the most efficacious way along a computerized highway. Each car traveling in single-file small groups will be equipped with instruments that provide immediate traffic advisories from central computers and satellites. Best-route suggestions will eliminate wasted gas and reduce the possibility of accidents.

The biggest motivator in changing our concept of being a car-centered society will probably come at the gas pump. While paying the lowest price per gallon in the world, Americans are nevertheless sensitive to price hikes. The Clean Air Act in 1990 mandated modifications in gasoline to reduce the amount of greenhouse pollutants. This, plus local and state regulations, put the burden on refineries to produce so-called "reformulated gasolines" designed to emit less noxious gases, linked to different seasons and locales in the country. "Designer fuels" hiked up costs to the refiners, who responded by reducing inventories. Any change in the weather—cold winters, hot summers (linked ironically to greenhouse gases)—strains refinery supplies, which raises the price at the pump. The pump price reflects local, state, and federal taxes, plus the price of crude oil. To deflect criticism from the unaccountable differences in pump prices, local gas stations offer accessible credit-card and ATM payments at the pump itself, as well as convenience store items, and in some places, cappucino bars.

In 1995 more than 30,000 drivers used alternative fuels, such as natural gas, methanol and ethanol (from alcohol), and biomass, from fermenting farm products such as wood and corn. The problem is, where do you fuel up? The Clean Air Act also encouraged people to buy cars that were more fuel-efficient, but the market had a disconnect: the Geo Metro, for example, got 55 miles per gallon, but the popular Suburban got only 13.

Battery-powered cars have been on the drawing board for a couple of decades, but the Partnership for a New Generation of Vehicles, initiated by President Clinton in 1993, challenged the auto industry and academicians to design a truly fuel-efficient vehicle by 2004. While they may emit no harmful exhaust, electric vehicles have batteries, probably made of lead, which need to be recharged from electrical sources provided by plants that burn coal, which is one of the worst air polluters around. The other problem is that they run only for a certain number of hours and then must be recharged for several hours.

An ideal energy source is a fuel cell, which creates an electrical charge from the conversion of hydrogen and oxygen into water. Space engineers perfected them for use on the Space Shuttle in orbit, where the water byproduct can be recycled and used. Hydrogen is expensive, but only a small amount is required. The problem in using them for cars is that they are heavy until they can be made in a lightweight composite material.

Nevertheless, the "Big Three" are gearing up for mass manufacture of some kind of electric vehicles (EVs) by 1998. Some models will retrofit existing models because, as an industry spokesperson said, car design is what Detroit has a lot of experience in. General Motors Corporation's EV-1, for example, is a $30,000 electric Saturn Coupe that gets 70 miles per gallon in the city, 90 miles per gallon on the highway, weighs 2,970 pounds, runs for 50 to 55 hours, and takes 15 hours to recharge. It's clean, it's familiar, but it requires a paradigm shift to run.

Hybrid vehicles, which are powered by a combination of electric motors and some kind of liquid fuel, may be the smooth transition in the paradigm shift. By using a tiny internal combustion engine that powers motors on the wheels, hybrids eliminate the need to carry heavy batteries that need to be recharged, and their air pollution is next to minimal. Several universities are working with the "Big Three" to make hybrids truly marketable.

The paradigm shift is what Amory Lovins and the Rocky Mountain Institute are all about. A physicist who runs the "resource policy think tank" with Hunter Lovins in Snowmass, Colorado, Lovins argues that the "really efficient car can't be made of steel for the same reason that a successful airplane can't be made of cast iron." Using lightweight but strong composite material that can be molded and recycled, Lovins's "Hypercar"—a hybrid with a fuel cell—is 65 to 75 percent lighter and so "slippery" it eliminates 60 to 80 percent of drag on the highway. Manufacturing it would mean rethinking the whole auto manufacturing process, Lovins says, "changing a die-making, steel-stamping culture into a molded-not-shaped materials/electronics/software culture." The car would be a marriage of materials and physics: special electric motors with converters on the wheels, for example, would convert downhill motion into electricity and operate electronic brakes. Supersmart and sexy, the Hypercar could even use its downtime constructively: Lovins imagines turning on the car at night and plugging the fuel cell into the home electrical system for power. And Lovins speculates that the Hypercar could be bought on the internet, thus eliminating the middleman, and because it consists of molded parts, the buyer could choose whatever color he wanted and have the car delivered overnight.

Other alternatives to using cars are bicycles or rollerblades, but cities without special bike or blade paths are dangerous places. Nevertheless, the move to eliminate urban sprawl—houses built in suburbs that require cars to visit malls, to drive kids to school, to go to work, etc.—has taken hold. Some builders have responded by creating so-called neotraditional communities that combine energy-efficient systems, like solar or wind power, with small-town architectural treatments. Places like Village Homes in Davis, California, have solar-powered homes with organic vegetable and flower gardens and vineyards that face narrow streets designed for bikers and walkers to encourage sociability. Cars are stashed behind houses and used only for long-distance trips. Most daily needs can be met on foot or by bike.

Telecommunication has spawned home businesses, usually begun by people who quit their firms and become consultants or subcontractors. Connected telephonically, they eliminate daily use of the car completely if they live close enough to schools and shops to walk or bike.

Ultimately it comes down to a redefinition of where we put ourselves: do we *need* to be a physical part of a huge office building by day and a suburban dweller by night, our spaces separated by a slow ride through poisoned air? One home-office subcontractor said he doesn't even miss the water-cooler chatter because of the freedom he experiences being in charge of his own life and being part of the wider internet community. "Now I select who I want to be with and what groups I want to join," he says.

Until we can all toodle around quietly and cleanly in our superlight superefficient hybrids, staying home might not be a bad idea.

What You Can Do

Car Organizations
The Hypercar Sampler costs $7, gives all the information you need on Hypercars. Ask for a catalog: Rocky Mountain Institute, 1739 Snowmass Creek Road, Snowmass, CO 81654; (970) 927-3851; website: http://solstice.crest.org/rmi.

General Motors has information on its new EVs: (800) 25-ELECTRIC.

Auto History
Henry Ford Museum and Greenfield Village in Dearborn, Michigan, is a living history museum with an excellent Archives and Research Library. To use the library, call for an appointment. For specific information, send letter to archival research expert ($35 per hour). Center for Henry Ford Museum and Greenfield Village, 20900 Oakwood Boulevard, Dearborn, MI 48121-1970; (313) 271-1620.

Detroit Public Library's National Automotive Historic Collection is considered the best collection; (313) 833-1456.

Bicycle Organizations
League of American Wheelmen, 190 West Ostend Street, Suite 120, Baltimore, MD 21230; (800) 288-2453.

American Bicycle Association, P.O. Box 718, Chandler, AZ 85244; (602) 961-1903.

Air Pollution
The American Lung Association publishes *Health Effects of Outdoor Air Pollution* and other information; (800) 586-4872.

9 The Homeless

Invisible People

PRECIOUS REAL ESTATE. Sleeping outdoors in the city is perilous. Just finding a comfortable, quiet spot can wear you out; other people steal your possessions, like the transistor radio on this person's lap; then police arrest you for loitering. Photo credit: Roger Archibald.

East or West, nobody knows how many homeless street people there are in the United States. Boston had between 5,000 and 7,000 in 1996; San Francisco thought it had about 10,000. Like birdwatchers on an Audubon Society Christmas bird count, census volunteers go into the city streets one night a year to count the homeless. Like birds, the homeless move around a lot in a night, spending some time eating in a soup kitchen, sleeping in a storefront, and slipping into a subway station or a shelter when the dark pre-dawn turns bitter cold. And they often give false names, volunteers report, making a true census impossible.

Nevertheless, numbers are a comfortable way of getting a handle on something many of us don't understand, even if the total national count ranges wildly from 300,000 to several million. We call them homeless, but what census takers see when they shine their flashlights on a tattered, layered mound sleeping on a grate is the startled face of poverty. Homelessness is only one of their problems.

"Alcoholics with money don't become homeless, rich drug addicts don't become homeless, and the wealthy mentally ill go to hospitals," says Linda Johnson, Director of the Boston Coalition for the Homeless. "The bottom line is, the homeless lack the resources to afford decent housing."

Who Are They?

To unbundle the homeless is to make discrete the threads of an unraveling society. Some are there because alcohol, drugs, or mental illness took away their ability to function in "common" society and no one in their life is able to care for them. Others are there because they are the victims of global economic change: companies have downsized, the labor market is "flexible," which means workers have zero job security, and low-paying unskilled jobs have been wiped out by technological changes and illegal workers who will work for slave wages.

In fact, the homeless subculture is as diverse as the general population. Many homeless have low-paying jobs (a spot check one week in Boston in 1995 found that a quarter of the people on the street were employed). Some fought in wars; some are ex-convicts; some lived in middle-class homes and had loving partners or caretakers who died; some lost their mortgages or their jobs. Some are teenagers; many are elderly; there are women, young children, and men; people with or without families; those who are ill; and those who, despite indescribable hardship, are healthy. Always subjected to public rejection and systems that often fail to understand, the largest percentage are young able-bodied men who would work if they could. But jobs are scarce, and job-training is scarcer.

Few Really Want to Be There

Two weeks or less is enough for most. Many of the short-term homeless often find themselves on the streets suddenly when landlords shut the doors, or a final family argument or intolerably cramped quarters make staying home impossible. Many are plowing through the red tape of applying for temporary housing or waiting for welfare checks or money from jobs before they move on. Lack of cooking facilities and money to buy food and embarrassment about eating in soup kitchens can cause families to live on junk food. The psychological trauma of living out of a car or on the streets can have generational effects on children. A study by nurse Karen Heusel in West Virginia found that newly homeless school-age kids suffered from depression and anxiety, had irrational fears of losing their parents, and deeply missed their friends and being in school. Several studies profile homeless adults as having been homeless as children.

Many of the long-term homeless have adjusted to life on the streets. They know where to eat, sleep, and, above all, they have a social network. Some will leave to stay with friends or family, but they tend to go back. A study in Minneapolis found that 50 percent of the homeless were not homeless for the first time. Several studies have found that many long-term homeless opt to stay within their homeless network even if they have an opportunity to end their homelessness. Although some in northern cities are as weathered as mountaineers, they get little credit for surviving the rigors of severe cold.

Many entrenched homeless, like those, for example, in Santa Monica, organize politically and elect a leader in charge of augmenting their rights. Homeless activist Andy Raubeson, a former runaway, for example, raised enough money to refurbish more than a thousand rooms in skid row hotels in downtown Los Angeles. Several organizations register the homeless to vote, a right that is theirs even if they have no address.

In the 1980s, a period of so-called deinstitutionalism, thousands of former patients with mental illness were released from sometimes squalid hospitals to halfway houses and the streets. Underfunded state governments believed closing the institutions and giving the patients medicine would solve a budget problem. But over time, the ex-patients stopped getting and taking medicine. The most violent went back to hospitals, but most stayed on the streets. A survey of 29 major cities done by the U.S. Conference of Mayors in 1995 found that 23 percent of the street homeless were mentally ill.

Being on the streets itself challenges mental health: coping mechanisms for finding food and bathrooms, privacy, cleanliness, clothes, healthcare, a place to sleep, and, above all, safety, plus having to do it daily in an atmosphere of public rejection, can produce unusual behavior. Violence, rape, battery, and murder among alcoholics and drug-users extends to nondrug-users, who, as victims themselves, may elicit little sympathy. In Boston, a homeless woman with a broken hip was sold for sex by her boyfriend during her recuperation. Rescued when her boyfriend left, she had never gone to a doctor. A recent study found that homeless women in most major cities were reluctant to seek healthcare because of nurses' negative attitudes toward them. Yet cases of tuberculosis continue to rise on the street, and the homeless suffer from colds, viruses, problems related to vision, teeth, pregnancy, and HIV as much as the general population. A novel approach in New Haven enlisted Yale University medical residents to deliver care, including drug and alcoholism counseling, to the homeless in a mobile van.

The Unexploded Bombs

Street people are the visible homeless. But tucked away in friends' apartments and relatives' homes are the transitional homeless "without a deed or a lease," thought to number in the millions. Many of them are between school and a job, or between jobs, or have been recently released from jail or the hospital or an institution.

Sometimes families explode, and battered women run to shelters; or families decay, and divorce leaves a parent and children without a job and evicted from their apartment; or families war internally, and grandparents kick out their children and grandchildren; or a stressed mother ejects a troubled son. Sociologists also count as vulnerable the marginal whose paychecks will not cover a hospital emergency or an automobile accident.

Chapter 9: The Homeless

Needed: Jobs, Houses, Public Help

In the mid-1990s Congress, eager to cut the budget, sought to eliminate welfare programs that directly helped the poorest. States were encouraged to impose a two-year time limit on welfare, a condition that some critics say will only swell the homeless on the streets because so few jobs are available. Accused of draconian measures, Congress nevertheless reflects a tired sympathy among its constituents. "Most Americans want the homeless off the streets," says sociologist Christopher Jencks in his book *The Homeless*, "but no one wants them next door."

"The worst thing about being homeless," said one gentleman of the Washington streets, "is that people walk by you as if you don't exist." A famous street person in San Francisco dramatized his nonpersonhood when he struck and held for hours the pose of a black servant in red jacket and white pants, resembling "lawn jockeys" placed on many southern white middle-class lawns in the 1950s. Outside Union Square's 5-star hotels, many tourists never realized he was flesh and blood.

"The attitude now is becoming more punitive," said Linda Johnson of Boston's Coalition for the Homeless, one of many nonprofit organizations that act as advocates for the homeless. In San Francisco, a particularly brutal mayoral dictum enlisted the police to enforce laws forbidding anyone to sleep in parks or obstruct sidewalks. Part of the punitive response is that the public funds have been mismanaged. In 1996 San Francisco's new mayor, Willie Brown, called in the U.S. Department of Housing and Urban Development to clean up not only the grossly mismanaged local department, but the shambles it had created in the low-income and temporary public high-rise housing units, which were filthy, without water, and denizens of crime. Caught in the middle, the homeless often only shrug: a woman in a crime-infested New York high-rise, smiled weakly for an interviewer who asked why she continued to stay. "It's got a roof," she said.

Federally, the response is to demolish the high-rise buildings, built originally in the 1950s and 1960s. Started in 1981 with a budget of $2.5 billion, the demolition in all cities (except New York) nevertheless precedes and overlaps the construction of low-rise suburban-type housing units designed to accommodate families, with strict rules to exclude members of the crack and cocaine culture.

87

Management is still the problem, as well as setting unfair rent. Currently, an affordable rent is considered to be 30 percent of income. A 1991 American Housing Survey, however, found that 50 percent of below-poverty households spent at least 50 percent of income on housing. The survey also points out that 30 percent of an annual income of $100,000 leaves $70,000 to spend on other things, while 30 percent of $10,000 leaves only $7,000 a year.

HUD's voucher system—giving homeless families cash vouchers with which they can seek private housing—is applauded by social workers because it keeps the rental market competitive and gives people a sense of being in charge of their lives. The trouble is that most rents exceed the value of the vouchers. Several groups try to prevent more homeless by intervening and mediating when landlords threaten eviction.

Habitat for Humanity enlists volunteers to help low-income families, many on the verge of becoming homeless and who definitely do not qualify for any traditional mortgages, to build their own modest homes, financed by low-interest loans. In its 1,100 affiliates in the United States, they average 35 houses a day. Recently, in conjunction with the Rocky Mountain Institute and other environmental organizations, Habitat has begun building environmentally sustainable housing, using appropriate technology, recycled materials, and incorporating resource efficiency. "Our goal," says senior advisor David Ewing, "is to provide decent sustainable housing which will have a minimal adverse environmental impact."

Most sociologists agree that the answer to homeless families is to increase public subsidy. In Boston, for example, when a family is evicted, what they can't carry with them is put into storage. Because the family will be in temporary housing, storage fees are charged by the day. There are stories of companies charging as much as $25 a day to store a family's possessions. When the family is finally approved for permanent housing, the evicted, unable to afford the cost of storage, must sit through the auction, hoping to get back personal items like family photo albums.

Truly affordable housing takes off pressure from a lot of areas within the family. Children especially have a place to come home to from the challenges of their business of growing up. When they lack this, the public sector has to take up the slack.

Of the long-term street homeless studied by sociologists in Minneapolis, 100 percent were high school dropouts. Adult education programs exist in most communities, but in many cases, dropouts perceive the whole system to be unresponsive and fruitless. The only way to get to the young people in housing project courtyards is to go after them. In Cambridge, Massachsetts, for example, a nonprofit organization called Positive Edge works with teenagers from projects who hang out with nothing to do. "They're effectively homeless," says director Edward Harris. "They dropped out of school, they can't go home, they have no place to be, so they have no connection to the community. We try to explain to them how the systems work, why they need a high school diploma, how they can train for a job," he says. "And we give them a place to be."

Sociologist Peter Rossi stresses that the short-term and long-term homeless have different needs. "Short-term homeless are easier to connect to labor," he says, "but the long-term have problems and need care." Rossi believes in reviving old skid row hotels and cheap YMCA rooms to give long-term homeless private, individual spaces. "Shelters warehouse the homeless and are a disgrace," he says. New York City, for example, shelters more than 7,000 people a night. Rossi suggested to Congress, when he testified on the homeless in 1992, that federal aid be given to people who house dependent adults with zero income. "It was met with resounding silence," he said. "But it's cheaper than mental institutions."

Labor

Skid row hotels were built to absorb the homeless generated by the failure of the economic system in the 1930s, when some of the many jobless fell into chronic alcoholism and took to the streets. When the stock market crashed in 1929, hundreds of thousands were out of work. Cities set up transient camps, called Hoovervilles, where 18- to 22-year old men stayed as they followed jobs around the country. Riding the rails and staying only as long as the fieldwork or construction job lasted, "hobos," as they were called, became romantic figures, remembered in song and film, notably Charlie Chaplin's *The Tramp*.

During the Great Depression of the early 1930s, President Franklin Roosevelt's New Deal provided public works projects, such as the Works Progress Administration (WPA) and the Civilian Conservation Corps (CCC), which provided work, meals, and a place to stay for thousands of workers who organized national parks and built bridges, sea walls, schools, public buildings, and roads.

Sociologist Christopher Jencks suggests instituting public day-labor markets in cities in which the young able-bodied homeless work in return for vouchers for a private cubicle room, plus meals and spending money. More job-training programs would direct a whole cadre of homeless willing to work but uncertain of how to go about it. Full employment would abolish homelessness in 10 years, says sociologist Rossi.

Several psychologists note that many homeless tend to be "disorganized": they have some resources but lack the knowledge of how to use them most efficiently. Courses and counseling in daily life skills—how to organize time, plan for the future, even how to get up and dress for a job—are offered by several groups, such as the National Alliance to End Homelessness.

The Future

Altogether, the homeless are the emblems of a culture in the process of dissolving and restructuring, as companies and government agencies downsize, as families reinvent themselves, as the population grows, and as social welfare programs reflect a restrained compassion. There are more people to fall through cracks that grow ever wider.

Homelessness is global. Around the world, as more people move to cities, economic imbalances will insure that a certain number of the population will not find work and will never be properly housed. The example in Brazil of some street children, in and out of homes, making a little money in prostitution, and being hunted and shot by police in periodic thinning-out raids is a horrific proof of systems gone wrong.

Economic, environmental, and political refugees, notably in Africa, fleeing ethnic cleansing, drought, and brutal dictators, fill tent cities the size of Washington, D.C. In this country, with restrictions on welfare, no unskilled labor market, and lack of affordable and decent housing, many sociologists predict that homelessness could become an epidemic.

What Makes a Home?

The idea of a home is the kernel of the American dream. The little house circumscribed by a fence most often drawn by homeless children is the place of safety, privacy, and comfort.

But home is above all a sense of connectedness, even for those who prefer to be homeless, such as yogis, adventurers, chronic travelers. Christopher Jencks notes that before 1960, a home was where the family was. After the 1960s, a home became a fixed address to which one could come and go and "sleep in peace." Now, Jencks says, a home can be defined as any private space to which one has a legal right.

Peter Rossi defines a home as a place from which social networks can be formed because people are able to reciprocate socially. Sister Mary Rose McGeady of the Boston Sisters of Charity says home is a sense of belonging somewhere. With or without a roof, she says, "the most desperate situation in life is feeling there is nobody who cares."

❓ What You Can Do

National Alliance to End Homelessness will put you in touch with other nonprofits helping the homeless, whether working in soup kitchens, volunteering legal help, giving healthcare, or teaching life skills. NAEH, 1518 K Street, NW, Washington, D.C. 20005; (202) 638-1526.

Habitat for Humanity has more than 1,300 affiliates in the world; they welcome volunteers to retrofit existing buildings or build new ones for people otherwise on the streets. Their goal is "to eliminate poverty housing from the face of the Earth." Habitat for Humanity, Habitat and Church Streets, Americus, GA; (912) 924-6935.

The City Summit: Habitat II is a global effort of the United Nations and HUD to address the problems of making crowded cities livable and economically viable. The City Summit: Habitat II Clearinghouse, P.O. Box 9060, Gaithersburg, MD 20898; (800) 248-8180; website: http://huduser.aspensys.com:84/habitat.html; e-mail: habitat2@aspensys.com.

The U.S. Department of Housing and Urban Development offers three reports on urban problems at $5 each. HUD USER, P.O. Box 6091, Rockville, MD 20849; (800) 245-2691; fax: (301) 251-5767. Or download from the Net for free: gopher://hudser.org:73/11/2/h2info.

10 Deteriorating Infrastructure

If It Ain't Broke . . .

FACTORY WINDOWS ARE ALWAYS BROKEN. When industry moves away, empty factories become playgrounds for gangs, dumping grounds for trash, and hangouts for addicts. But they can be saved. Investment money often transforms the valuable square footage into a mall or luxury condominiums. Photo credit: Roger Archibald.

Fortunately, Mrs. Anne Hammel, grandmother and retired seamstress, never knew what happened. Preparing for her Wednesday night bingo game and a grandson's birthday barbecue in Yonkers, a suburb of New York City, she was shopping on the block that housed her neighborhood deli and Woolworth's when a 50-foot-long decorative concrete parapet above the dry cleaner's and the Chinese restaurant suddenly collapsed and crumbled into chunks of debris and billows of dust on top of her. The cause (according to fire and building inspectors): softening of the mortar due to accumulating water on the roof from melting winter snows and excess spring rains; plus the constant rattle of car, motorcycle, and truck traffic past the 50-year-old buildings; plus age; plus patchwork maintenance over the last 30 years.

In other words, Mrs. Hammel's killer parapet could describe any of the thousands of neighborhood-block facades throughout the country. Never built to last forever, they are reaching the end of their structural life.

The word *infrastructure* was borrowed from the military in the 1950s to expand the concept of public works, a term that encompasses the civilizing grids that connect people in the commerce of everyday life: shopping centers, roads and highways, bridges, water supply and sewer systems, electrical, gas, telecommunications and cable lines, garbage and waste removal, landfills, parks, playgrounds, public buildings, subways, railroads, and airports. These are the elements of living together that urban planner David C. Perry says, "work best when they are noticed least or not at all." Only after the damage is done, he adds, do we focus on them.

More damage can be expected. Much of the infrastructure we live with today was built either in the early decades of this century or in the 1950s and 1960s. Lots of use, no money for maintenance, and poor workmanship and mismanagement are now leaving us with fallen bastions of support.

- In the first five months of 1996, four New York City water mains burst, sending cascades of water into city streets and subways. The cause: age and faults in the steel pipes.

- In Milwaukee in 1993, 400,000 people became violently ill when the city's drinking water filtration system failed to trap the infectious cryptosporidium bacteria.

- In Chicago in 1992, 250,000 people were evacuated from downtown businesses at a cost of $1 billion, when the Chicago River rushed through a "$10,000 patch job" crack in an underground tunnel.

And there are other glitches in the system, too: in Boston, an escalator in a major downtown office building suddenly reversed direction, sending riders tumbling backwards on top of each other. The cause: no maintenance. A wheel fell off a roller coaster in Coney Island, injuring two riders. The cause: missing bolts and failure to have metal-fatigue inspection. In all cities, bad air takes its toll on the ill and the elderly, eating away at public buildings as esteemed and eternal as the Parthenon in Athens. In orbit in the outer atmosphere,

Chapter 10: Deteriorating Infrastructure

a silent swirling collection of dead satellites, old rocket debris, and spent fuel tanks clutters areas we never even think about.

Across the United States, evidence of age is beginning to show: in vertical cracks in highway overpasses, in overfull landfills, in rusty bridges. As the New York City socialite is reputed to have remarked upon turning a critical age, "Maintenance is all." While abandoned farmhouses in the middle of Midwestern farm fields simply tilt, then collapse, benign neglect in the city has a higher price in places where abandoned buildings on public and private land create fire and health hazards or simply hide drug users.

As older cities in the East hear the swan's song, cities in the West must deal with the challenges of natural disasters like earthquakes and mudslides. Earthquakes tear up underground lines, sending natural gas into the air and water and sewage gushing through the streets. Many buildings in the 1992 Northridge, California, earthquake, for example, could have been salvaged if building inspectors had forced builders to adhere to strict earthquake building codes. Instead, the city was left with piles of rubble.

A hundred years ago, grand and glorious public works projects were the celebration of the country's prosperity. We built dams almost as big as the Grand Canyon, changed the course of rivers, laid rails that connected the coasts, and strung bridges that sent poets into ecstasy. Politicians then, as they do now, routinely cut the ribbons that signal the beginning of new economic endeavor.

But building major projects is a lot sexier for politicians than imposing taxes or user fees for future maintenance. Playing catch-up now is harder, with the U.S. Congress paring federal funds and competition for state and local tax money growing ever fiercer. A recent private study of New York City revealed that Manhattan was $2 billion in debt and badly in need of a core city overhaul and transportation improvements.

Mayor Rudolph Giuliani proposed dissolving the Department of Transportation and remaking it into several departments designed to handle specific problems, such as traffic fines and trucking, a move that critics said would save a dollar and create management nightmares. Meanwhile, the governor of New York, George Pataki, has couched a $1.3 billion wish list of infrastructure repairs in a proposal for an environmental bond designed to improve drinking water, clean toxic wastes out of the harbor, and find badly needed landfill areas away from human habitation.

Typically, money for maintenance comes from local real estate and gasoline taxes, state highway and user taxes, some federal funds, and private investors. Realizing return on investment, however, is slow. Urban rapid transit, for example, has never been profitable: to attract more users, the fees must be low, and low fees do not generate enough money to pay for the repairs necessary in a system with a lot of use.

The only people for whom public works projects are profitable are the suppliers of materials and labor: bricks, asphalt, and concrete; dump trucks, heavy machinery, and their operators. The supply area is also where graft can grow, when building codes are violated to cut corners and inspections are made on paper only. New York's Mayor Giuliani suspended 42 elevator inspectors after an investigation found they had taken bribes to look the other way as safety work was not done. City potholes are another bonanza for crooks: suppliers and road crews cherish shortcuts on materials or techniques of road repair that will guarantee future work.

Despite inevitable human foibles, the failing infrastructure might be saved by technology. Satellites, computers, and electronics have come to the rescue in the nick of time.

Roads and Highways

Sixty percent of the more than 3.9 million miles of American public streets and highways need repairs, according to the U.S. Department of Transportation. According to the American Automobile Association (AAA), 80,000 miles are in "poor" condition and 160,000 miles are "mediocre." Six hundred and fifty-one thousand miles of highways were built by the Works Progress Administration (WPA) in the 1930s. The 44,000 miles that comprise the interstate highway system were begun in the 1950s.

Not all repair needs are as obvious as potholes or frost heaves. A lot of it is damage waiting to happen—subsurface holes, hairline cracks, excessive damp areas, and other trouble spots that have been hard to locate until a few years ago. Now with computer and satellite assistance, the orange Department of Transportation Automated Road Analyzer trucks—outfitted with lasers, cameras, and sensors coordinated with GPS (Global Positioning System) satellites—travel at normal speeds while they read and map the subtle features of a highway, identifying areas in need of repair.

Chapter 10: Deteriorating Infrastructure

The trouble is that federal funds are scarce. Noting that the government does not spend all it is expected to spend on roads and highways, the AAA recommended that all driver taxes be used for highway maintenance and a trust fund be set up for future care. Trapped in deficit reduction, the federal government looks to the private sector to help in projects like the Adopt-a-Highway program in which groups or individuals raise money to care for sections of a highway, which is posted with signs of the donor's name.

For city streets, a smooth infrastructure means regulated traffic that accommodates rush-hour office workers and downtown businesses. Most American city streets are laid out on a rectangular grid system, with the exception of Washington, D.C., which follows a radial grid, and the oldest parts of Boston and New York City, which are labyrinths of winding former cow and Native American paths. The in-and-out flow of commuter traffic weaves through the design of one-way streets and rotaries, timed traffic lights, and clear signage, all of which should contribute to an automated ballet. To avoid gridlock, like the famous one that paralyzed Boston in 1956, when cars were hopelessly checkmated (and people got out of their cars and made friends), transportation safety officials are working on an "intelligent highway." Embedded with electronics, roads would link up to in-car computers, giving the best possible route and taking into consideration reported accidents and the density of rush hour traffic.

Bridges

Of the 578,000 bridges over waterways, railroads, and highways in the United States, the Department of Transportation has classified 170,000 "structurally deficient" and 80,000 "functionally obsolete." Of the 25 worst bridges in the United States, 11 are in New York State.

Each year 120 bridges collapse. Not all collapses are as dramatic as the fall of the Silver Bridge over the Ohio River in 1967, which sent cars like toys into the river and killed 46 people. Bridges usually decay slowly and secretly. The Schoharie Bridge, for example, part of the New York State Thruway, had subtle problems from its inception in 1954—vertical cracks on its piers, surface joints out of line—but it always passed regular inspections because inspectors usually can't predict when a problem will topple a bridge. Slated for an overhaul in 1987, the bridge one day simply buckled and fell. The cause: the soil around its piers had washed away.

Doomsday Denied: A Survivor's Guide to the 21st Century

Suspension bridges are structurally complex and require huge amounts of maintenance in their spanning cables and wires, towers, and underwater supports, as well as in their paved roadway surface and steel-beam reinforcements. Bridges corrode and rust from weather and salty fogs and need to be painted often with special paint; they get dirty from steady vehicular traffic and need to be kept clean; and they must weather storms and violent winds. Ships ram into their piers, and trucks collide with road underpasses.

Because bridges are subject to lateral and vertical as well as oblique forces, they can develop problems in a lot of areas. To identify breaks in the reinforcing steel embedded in the concrete of a roadway, engineers traditionally have dragged a chain across the surface and listened for a telltale thudlike sound. But now a technique called *horizontal photogrammetry* can photograph and map a bridge's internal movements. With computer imaging programs, engineers can pinpoint real and potential trouble areas.

Bridges are not cheap. Maintenance funds usually come from gasoline taxes and traffic fines, as well as tolls. The Manhattan Bridge (one of the country's 25 worst), which spans the East River from New York City to Brooklyn, took seven years to build in 1909. Closed for repairs in 1982, the bridge is expected to take a total of 16 years to repair, at a cost of $452 million.

Water Supply

A hundred years ago typhoid and cholera, both water-borne diseases, plagued cities, and households were required to boil drinking water. Providing clean water for cities and suburbs is a primary concern for all metro areas. Allowing 100 to 200 gallons of water per day for each person, engineers design systems in which pumps draw water from treatment plants where it is filtered and purified, then sent through pipes buried beneath city streets into buildings and homes.

But the system is not perfect. New York City, which pipes 1,300 million gallons of water a day, has on average 550 water main breaks a year. Brittle steel, a fault inherent in the material of one of New York City's broken water mains, was not detectable until it broke in 1996. Simple age caused a 94-year-old, 48-inch cast-iron water pipe to give way. Officials noted that other water main breaks were caused by the pressure of the weight of the other pipes that are part of the underground infrastructure labyrinth: cable, telephone, gas and sewer lines, as well as old trolley tracks that had never been removed.

Lead from older pipes and bacteria that can collect inside faucets are a constant municipal problem. Water that comes from aquifers—layers in subsurface rock—can be tainted by seepage from garbage in landfills, by pesticides and herbicides in runoff from farms, or by sea water that seeps through coastal barriers.

Occasionally, deadly bacteria occur in surface and spring water sources and break through public filtration and chemical systems. Public health officials found that the cryptosporidium bacteria that infected so many people in Milwaukee, Wisconsin, in 1993 were not only resistant to chemical disinfectants, but so tiny they penetrated the filters. The source of the bacteria was thought to be feces from cattle near the Milwaukee water sources, but officials at the Centers for Disease Control (CDC) found that the bacteria were present at low levels in the tap water of most cities, including New York, Boston, and San Francisco. With that startling information, the CDC recommended increased vigilance of city water and the installation of finer water filters at water treatment plants.

Sewage

Like everything else, sewers are decaying. Sixty percent were built before 1950, and city officials hate to have trouble with them because repair usually means tearing up streets with pneumatic drills, interrupting business and traffic, and not always finding the source of trouble. But engineers now can identify where the breaks are by using nonintrusive ultrasound seismic resonance testing. A new technique called *trenchless technology* then allows them to replace sewer mains without digging wide holes. It's especially useful in historic districts where old houses always teeter on the verge of collapse. Called microtunneling, the computer-controlled technique uses laser and video aids to dig and destroy the old sewer mains and install new ones. In Boston's recent mammoth $7.9 billion urban renewal project, engineers were able to protect antique buildings and not interrupt the city's tourism industry by using microtunneling to install new sewer mains.

Biotechnologists are discovering that sewage can be reused if it's properly treated with appropriate bacteria in sewage treatment plants. Biosolids from septage treatment plants in Island County,

Washington, for example, are being used as fertilizers. Other experiments with oxidation and super blue algae are successfully rendering pure otherwise contaminated and hazardous wastewater.

Solid Waste

Each person produces an average of 4 pounds of solid waste a day. Most of that is household waste, most of which is paper goods—the package wrappings and junk mail of daily life. Add that to commercial and construction solid waste, and you come up with about a half a billion tons of stuff carted off to landfills and incinerators each day. Most of it is carried to packer transfer stations, compacted, and loaded onto trucks that carry it to dumps where it is burned or left to become compost.

Landfills are supposed to be lined to prevent contamination of groundwater. Hazardous waste dumps are supposed to be double-lined. Gas stations, dry cleaners, and hospitals must pay to get rid of toxic waste, but not all bother to do so. Used hyperdermic needles and other medical paraphernalia that turned up on beaches in the Northeast a few years ago were obviously dumped into the ocean—free of charge.

New York City is famous for having put its commercial solid waste (mostly paper) on a barge a few years ago and sent the barge out to several foreign ports, which rejected it. With 13,000 tons of garbage a day, New York's only remaining landfill, at Fresh Kills on Staten Island, which has made neighbors sick from its odors for years, is scheduled to be closed in 2001. The future of the city's garbage? Mayor Giuliani recently cut funding for expanding the recycling program, which could account for at least a third of the garbage, and is planning to ship it to private landfills in neighboring states, which have some reservations about being municipal dumping grounds.

In the United States there are an estimated 170,000 industrial dumps. One way to reduce landfills is *industrial ecology*, a new practice that seeks to recycle one company's waste into another company's product. For example, Eco-Industrial Park, outside of Baltimore, separates the waste from a petroleum-based industry into oil and water, which can be reused. Making the connections between producers and users, managers encourage companies to recycle. At MIT and other research centers, computer programs are being designed for city managers to better understand the various components of municipal waste management to find optimum solutions to the landfill problem.

Railroads and Airports

The rails that were laid in the first few decades of this century will not, despite the strength of the steel and the endurance of the builders, service the next century. The reason is not that they are all aging and unusable, but that they cannot accommodate the speed at which trains must go to compete with airplanes. Charging approximately the same fare to travel between New York and Washington, for example, trains take three times as long. For this reason and because most Americans prefer to travel by car, the average person travels only 49 miles by rail a year, compared to 7,800 miles in other vehicles, according to World Road Statistics.

Fast maglev (magnetic levitation) trains, such as those in use in Japan, travel about 300 miles per hour, but require special tracks, an expense that would take another century for the railroad to recoup. However, several maglev trains that use conventional tracks, such as Sandia National Labs' Seraphim that travels on wheels at about 180 miles per hour, are on the drawing board both here and abroad.

Air Travel

Passengers rushing to catch a flight call automobile traffic congestion the key airport problem in most cities. But federal safety officials worry about the aging conditions in airport control towers. Aircraft takeoff and landing are guided by often overworked air traffic controllers using binoculars and computers. The trouble is that the computer programs need to be updated to match the increased volume of traffic, but problems with funding caused delays that have put off modernization until 1999. In that year, controllers will have access to smart computer programs and ground radar that will greatly increase air safety and minimize or eliminate delays and accidents.

Some airlines have installed some state-of-the-art technologies, such as an inflight data recorder—the famous black box—which gives 150 readings eight times a second; a terrain guide, using radar altimeters, which warns a pilot if he is approaching a mountaintop; and an inflight program developed at the National Center for

Atmospheric Research, which alerts pilots of conditions for airplane wing icing. Travel experts predict a 50 percent increase in travel in the next decade, so safety is paramount as the aircraft fleet ages and must be overhauled.

Telecommunications

In 1993 the architects of the National Information Infrastructure, called the Information Superhighway, envisioned towns, schools, and individuals being able to access the best: 911 would be augmented by a program that would distinguish instantly among fire, medical, and police needs; students would interface with superstar teachers on line; people would quit their jobs and work at home, where banking, shopping, and library searches would be done on computer. Everyone would access the internet; most would have web sites to set up a global town meeting.

Ironing out the wrinkles in this infrastructure, however, challenges the brightest. Not everyone has access to a computer yet, although some thinktanks have suggested opening e-mail centers, like copy centers, where everyone could be online. Viruses and privacy invasions wreak havoc with users' checkbooks, credit cards, and ideas; not all career jobs can be done online; and a major disaster, such as an earthquake in Los Angeles, could wipe out critical global financial data.

Nevertheless, cable and fiber optics link up people as never before. But as users refine their telecommunications skills, most businesses and universities are grappling with what's been called the "millennium bug." It was introduced innocently into mainframe programs a quarter of a century ago, when programmers referred to dates by the final two digits only, in order to save disk space. This would be no problem in any year other that the turn of a new century. Now the two zeros of the year 2000 loom ominously, compromising everything from social security birthdates to bank records. To fix, businesses estimate it will cost the country in the hundreds of billions of dollars.

Cities

As the United Nations and the U.S. Housing and Urban Development agency call a conference to discuss the problems of the city in

Chapter 10: Deteriorating Infrastructure

the next millennium—predicting that 80 percent of the world's population will live, for better or worse, in cities by 2000—most urban areas, like New York, struggle to keep up with the abuse created by the residents they already have: used drug needles and crime in public parks, trash on sidewalks, etc.

But underfunded local governments are getting help throughout the country from neighborhoods that form urban grassroots coalitions to do simple beautification projects, such as planting and caring for flowers and trees. Since 1977 in the South Bronx borough of New York City, the Banana Kelly Project (named after a street) has rebuilt 2,500 homes rescued from the rubble of urban abuse. The neighborhood group turned tenement blocks into a tree-lined street with fresh rehabbed apartment buildings.

Urban Wildlife

Nesting in buildings, storm drains, sewers, wharves, dumps, and parks, and very much a part of the infrastructure, are several species of animals that have come to depend on human garbage: pigeons, seagulls, raccoons, possums, skunks, squirrels, feral dogs and cats, coyotes, and rats. In the West, bears raid dumpsters; in the East, Canada geese have given up migrating to settle year-round on the smooth green lawns of suburban industrial parks. Canada geese, once a favorite of birdwatchers, leave so much spoor some communities have begun trapping them as food for the homeless. And tapping their way across the country's utility poles are woodpeckers, drilling holes for nests and food storage caves that are so labyrinthine they occasionally topple the poles.

❓ What You Can Do

EPA publishes data on Home Water Testing and national primary drinking water standards. Call the Safe Drinking Water Hotline: (800) 426-4791.

Food and Water in an Emergency is a free pamphlet published by Federal Emergency Management Agency and available at your local American Red Cross center.

Habitat II is studying problems of city dwelling. For information contact Habitat II Clearinghouse, P.O. Box 9060,

Gaithersburg, MD 20898; (800) 248-8180; website: http://www.huduser.org/habitat.html.

Indoor Air Pollution in the Office is available from the American Lung Association: (800) 586-4872.

Sick Building Syndrome: call the EPA Indoor Air Quality Information Clearinghouse: (800) 438-4318.

Global Recycling Network is a key resource for recyclers; website: http://grn.com/grn/.

11 Population

Adam, Eve, and the Condom

POPULATION BEGINS HERE. God said, "Do not eat the apples." The snake said, "Try one." Eve said, "Adam, one bite, you'll love it." This detail of a painting by Lucas Cranach the Elder chronicles a Biblical event popular during the last millennium: The temptation in the Garden of Eden and the expulsion from Paradise.

They're everywhere—other people—filling up the train before you get a seat, forming endless lines at the ATM, at the airport check-in counter, in the post office. They get the best tickets, the last hotel rooms, and they get sick and go to the doctor the same time you do. Life in the '90s has become a competitive jungle.

Population is a delicate issue because it involves our religious, philosophical, political, and social beliefs, as well as our bodies. Who should prevent pregnancy and who should decide? Who decides which and how many immigrants are allowed into a country? Do we believe each person is partly divine or merely a worker in an economic system? Do we believe in child welfare payments and orphanages? And population reveals our naiveté: If there are "too many people" on the Earth, will we feel it personally? Is "overpopulation" just a sport of the third world and a blight in California?

The fact is, there are so many of us around—5.7 billion and growing—that population issues these days concentrate less on keeping the numbers down than on reconstructing the ways in which we use our resources. While we tend to think that population, or overpopulation, is somebody else's problem, look around the next time you wait in a supermarket line or sit in weekend traffic crawling to the beach: everyone you see is the product of the sexual union of two people. On average in the United States, everyone you see eats 3.3 pounds of food a day; drinks and washes with 200 gallons of water; produces 4.3 pounds of garbage and paper trash; uses 15 pounds of fossil fuel to generate electricity, power the car, and heat and cool the house; and contributes 115 pounds of greenhouse gases to the atmosphere. That's per person, per day. The principal greenhouse gas is carbon dioxide (CO_2), which is absorbed by trees, which are felled to produce, among other things, newspapers (75,000 per *The New York Sunday Times*) and junk mail (17 trees per person per year).

Then multiply this person by 265 million to get an idea of the size and the impact of the population of the United States. The third most populated country in the world (after China with 1.2 billion and India with 931 million, and before Indonesia at 201 million and Russia with 149 million), the United States consumes about 25 percent of the world's energy resources each year. For the 24 million barrels of petroleum used each day by all of the 24 Organization for Economic Cooperation and Development (OECD) countries, the United States alone consumes 20 barrels. The United States also takes the prize for the most waste, both industrial and garbage.

Using the economic indicator of inanimate energy as an example of consumerism, Joel Cohen, director of the Laboratory of Populations at Rockefeller University, says that in 1860 the average person used one megawatt hour a year, "enough to fuel a lawyer or a teacher." If you think of each megawatt hour as a full-time personal slave, Cohen continues, "by 1991 the average person on Earth used the energy equivalent of about 19 full-time slaves."

Where Is Everyone?

A researcher at the Consortium for International Earth Science Information Network (CIESIN), an environmental research group, figured out that if everyone on Earth were spaced equidistantly, each of us would be 500 feet away from our nearest neighbor. Unfortunately, it doesn't work that way. Our "primary habitat," says Stephen Olsen, director of the Coastal Resources Center at the University of Rhode Island, "is the coast." More than 30 percent of the world's population of 5.7 billion are crowded onto or clustered within 50 miles of the coasts. And the coasts can't take it. When septic systems fail (and they often do) from age, neglect, or coastal storms, sewage pollutes ground and drinking water and sends contaminates into the ocean. Bacteria multiply into toxic algae in seaweeds and create conditions for epidemics like cholera, which is transmitted to humans from shellfish.

But the coasts are trashed in other ways too: from pleasure crafts dumping oil, from oil tankers running aground, from overfishing the seemingly boundless seas so that wild salmon, for example, have all but disappeared in the West, and cod in the East. Olsen points out that many factors have come into play at the same time: decade changes, such as dense house-building; 100-year changes, such as the ballooning population; and the relatively unknown changes that come over millennia, such as the natural elements of global warming and rising sea temperature that bring changes in weather patterns.

People are not only coastal dwellers—some scientists say 50 percent of the population will live on 10 percent of the land by 2050, but perhaps as much as 80 percent of the population will live in cities. Three-quarters of the population of the United States currently live in metropolitan areas. In 1950 New York and London were the world's largest cities with between 10 and 12 million people. Demographers predict that by 2010, seven cities will have populations exceeding 10 million: Mexico City, Sao Paulo, Rio de Janeiro, Buenos Aires, Seoul, Shanghai, and Calcutta.

The great migration to cities has already begun. Cairo already has 6.6 million inhabitants. The principal reason people migrate to cities is to find work. In Africa, for example, small farmers are forced to move because their land has been confiscated by the government to grow cash crops for export, or because the soil, used year after year, can no longer support growth. But when people move into the cities, they carry their rural lifestyles with them: interspersed in the dense parts of third world cities where the new migrants live are small plots of crops growing, enough to feed the family. Here water is the vital problem: the rich can have bottled water flown in from Europe; the poor struggle with small amounts carried back from public wells. Disease grows in the water, often creating infant diarrhea, the biggest killer of children in Africa, who die because there isn't enough clean water to rehydrate them.

Carrying Capacity

The optimum balance between resources and inhabitants—as many acres, for example, of topsoil regenerated as are planted, to provide enough crops to feed the number of people living there—is called *carrying capacity*. Carrying capacity depends on a number of shifting factors: weather and natural disasters, cultural habits, political structure and corruption, wise management of resources, and the level of wealth of a country. Sociologists say that in a crisis people adapt, migrate, or die. The Netherlands, for example, a country veined with canals and rivers and dikes, has 1,031 people per square mile, which far exceeds its carrying capacity, but it's rich enough to afford to import most of its cereals and other foodstuffs, and it carefully manages its water resources.

Poor people, however, usually migrate (if they don't die first). When drought turned farmlands to dust in the American Midwest in the 1930s, for example—the result also of the soil not having been allowed to regenerate—many people packed up for California and a new life. Today, overpopulation and limited resources send Mexicans across the American border, legally and illegally. Around the world, political and environmental refugees, such as the hundreds of thousands of Rwandans who fled to Zaire, are expected to increase. The U.N. Population Fund has called migrations the potential "human crisis of our age."

Why We Mate

Honeymooners visiting scenic wonders "make love"; when demographers describe the activity that brings Adam to Eve, it's called

Chapter 11: Population

"breeding." T. R. Malthus, a British economist, published a treatise in 1798 in which he said that people will stop breeding when they run out of food, which they will do if they breed without restraint. The famines and wars that follow keep the population in check, he said. Neo-Malthusians argue that this premise still exists, although it has been modified by migrations and technological advances in farming.

Other theories are based on the idea that people breed when they perceive a need to be cared for in their old age or when they need hands in the fields; but they will stop breeding when economic prosperity is high. But Worldwatch president Lester R. Brown believes that population in the third world is high because too many people waste the resources. When the soil is finished, farmers go to the city to find work, which causes disruption in the extended family and creates insecurity, which in turn is the genesis for more children. Others believe that insecurity from the loss of the extended family diminishes the desire to have children.

Population experts Anne and Paul Ehrlich argue that the causes of population problems rest in the self-esteem of the woman: if she is literate and enjoys some equal rights, such as being part of the work force, and has healthy children, she will prefer a small family because she has other sources of status.

UNESCO researchers have revealed the sad plight of third world women. Two-thirds of the 800 million illiterate people in the world are women; 80 percent of refugees from wars and conflicts are women; 1 out of every 4 women die in pregnancy. The children from these disrupted unions have it worse: 100 million live in the streets around the world; 150 million are child laborers; more than one-third of all children under the age of 5 suffer from malnutrition.

Contraceptives

Population physicians Malcolm Potts and Martha Campbell of University of California–Berkeley, report that "there is a worldwide demand for smaller families." In situations where people had access to a variety of contraceptive choices, they used them, the researchers found. Globally, people are having smaller families, according to the U.N. Population Fund, due to greater understanding of contraception and better health care. But foreign aid for family planning from the United States still amounts to a very small $1 million.

In the United States, raising a child from birth to 17 costs a low-income family $171,000; a middle income family, $231,000; and a high income family, $335,000. College is extra. For this reason, many people elect not to have children or to postpone having them until they have made some money. If abortion were not such a legal and political issue in this country, pharmaceutical companies long ago would have devised and marketed a swift, safe, and unobtrusive contraceptive. At mid-decade, the preferred contraceptive is the male condom, especially among those under 35. The FDA quietly placed the birth control pill on the Federal Register, authorizing its use as a morning-after pill; and RU-486, a physician-administered abortion pill, was approved after almost two years of debate.

On the drawing board and scheduled for the next century are injectable hormones and vaccines for men that will last from three months to a year. Genetic engineers are perfecting a way to hold back temporarily the genes that make sperm. For women, there will be biodegradable hormone implants that will last for up to five years and spermicides that also kill vaginal diseases.

The History

Women have long been controlling their pregnancies, both secretly and openly, with herbs, salves, contraptions, and magic rituals. In some cultures people threw babies over cliffs, controlling not only the population but the sex preference of the population (girls usually were the first to go). Recently, China limited the number of children its population could reproduce to one per family, with benefits to those who did, and approved eugenics on mentally or physically handicapped babies, or so-called inferior births.

On the other end of the scale, anti-abortion activists, composed of Catholics and fundamental Christians, Jews, and Muslims, have such a powerful political effect that candidates for public office—Republicans and Democrats alike—tread delicately on abortion issues. Some radical antiabortionists in the United States have killed workers at abortion clinics to register their opposition to the taking of a fetal life, which is legal.

Historically, failure to control populations has had dire consequences. The Mayans in Central America, for example, grew for 17 centuries, spread out over an area from Mexico to South America,

Chapter 11: Population

used and reused farmlands, wells, and coastal resources until one day in the ninth century their population maxed out and their society collapsed. Extensive droughts sent many migrating elsewhere; epidemics killed all but a few. The Mayans doubled their population every 408 years, archaeologists report. The United States in this century has doubled its population in 40 years.

About 100 years ago, the measure of a successful man was a big wife, a big house, and a big family. In the entire United States there were 76 million people, most of them between the ages of 20 and 44 (the majority were between 30 and 39 in 1994). There were 709,000 marriages and 56,000 divorces in 1900 (compared with 2.3 million marriages and 1.1 million divorces in 1993). Average life expectancy was 47 years (75.8 in 1994); but men outlived women: after the age of 45, there were 110.7 men to every 100 women (6.2 million more females over 65 in 1994). In 1907, 1.2 million immigrants came to live. (In 1994, 804,416 legal immigrants were admitted, with a suspected 3 million illegal aliens in residence.) Germans and Irish predominated minorities in 1900 (in 1994 the dominant minorities were African Americans, 12 percent; Hispanics, 10.5 percent; and Asians, 3 percent). Before automobiles, about 2,000 people died of accidents. (About 40,000 were killed in motor vehicle accidents in 1994). Many women died in childbirth; most people died of heart disease or pneumonia, influenza, or tuberculosis, against which there were no antibiotics. In 1995 heart disease, cancer, and stroke were the biggest killers, but public sanitation, vaccines, anesthetics that allow surgery, and technological advances, like heart pacemakers, kept people alive longer.

In the early 1900s Americans vacationed in national parks or traveled to more exotic places without leaving a trace. In 1995, 269 million tourists visited national parks; Yellowstone National Park has 2,300 hotel rooms and 1,864 campsites. Mount Everest still draws fewer than 100 climbers a year, but it's called the "world's highest trash pit" because visitors leave behind such refuse as used toilet paper. Population is not a problem until local resources can no longer sustain visitors. Underfunded ecotourism projects that try to preserve a natural wonder while encouraging tourist dollars are sinking some funds into making videorecords for inclusion later in virtual reality programs, when people can travel without leaving home.

Are We Doomed?

Once upon a time demographers believed that rising numbers coupled with global warming spelled the end of life as we know it. Famines, wars, and epidemics would result from lack of food. Some of those things will happen in some places.

But now researchers and policy makers identify consumerism as an evil force in population problems: remember, carrying capacity works when there is enough to go around.

Coastal resource manager Stephen Olsen witnesses coastal degradation around the world. "The 'me-first' syndrome of consumer-based values and behavior cannot be sustained," he says. Some demographers see change as being market-driven: scarcity will force prices up, which will inspire technological invention. Others see local solutions coming out of the local population. Farming the wet banks of Lake Chad, for example, during the dry season could produce enough food to feed a substantial portion of Nigeria if a transportation network could be arranged. Olsen says the problems don't lack excellent researchers and ideas; there are simply not enough connections being made between researchers and policy makers to make a difference.

In this country and around the world, small technological changes can have profound effects: recycling industrial waste, using refined sewage for fertilizer; installing solar and wind energy, sending soil experts to analyze farmland rather than sending tractors to farm more acres.

Future Shock

Population will not diminish in the near future. Low- and high-end predictions of the U.N. Population Fund range from 7.8 and 12.5 billion people in the world in 2050. The U.S. Census Bureau sees 394 million people in the United States in 2050. It doesn't take a rocket scientist to see we will have to change.

Globally, the 1994 U.N. Conference on Population and Development in Cairo identified several simple areas that would raise the standard of living and refine family size in developing countries: primary education for all, especially women in the workforce, access to contraceptives and family planning, healthcare for children especially. Population expert Joel Cohen adds developing economies to this list. In what he calls "Human Caring Capacity," he asks how people can go hungry when food is cheap. The "bottom billion"

Chapter 11: Population

make less than US$1 a day. "They have no money to buy food, so they cannot drive up its price," he says. "The extremely poor are economically invisible."

In the developed world, natural constraints and human choices, says Cohen, will determine the Earth's capacity to support us all, but for the next 50 years, expect to make "difficult trade-offs," he says, "among population size and economic well-being and environmental quality and dearly held values." These will manifest themselves in choosing cotton over polyester, bean sprouts over beef, and parks over parking lots, Cohen adds.

Population these days is a matter of abused resources and poverty. Solutions lie in finding the quality hidden in the quantity; to make better use of human resources and anything that raises the level of dignity, including resolving environmental problems; to give children a shot at growing up into decent adults.

What You Can Do

CEISIN has a variety of population information. 2250 Pierce Road, University Center, MI 48710; (517) 797-2700. For a map of world population: website: http://www.ciesin.org/datasets/gpw/globldem.doc.html. CEISIN's home page is: http://www.ciesin.org.

The City Summit is a project of the United Nations, HUD, and the Agency for International Development (AID) to study and design solutions for cities. The City Summit: Habitat II Clearinghouse, P.O. Box 9060, Gaithersburg, MD 20898; (800) 248-8180. website: http://www.huduser.org/habitat.html.

A number of population groups study aspects of population. The Population Council, One Dag Hammarskjold Plaza, New York, NY 10017; (212) 755-6052. Carrying Capacity Network: (800) 466-4866. Population Reference Bureau: (202) 483-1100. Population Action International: (202) 659-1833. Population Institute: (202) 544-3300.

For a sense of the effects of changing populations on global management and resources, request a catalog of software, maps, and games from World Game Institute, 3215 Race Street, Philadelphia, PA 19104-2597; (215) 387-0220; e-mail: wgame@libertynet.org.; website: http://www.worldgame.org/~wgi.

12 Cloning

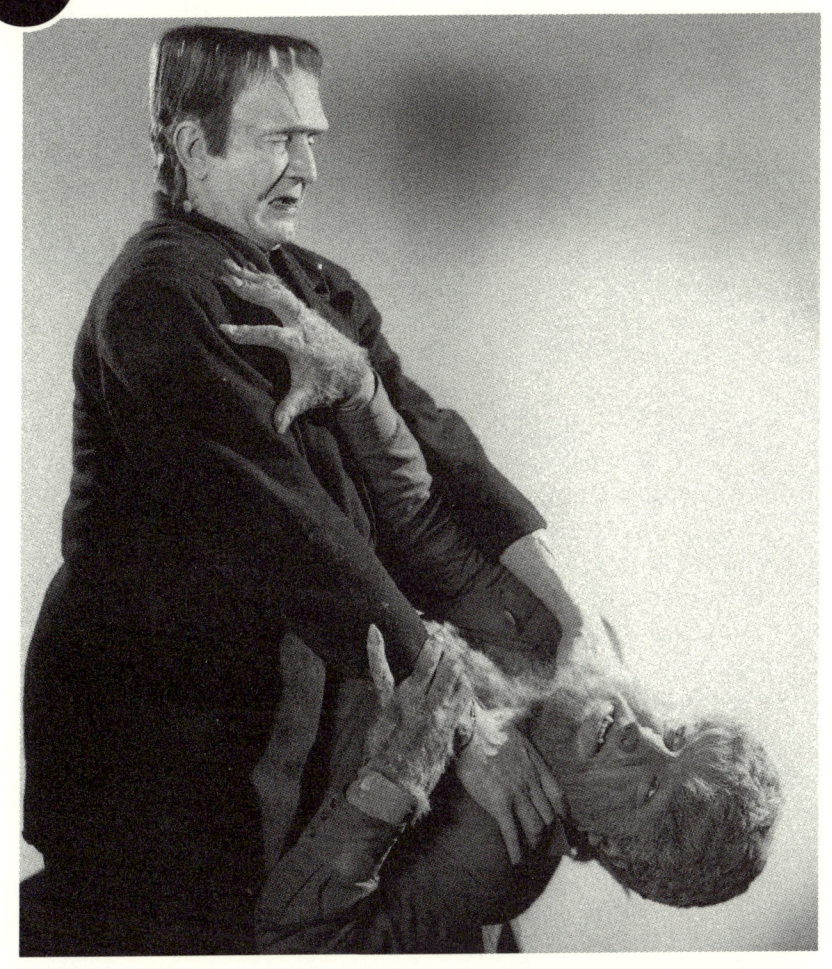

Downloading the Monster

GETTING IT RIGHT IS HARD. The fellow on the left is composed of parts from fresh corpses, animated by a jolt of electricity. His opponent on the right has a genetic fault that brings out the animal in him on moonlit nights. Bela Lugosi and Lon Chaney, Jr. face off in the 1942 movie "Frankenstein Meets the Wolfman." Photo credit: Movie Still Archives.

When biotechnologists talk about cloning an extra person at birth to keep as a backup for replacment organs as they are needed throughout the life of an individual, the problem arises of what to do with the second you. Should you keep it around for a conversational twin, or should you pack it away in a closet so you don't get too attached? Could it be useful to do the things you dislike doing, or would it have a mind of its own, distinct from yours, and be able to create a different lifestyle? What if it "got it right," and you never did?

Body doubles are not an option yet, but mice with human ears and herds of identical sheep are. Being able to decipher genetic blueprints coupled with fast computers has put us into the buffer zone of the weird. Rumors abound: drops of blood found in a mosquito's gut immortalized in a drop of Jurassic amber might provide the critical ingredient for re-creating a dinosaur. Tucked away in secret labs ruled by ruthless technicians, are there mice with the tails of foxes and wings of eagles? Cockroaches the size of rottweilers? Centaurs?

Genetic manipulation and science fiction go hand in hand. For example, scientists talk of creating organic nanocomputer implants that will give automatic access to an infinite number of databases and skills to make us not only informed but smart. When the right combination of genes is identified, geneticists should be able to manipulate those that give the body the signals to age, giving, if not immortality, then eternal youth.

But the possible—what is now being done—is almost as strange. The human ear on the mouse, for example, was generated in a biodegradable polymer scaffolding seeded with cartilage cells implanted under the skin of the mouse. Contour mapped on a computer by University of Massachusetts anaesthesiologist Charles Vacanti, the ear grew, regenerating the tissue as the genes dictated, nourished by the mouse. It's not intended to turn mice into freaks; it proved that genetic tissue engineering can regrow noses and ears, and soon hands and arms.

Cartilage for joints already is being grown outside the body, as is polymer skin to be used in grafting. Severed hands, fingers, arms, and legs can be reimplanted. Cloned herds of identical farm animals have been developed, and scientists look forward to genetically created "magic bullets" that will zap cancer, and greatly improved diagnostics, such as bedside blood tests.

Organs, however, are a problem. Surgeons are confident of their technical knowledge, but they lack a steady supply. Organs to be transplanted from the brain-dead must be put on ice within minutes to be transplantable, and the list of those waiting for donors is long. Rumors suggest there is a black market, and that some unknowing drunks in public parks and the sleeping homeless in third world coun-

Chapter 12: Cloning

tries awaken to find a kidney has been stolen. Recently, doctors in India, discovered to be selling organs for $30,000 for which they paid $1,000 from secret sources, were arrested.

Xenotransplants, organs from other species, such as the baboon bone marrow transplant in an AIDS patient in San Francisco, are often rejected by the recipient's body. However, genetic engineering, using sophisticated polymers, will allow organs to be grown in the lab. Until then, transgenic pigs are being bred with human protein specifically for the purpose of using their hearts and kidneys, close in size and function to humans'.

Genetic Engineering

Recombinant DNA, or genetic engineering, was first successfully completed in 1973 by Stanley Cohen of Stanford University and Herbert Boyer of the University of California San Francisco, when they spliced DNA (deoxyribonucleic acid) from a bacterium with a gene from a toad. Each of the two strands of DNA carries 23 chronomsomes that determine the genotype (the genetic makeup, what doesn't always show) and the phenotype (the physical manifestation, hair color, etc.) of an individual. Some chromosomes, or genes, are damaged. They can be inherited in a damaged state and skip one or two generations before becoming a problem, or they can be the product of a mutation in the individual. Diseases, some of which do not manifest themselves until later adulthood, lie latent in the gene. Recently, geneticists identified such behaviors as alcoholism and homosexuality with specific genes. Because behaviors involve a lot of cultural and psychological influence, these claims have been questioned, most recently by philosophy professor Philip Kitcher, in his book *The Lives to Come*, who calls such claims "genetalk."

Gene Therapy

Gene therapy—replacing a patient's defective genes with normal ones—has not been the bonanza cure it was originally thought to be. For one thing, it's expensive because it is disease- and person-specific. There's the danger that DNA segments, cut and replaced, can bond in the wrong place and create other problems. And new genes require corrected protein and chemical balances, which are a challenge.

Beyond this, there are ethical considerations: somatic cell genetic engineering simply inserts foreign genes into damaged cells to correct the defect. But manipulating so-called stem cells by inserting foreign genes into the genes that make sperm or eggs borders on playing God because it can create whatever you want, and that will continue to be passed on for generations to come.

A famous somatic gene therapy experiment was done apparently successfully in 1990. W. French Anderson, professor of biochemistry and director of the Gene Therapy Labs at the University of Southern California in Los Angeles, extracted white blood cells from the defective immune system of a 4-year-old girl who had inherited the damaged genes from both parents. Her inoperative T-cells rendered her unable to fight disease. Anderson made normal copies of the defective gene, returned the corrected cells to her body, and after four infusions over four months he cured her. He says that she went from being a child who was always sick to a vibrant 9 year old "who does everything."

The Big Gene Database

The Human Genome Project, a 15-year, $3 billion federally funded project, was begun in 1990 to analyze human genetic heritage. With the help of fast computers, the project, designed to map the hundreds of thousands of sites on the DNA strings, will be ready in 2003. This means that researchers will know, within a decent probability, where genes are that control specific traits, what each gene carries, and what it doesn't. Then everyone in the world, from a drop of blood or even from the remnants of saliva on a licked envelope, can have a DNA analysis to know what potential weaknesses and diseases will be a problem, which ones are more likely than others to manifest themselves, or if one is musically gifted or has a propensity for mothering.

Privacy

A personal databank, however, could be a Pandora's Box.

It's one thing to have your bank statements on the internet; it's quite another to have all the secrets of your body available to anyone who might be curious about you. Knowing that you will develop, say, Alzheimer's after the age of 45, for example, can be of interest to your insurance company who could deny you long-term medical coverage or hit you with a whopping premium because of a "pre-existing condition." It could also turn away a job with a company that did not want to provide extended medical coverage or lose a worker at a critical career point.

Several observers strongly recommend legal protection before so much genomic knowledge is amassed. Currently, seven bills in Congress deal with genetic privacy. One of the bills, sponsored by Representative Jim McDermott, would give a patient the right to forbid access to all private medical and genomic data without the patient's consent. Political activist Jeremy Rifkin of the Foundation for Economic Trends called for support of several privacy bills currently in Congress, emphasizing the importance of limiting access to one's gene records by anyone in commerce, research, or medicine.

Until then, the curious can be tested anonymously or under an assumed name. But do we need to know? Doctors warn that knowing, for example, that you have a 90 percent chance of developing some debilitating disease can create depression and certainly cause you to reconfigure your future plans. The hopeful thing is that gene therapy rides concurrent with developments to cure diseases for which there are no present cures.

Gene Patents

Approved by the Supreme Court in 1980 that companies have a right "to patent novel forms of life" created outside the body, gene patents, freely issued by the Patent and Trademark Office—1,500, 500 of which are human genes in 1995—usually take formerly hospital- or university-associated researchers into their own very profitable, soon-to-go-public genetic engineering companies. Several people oppose gene patents on the grounds that, as former breast-cancer patient Bella Abzug has said, "Human genes are not for sale or profit." For the past several years, Jeremy Rifkin has opposed gene patents, petitioning the Patent Office to forbid patenting of genes.

Eugenics

Aside from the fact that your genes can be profitable for your doctor, there are dark sides to genetic manipulation, what *The New York Times* science writer Nicholas Wade has called "biology's demiurge powers."

Genetic mutations are bound neither by species nor by time: recent lab experiments, for example, created a mouse with a backbone from an evolutionary time slot 200 to 300 million years ago. DNA from bacteria can be spliced with just about any other species' DNA to produce a new entity. Rapidly breeding fruit flies have been designed with eyes on their wings and legs on their heads.

If freaks can be produced genetically, so can the perfect. Tests done routinely on fetuses of pregnant women can reveal not only the sex but any potential birth defects. If the parents decide they do not want a damaged child, the fetus can be aborted. There is a thin line between this and eugenics, the word that resounded in Nazi Germany in medical experiments to create a "master race." In the film *The Boys from Brazil*, former Nazis track down young cloned Hitlers grown from his cells at the end of World War II. Selecting for particular eye, hair, and skin color, and other genetically determined characteristics is right around the corner.

Eugenics was suggested in 1883 by mathematician Francis Galton in a treatise, *Enquiring into Human Faculty*, in which he recommended "judicious matings" to promote what he called "the science of improving stock." Even in this country, as Jay Varmus has pointed out in an article in the *Journal of the American Medical Association*, the notion of eugenics lurks latently in the shadows. The Immigration Restriction Act of 1924, Varmus reminds us, sought to impose quotas on immigrants from countries perceived as "inferior."

The Good Genes

On the bright side, genetic engineering is improving life by creating vaccines and eliminating disease. Mosquitoes are being bred to be malaria-resistant. Special oil-eating microbes help clean up oil spills. Plant seeds can be designed to be drought-resistant and to yield bigger crops faster. Since the 1970s, one company, Monsanto, has sunk $2 billion into genetic engineering experiments to come up with genes for an insect-resistant cotton, to reduce the use of pesticides, and is working on a strain of corn that will repel weeds. Researchers are experimenting with the genes of metal-absorbing plants, called *hyperaccumulators*, to mix them with faster-growing plants and other absorbers to produce a plant that will soak up several metals, such as nickel and zinc together, fast, at polluted sites.

And DNA sequencing can also go backwards to our original mitochondrial mother. Using computers, DNA detectives, working for archaeologists, can track the origin of, for example, Native Americans, from a single strand of DNA, and identify at which points they mutated, giving a suggested date for their migrations across the Bering Strait.

And DNA can be used as an identification tool in criminal cases (the O.J. Simpson Trial for example), to reconstruct forensically from blood and semen the presence of the killer, not only contemporaneously but in the past.

A Future Like No Other

We can preserve our DNA to be recreated in the future. Or, if the world doesn't need another exact copy, we can preserve our sperm and eggs for reproduction in the future. We can have our whole bodies frozen cryogenically to be revived and cured in a better time. And sperm cells can be frozen and grown later in another species.

Real dangers abound, of course: experimental viruses can simply escape and if they are airborne, cause a global catastrophe. And some evil geneticists can design smart and lethal viruses to attack genes specific to a whole race. As in science fiction movies, something very large and without a reproductive control could seep through the laboratory walls and create havoc in a community.

In an article in *The Futurist*, Gene Stephens of the College of Criminal Justice at the University of South Carolina worries about law enforcement in a society with a large number of clones and laboratory humans. "Is it murder—or just lunch?" he asks, if a human, genetically altered with bird genes, eats a small green man with gills. "Will the protections of the U.S. Bill of Rights and the U.N. Declaration of Human Rights be granted to semi-humans?" he wonders. But if criminals could be outfitted with nanocomputers containing bank statements, they could, if caught, also be implanted with microchips giving constant messages that they must avoid criminal behavior.

Will cloning be commonplace in the next few years? Is it already? Cyborgs, humans outfitted with bionics, are already among us, some with microchip-aided vision. Isaac Asimov's imagined ideal robot looked and acted like a human. "Father of robotics" Joseph F.

Engelberger, speculates that robots in the twenty-first century will not only act as companions for the elderly, but they will shop, cook, clean, and go to Mars. Outfitted with voice synthesizers and recognition, they will be programmed to receive Global Positioning System signals and will never get lost. Designed by animatronics experts, perhaps your personal robot could be programmed to dance like Fred Astaire or Ginger Rogers to keep your clone occupied while it waits to outfit you with a new spleen.

What You Can Do

To preserve your DNA for $55, rub your finger on a piece of gauze, send it off with your check, and this company will send it back preserved in a glass capsule: Immortal Genes, Third Millennium Research, Inc., 5739 33rd Avenue NE, Seattle, WA 98105.

13 Plutonium

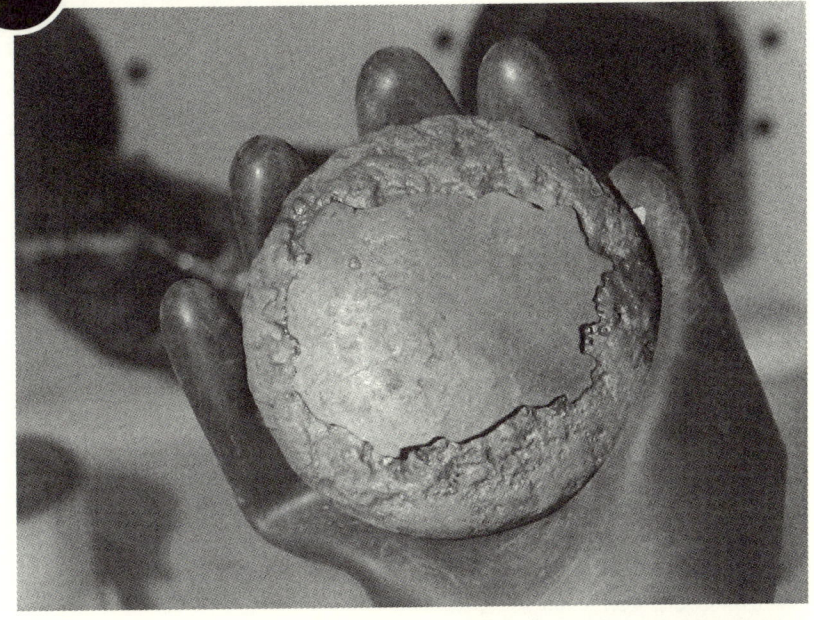

A Clear and Present Nightmare

DO NOT TOUCH THIS. A palm-sized plutonium "button" looks a little like dull gold and is very heavy. Several of these create a plutonium "pit" used in nuclear energy and weapons. It is highly radioactive; its dust can be inhaled; and it can cause vomiting, disorientation, and, over time, cancer. Photo credit: U.S. Department of Energy.

Nuclear reactor tanks look like swimming pools except for their blue glow. It's not a Hollywood swimming pool–emerald blue glow; it's closer to the ethereal, alien, mysterious blue that cartoonists give to crystal balls when fortune tellers see something in them. Nuclear reactor pools are in fact deadly lagoons: The water is blue because it is highly radioactive. Energy is generated by the interaction of thousands of neutrons of uranium atoms that create enough heat to power generators strong enough to light up whole cities. What's left are bits and pieces of chemical power quickly transforming themselves into radioactive elements. Nuclear reactor pools are the birthplace of plutonium.

Conceived for a war by warriors and scientists, plutonium was appropriately named after the god of the underworld. Packed into a bomb on August 9, 1945, and named "Fat Man" by scientists gone loopy with their isolated task of creating a weapon of mass destruction, plutonium triggered an explosion over Nagasaki that killed tens of thousands of people instantly, leaving as many to die shortly from radiation sickness. Those removed from the target zone later suffered rare forms of cancer. Many were permanently blinded, and their babies were born malformed or without limbs or organs.

Its companion bomb, "Li'l Boy," was a uranium bomb dropped three days earlier on Hiroshima. Both bombs sent up mushroom clouds that billowed like dandelion crowns above thousands of square kilometers of devastated waste.

Japan surrendered to the United States, and World War II ended. But when governments realized the terrible power and the range of misery of nuclear bombs that could spread radioactive dust around the world forever and could cause genetic mutations in future generations, arms limitations treaties became paramount. During the Cold War from the 1950s to 1990, the Soviet Union and the United States agreed to use nuclear weapons as deterrents and to limit their use, but weapons of mass destruction were nevertheless built, tested, and stockpiled—just in case.

In 1991, when the Soviet Union devolved into non–Communist Russian states, the so-called Super Powers agreed in two arms reduction treaties—START I and II—to dismantle their nuclear weapons, ending the threat of global destruction. But it was like letting the lions out of their cages, having forgotten why they were in the cages in the first place.

Leaky Storage

In 1992 Russia agreed to let the United States buy most of its plutonium, but weapons in the former Soviet Union are scattered among its states, not all of which want to give up their power. But that was only one problem. Suddenly faced with enough radioactive hotcakes to fill all of Utah and most of Nevada, the plutonium clean-up crew discovered that weapons plants in the United States, the likely repositories for plutonium, were suffering from two or three decades of neglect, abuse, and careless handling of toxic waste.

Black Market

The second problem was that plutonium slipped into the criminal world and became a big item on the global black market. Police in East Europe have confiscated plutonium hidden in metal coffee cans in apartments and tucked under seats in parked cars. Other elements of nuclear reactors have turned up in this country: in 1995 three men were arrested in New York City trying to sell 3 tons of zirconium that they had smuggled in from Russia and stored in a warehouse in Queens. In 1993 startled inspectors from the Department of Energy discovered an Idaho man building nuclear reprocessing equipment from a manual in his garage out of parts bought for $150,000. He hoped to render uranium from spent fuel rods into weapons-grade plutonium to sell.

In 1994 airport security personnel found 60 grams of weapons-grade plutonium in a suitcase in Munich. It was flown in on a Lufthansa flight from Moscow, as part of a secret deal to sell stolen plutonium to global arms dealers, in this case, a company in Bulgaria. The suspected buyer was Iran; the suspected seller was Russia. The price was $2.1 million.

Plutonium has always been a hot-ticket item. Since 1946 defense experts figure the United States and the former Soviet Union have spent $5 trillion keeping themselves defended. Just storing the surplus plutonium, the Department of Energy expects to spend between $500 million and $1 billion a year.

Designer Bombs

Officially, six countries have nuclear weapons: the United States, the Russian states, Great Britain, France, China, and India. Unofficially, Israel, South Africa, and Pakistan also have The Bomb, and enough suspicion exists to believe North and South Korea, Taiwan, Brazil, Argentina, Iraq, Iran, and Libya are building bombs. But loose highly enriched uranium and plutonium, out-of-work scientists, and spare parts can be bought by any individual, rogue nation, terrorist organization, or small country with a gripe against its neighbor. What they can't afford, they can steal. Experts estimate it would take 10 years to build a nuclear bomb, and one year to build a small one. Minimum personnel include a nuclear scientist, a mathematician, a chemist, a mechanical engineer, and an explosives expert.

Doomsday Denied: A Survivor's Guide to the 21st Century

The Nightmare

Everyone who has anything to do with plutonium uses the word nightmare. John H. Nuckolls of the Lawrence Livermore Nuclear Laboratory sees four nightmare scenarios: Cold War II; escalation of a conventional war into a nuclear war; instability from "proliferating epidemics" of nuclear weapons; and nuclear terrorism. Seeing "instabilities managed by fallible human beings," Nuckolls sites a desperate need for increased intelligence and security technology, including a device that would cause a nuclear weapon to self-destruct if stolen, to avert disasters caused by "power-hungry, irrational, or even truly 'mad' leaders—unpredictable and undeterrable."

Not a Toy

One pound of plutonium equals 7,500 tons of TNT. The bomb that decimated Nagasaki used three pounds of plutonium to get a blast equal to 22,000 tons of TNT; but modern-day nuclear designers claim they can achieve a similar blast in warheads with 2.2 pounds (1 kilogram) of plutonium. Invented by Glenn Seaborg and three other physicists in 1940 by bombarding uranium-238 with a hydrogen isotope, plutonium melts at 640°C (1,184°F) and boils at 3,460°C (6,250°F). It produces a fission bomb, which means that when plutonium-239 is hit by neutrons, the atoms split in two and produce more neutrons, and these hit others that cause a chain reaction, which, with an infusion of highly enriched uranium, produces a blinding flash of light and the telltale mushroom cloud.

A palm-sized buttom of plutonium metal held in a gloved hand is golden in color and heavier than lead. Plutonium isotopes can float around in dust and enter the body through a cut or in a breath of air. They are insoluble, invisible, and odorless. In the body, they seek bone marrow or the soft tissue of the prostate, lymph glands, breasts, and the throat where they cause chemical changes in the cells that lead to cancer. In the lungs, the isotopes settle forever. An army colonel who flew a helicopter over the fire in the Chernobyl nuclear reactor in 1986 said he believed he saved himself by smoking cigarettes. The radioactive isotopes, he said, "got absorbed in smoke particles and were exhaled along with them. I always had a cigarette in my mouth, believing that nicotine would be less dangerous than radioactive isotopes."

Chapter 13: Plutonium

Plutonium has a half-life of 24,000 years, which means that half of an amount decays in 24,000 years, and one-half of the remaining amount decays in 24,000 years, and so on. Extreme sudden exposure after an explosion causes internal bleeding and death; milder exposure causes hair loss, vomiting, and severe headaches. Nikolai Gorbachenko, a radiation monitor at the Chernobyl station the early morning of its explosion, found a co-worker lying unconscious in radioactive water in the dark steamy pool room. He had "bloody foam coming out of his mouth making bubbling sounds. We picked him up and carried him down. At the spot on my back where his right hand rested, I received a radiation burn." A couple of hours later, Gorbachencko went to the hospital with radiation sickness, where the doctor gave him 500 grams of pure alcohol. Feeling a lot better, he went home, but the deaths of his co-workers in the days that followed left him anxious. "You go to sleep at night not knowing whether you will wake up in the morning."

"We will have to learn to live with nuclear weapons," the Harvard Nuclear Study Group concluded in 1995. Rough Defense Department estimates indicate that 52,000 nuclear warheads containing more than 270 metric tons of plutonium are stashed around the world. Some of it is stored in the stockpile of on-hand weapons; some of it is in temporary storage, waiting to be buried or dumped; some of it is simply unaccounted for.

But plutonium is born every time uranium atoms create energy in each of the 450 or so nuclear power plants around the world. A nuclear reactor pool has vertical fuel rods hanging over it. One-half are uranium-238, which is a natural element; the other half are control rods with boron or cadmium that absorb the U-238 neutrons and keep them from becoming fissionable. To manufacture power, the control rods are slowly removed, increasing the number of fissionable neutrons in the pool. The result: the energy of the moving neutrons heats the water into steam that drives the turbines that produces electricity. It takes a few days for plutonium to appear: The neutrons hitting U-238 cause it to turn into U-239, which decays into radioactive neptunium-239, which decays into plutonium-239.

In 1993 global supplies of highly enriched uranium from spent fuel rods (which can be converted into weapons-grade plutonium, or Pu-239) were thought to be 1,700 metric tons. Two-thirds of the 1,100 metric tons of Pu-239 were from civilian storage. (A metric ton is 2,205 pounds, enough to make 125 to 1,000 warheads.) Some figures estimate that another 400 metric tons of potential weapons-grade plutonium from spent fuel will exist in 2010, enough to make 100,000 nuclear weapons.

Spent fuel rods are everywhere, but to make Pu-239 from them, they have to undergo a special process in a reprocessing plant. How can this be policed? The international Nuclear Nonproliferation Treaty, renewed in 1995, seeks to control weapons manufacture and to ensure safeguards of nuclear materials through monitors provided by the International Atomic Energy Agency. But without one world authority to oversee superpowers and "little guys" alike, "enforcement is largely a do-it-yourself proposition," says Konrad Kressley, political scientist at the University of South Alabama. Hidden facilities visible from satellites, such as those suggested in North Korea and Iraq, are not always easy to inspect in person, he adds.

What Do We Do with It?

Safe Temporary Storage

The nightmare here is that most nuclear weapons manufacturing plants—those in guarded military bases where plutonium would be safe from thieves—were closed in the 1980s because they were considered to be "dilapidated and hazardous," according to a U.S. Department of Energy (DOE) report. Plutonium had been stored as powder, liquid, and solid in plastic bags, metal canisters, and glass bottles, many ruptured or unsealed, or simply broken. Plutonium had seeped into air filters and collected in pipes, and had polluted groundwater and soil. Rocky Flats, a few miles north of Denver, was raided by the FBI in 1989 for storing plutonium in the open and for spraying wastewater into the air. The Hanford facility in Washington state dumped waste into the Columbia River. The Pantex plant in Texas, the major site of the weapons dismantling, is an EPA superfund site.

Nuclear energy has occupied people for a half century, slipping from its sparkling original vision of cheap power for the world into the muddy toxic hell of the Chernobyl explosion caused by design faults, mechanical failure, and personnel errors. The reason for the storage mess at weapons plants, according to the DOE, is that scientists who created nuclear weapons quickly to end a bloody war in the 1940s left storage and disposal problems of radioactive waste for

Chapter 13: Plutonium

personnel who were neither educated nor funded to deal with something so lethal and long-lasting.

Now enter several tons from dismantled warheads, and the nightmare won't go away. "Nobody has any good overall solution to this mess, including us," said Arjun Makhijani, president of the Institute for Energy and Environmental Research in Takoma Park, Maryland.

Some Storage Ideas

Bury It—Currently the DOE is planning to bury plutonium in metal cases in the concrete galleries of Yucca Mountain in Nevada, which is a volcanic ash mound. Congress has approved the site over the objections of some scientists who claim that any water leakage—from an underground aquifer, or rain breaking through the ash—could trigger an explosion or leakage of the plutonium into the water systems. Plutonium is highly volatile and will explode if kept in anything other than tiny amounts. Water and any kind of earth movement could trigger its unique chain reaction, causing an explosion that would release dense radioactivity into the air.

One state over in southern New Mexico is the Waste Isolation Pilot Plant, an underground storage unit 2,150 feet down. Built five years ago, it has never been used because the state of New Mexico objected to the risk of the presence of plutonium. But nearby, the Mescalero Apache Indian Reservation, home to a prosperous casino and luxury hunting resort, has agreed to accept temporary storage in the form of glass logs.

Bury It as Glass Logs—Storage in vitrified logs—plutonium blended into molten shiny black borosilicate glass—would be relatively safe for several decades. The cost, $100 million for 100 metric tons, is considered to be reasonable. At the Defense Waste Processing Facility at the Savannah River Weapons Plant in Georgia, sludge from reactor pools is mixed with molten glass into 10-foot cylinders, which, when they cool, are put into stainless steel canisters then jolted with electricity to seal. The canisters will be stored several hundred meters underground. The only problem is time: workers believe it will take 25 years to seal 36 million gallons of sludge.

Burn It for Electricity—Another proposal is to convert plutonium to mixed oxide and sell it as a fuel for utilities. This idea is popular, what Nobel physicist Carlo Rubbia has described as "transforming a liability into an asset." The problem is that the special plant designed to burn plutonium would consume only 12 tons in 40 years—cheap electricity, but still a pile of problem plutonium.

Bury It at Sea—Burying it in sea mud in titanium casings dropped from ships has been controversial. There is some indication that sea mud has qualities that uniquely absorb radioactive material. Until this is proven, this solution has its detractors. Others suggest putting it in deep ocean trenches where it will be pulled into the Earth's mantle. This has serious detractors.

Shoot It to the Sun—Another permanent solution is to shoot it at the sun, where its volatile tonnage would be right at home. But scientists groan when they think not only of the expense but of the results of a possible accident.

Dissolve It into the Oceans—Some believe radioactive material will dissipate over the Earth's oceans in time so that it is no longer dangerous. This was banned in 1983.

Bury It Under the Ice Caps—Yes, it might melt the ice. Then what?

Transmutation—This theory developed by Charles Bowman of the Los Alamos National Laboratory uses a particle accelerator to bombard plutonium with neutrons. This will reduce its ridiculously long half-life and render a substance that would still be radioactive but only for a few decades. A few nuclear experts are banking on this solution.

No elegant solution is in place. What's needed instantly is a secure way to store an abundance of weapons-grade plutonium from dismantled warheads and spent reactor fuel. The only requirements are that it has to be safe, cheap, and foolproof to keep it from polluting the environment or falling into the wrong hands. No idea is too off-the-wall. Geneticists are busy developing appropriate bacteria to devour plutonium without leaving a trace. Someone suggested shaping it into bricks, wrapping it in gold (which is heavier than plutonium) and storing it in already-guarded Fort Knox.

Rumor has it that Russia is sinking much of its foreign aid for restructuring into building a complex the size of Washington, D.C.,

Chapter 13: Plutonium

in a mountain in the Urals as a safe bunker against nuclear war. Some believe we should consider the possibility of an accident and, at the very least, have an ample supply of potassium oxide available. It's the best protection for the vulnerable thyroid against radioactivity.

We've come a long way from the duck-and-cover era of the 1950s, but there is no escaping the fact that plutonium will be a reality check not only for us, but for more than 3,000 generations to come.

What You Can Do

For a fact sheet on plutonium, contact the United States Nuclear Regulatory Commission, Office of Public Affairs, Washington, D.C. 20555; (800) 368-5642, x415-8200; fax: (301) 415-2234.

For a free copy of *Closing the Circle on the Splitting of the Atom* (1995), contact the U.S. Department of Energy, Environmental Management Information Center, P.O. Box 23769, Washington, D.C. 20026; (800) 736-3282; (202) 863-5064.

For information on what to do during and after a disaster, contact your local Red Cross chapter. Write for a package on disaster preparedness: FEMA, P.O. Box 2012, Jessup, MD 20794-2012; (800) 480-2520; website: http://www.fema.gov.

American Red Cross; website: http://www.redcross.org.

14 Soil Degradation

Ciao, Garden of Eden

WHEN IT GOES, IT GOES. Soil works until it drops. But overworked and dried out, it turns into sandlike granules that are so fine, the wind gathers them up into huge black clouds that rain down a choking dust. This Kansas farmer during the Dust Bowl of the 1930s digs out the fencepoles of his once fertile farm. Photo credit: National Oceanic and Atmospheric Administration.

One of the most puzzling fertility myths concerns Demeter, the ancient Greek goddess of staple foods—grains and cereals. According to Hesiod, Demeter made love with "the Hero Iasion" in a "thrice-plowed fallow field," and from their union came the god Plutos, who brought great wealth to everyone he met.

What scholars have pondered is why great wealth should have come from a metaphorical romp in a symbolically barren field. The answer lay in the farming practices of the Middle Ages, when farmers plowed their fallow fields three times a season to keep down the weeds. The final plowing of the weeds left the soil at its most fertile, ready to be planted for the next season.

The trick is in the weeds: they decay into humus that brings nutrients to feed the microbes that keep soil "alive" and that nourish the seeds and render crops nutritious. What ancient Greek, medieval, and more recent farmers cared about was the soil: No soil, no lunch. In the 1990s few fast-food diners, wolfing down a microwaved sandwich, know that the bread that is glued to their piece of meat came from grains grown in a field probably somewhere in Iowa or Kansas or Oklahoma.

After World War II, when industry produced megamachines and technology created pesticides and artificial fertilizers, farmers also suffered a dangerous disconnect from the soil. They no longer had to wait for the soil to rest: they pumped it up with vitamins. They no longer had to vary the crops to keep the soil nutrients alive: they could plant the same crop year after year. They no longer had to plant only small plots: they could sow mega acres. And they could export their agri-knowledge around the world in agri-business.

Sterilized with insecticides, hermetically sealed from weeds, fed a choking diet of nitrogen, phosphorus, and potassium, and waterlogged with zealous irrigation techniques, the soil lost its ability to stick together. It couldn't hold water or hang onto roots, and the all-important earthworms that bring aeration into the depths of the soil died or went elsewhere. Enter a drought or heavy rains and the soil blew or ran away to clog rivers and reservoirs, slipping into groundwater and carrying with it all of its "killer-cides" and chemicals.

Farmers meant well: countries have to feed their people. But much of the soil quit. Since 1945, according to a study done by the United Nations Environment Program (UNEP), the Earth has lost 11 percent of its arable land to human-induced soil degradation. Another study done by the World Resources Institute found that 4.9 million acres of cropland in the world were degraded by abuse and overuse. Of total arable land area, 23 percent has been lost in Europe, 22 percent in Africa, 20 percent in Asia, 14 percent in South America, and 8 percent in North and Central America, according to UNEP.

Three Big Problems

Farming is more high-risk than playing the tables in Vegas. Wholly dependent on the climate, the timing, the size of the crops, even whether there will be a harvest or not are the result of the optimum combination of healthy soil and gentle weather. Global climate change, ozone depletion, and growing populations cast an ominous shadow. Thomas Karl, director of the National Climate Data Center, speculates on changes produced by several degrees' rise in global temperature. Even with a 1/2°C (or 1°F) rise in Des Moines, Iowa, which he uses as an example, the number of hot days above 90°F will increase by 5 percent. Precipitation will almost certainly increase, he says, "with more heavy convective events," or violent rushing rains. Karl and others theorize that rising global temperatures will affect the temperature of the midlatitudes to the extent that the Corn Belt could move north to Canada, for example. One certain change is insects: they will be a force to be reckoned with.

Ozone is a worse problem: intense UV rays cook leaves on the vine and dessicate soil. Already it has damaged the photosynthesis of staple crops in Australia, near the hole in the ozone layer over the Antarctic.

Add 130 million more people in the United States in the next 50 years, and 2 to 5 billion more people on the planet, and we are in deep trouble.

The Sahara Was Once Green

Two thousand years ago, the Sahara was green and fertile. Over the years, changing weather patterns eliminated rain from North Africa. Then, in the 1900s a booming European business in gum Arabic, a sap from acacia trees used in everything from medicines to glue, wiped out the trees that anchored Saharan soil and created desertification and subsequent vast acres of windblown sand.

Desertification is a condition in which topsoil loses its anchors from overgrazing and overuse, erodes, and blows away; what's left is unplantable.

Because everyone on Earth farms in one way or another, most of the alterations of the Earth's surface are due to farming. Most of the world's fresh water goes to farm irrigation. Any changes on the surface of the Earth—for example, when a once-green area suffers from drought or deforestation—affect the atmosphere. Wind and precipitation patterns change, and these changes are experienced around the globe.

Those who survived the Dust Bowl of the 1930s in the American Midwest remember desertification. Huge black clouds moved across the Plains like a tidal wave, full of topsoil. Desolate fields of dry soil were still neatly bordered by almost buried farm fences. A lot of problems brought the soil to that point, but one of the biggest was growing cash crops, the same thing year after year, in order to satisfy a market demand.

In the 1990s much of the third world, suddenly faced with mega-agriculture, has created mega-problems. With tractors and harvesters provided by foreign investors and with ready markets in the developed world, third world countries grow cash crops, such as tobacco or coffee, purely for export. Old harmonies are upset. In Nigeria, for example, small farmers traditionally work with pastoralists: they let cattle eat the weeds on their fallow field, and the cattle's manure fertilizes the resting soil. But when the soil was put into full-time use by state cash crop programs, which pumped out products for export, the soil worked until it died. And without fallow land, the cattle grazed on scrub brush on unused land, pulling out the roots and drying out the soil.

Plant a Tree, Please

Deforestation on small and grand scales happens everywhere. In the tropical rainforest belt around the belly of the globe, major corporations in league with the local governments clear cut forests for timber, leaving unprotected slopes whose soil washes away with the first rain. This clogs rivers and causes floods downstream, which, if the water mixes with phosphates from fertilizer, deprives fish not only of clear water but of oxygen.

In the American Midwest, where forests were leveled for cropland a hundred years ago, the soil was inadvertently exposed to wind and rain erosion. Today as much as 2 billion tons of topsoil are lost a year, according to one study. In 1995 Cornell soil scientist David Pimentel figured out that the United States spends $44 billion in damaged land, waterways, infrastructure, and health each year because of topsoil that is carried away by wind and rain.

Farmers, such as the tiny tribes of Pygmies in East Africa, have always cut down a few trees for firewood, building timber, and to plant some crops. But now increasing populations carve into the forest to plant food crops. But forest soil is arable only for a few years because it lacks the nutrients to grow crops, and because of this, the farmers are forced to hack away more acres of trees to plant in new soil.

Trees absorb carbon dioxide and the exposed forest floor gives off carbon dioxide, and so the whole process of deforestation sends more CO_2 to the greenhouse gases in the atmosphere. This creates global changes: the exposed unplanted land reflects the sun, which affects the temperature of the Earth, which influences the formation of clouds and weather patterns, which determine where rain falls or doesn't.

Water: The Oil of the Next Century

"I'd sell my wife before I'd sell my water rights," said a California farmer during the drought in the early 1990s. All the water we currently have on the planet is all we will ever have. And of all that water, only 2 percent is fresh. Desalination projects, making fresh water out of the ocean, currently service some resort hotels on dry Caribbean islands; some cities like Santa Barbara, California; and much of Saudi Arabia. But they're pricey.

A lot of irrigation water is wasted. Spray irrigation in hot countries sends more water into the air than onto the crops. But it's cheap. Farmers who can afford drip irrigation—it costs about $1,100 to $1,200 an acre to install—instead bury pipes with little holes next to their crop rows. It uses a third of the water that spray irrigation uses.

Over-Irrigation

A lot of water was pumped into farm crops before farmers realized that it contained salts and minerals that plants do not absorb, but that soil does. To unclog the soils, some farmers install pipes that flush the salts out of the soil. But it just passes the buck. An infamous example was revealed in the Kesterton (California) Wildlife Preserve (and agricultural dump) in 1983 when birds that visited the area began hatching babies with deformities, such as two heads or legs instead of wings. Preserve officials fired guns to scare away the birds while their investigation disclosed that in the ponds a high concentration of selenium built up from farm chemicals was passed on to the plankton that was eaten by the insects that were eaten by the birds.

A newly developed technique called *electroosmosis*, in which electrically charged plow blades repel the electrons in water, is being used to dry out waterlogged soil. It is also being tested to eliminate pollutants.

As people around the world move into cities, the demand for water exceeds farmers' demands. Many farmers will be forced to sell some of their water to cities and to get by on less by installing as many water-saving devices on the farm as they can. This has been the case in California since 1991 when the legislation decreed that farmers in the San Joaquin Valley were obligated to sell some of their water to dry Los Angeles.

More than Swatting

A report by the EPA in 1995 revealed that the United States had used 1.25 billion pounds of pesticide, a quarter billion more than what was used in 1993. Pesticides include insecticides, herbicides, and fungicides. What are we killing? Insects, crop nutrition, soil, and us. A National Research Council study in 1993 found that children, because they consume more calories per body weight and eat a less varied diet, are especially big consumers of pesticides, such as those, for example, found in apples a few years ago. Recent studies of sperm counts in American and British men that found reductions of as much as 25 percent among those born in the 1970s blamed pesticides as the cause.

In the 1930s and 1940s the pesticide DDT was sprayed everywhere indiscriminately until birds, including eagles, were no longer able to produce hard-shelled eggs. Traces of the chemical are still found in deep-ocean fish; and no one knows how many human cancers resulted from it. But the insect quickly mutated resistance: houseflies by 1947; 203 other species by 1975. DDT was officially banned in the United States in 1971 but is still used in some developing countries.

To reduce pesticide use, in what is known as Integrated Pest Management (IPM), analysts use vegetative index satellite data that can isolate exact areas in crop fields where insects are active or pinpoint breeding areas of disease-carriers, such as malaria mosquitoes. Millions of locusts, for example, swarming in a swirling cloud while looking for food, are uncontrollable. But on the ground before they fly off (visible from satellites), they are containable. This allows for controlled spraying in specific target zones.

To replace insecticides, scientists now are experimenting with biochemical pesticides made from insect hormones, like neuropeptides. (Long-term residual effects of these, however, are unknown.) Researchers have also isolated fungi that live on locusts, manufactured them into a liquid, and used them as an insecticide against their hosts.

Desperately Seeking a Breadbasket

A hundred years ago 37.5 percent of the total population, or about 11 million people, worked on farms, the average size of which was 137 acres. In 1994 only 2.5 percent of the population worked on farms, with an average acerage of 471, leaving a large population of unemployed rural poor. Large corporate farms employ thousands of migrant workers seasonally, paying them minimum wage (or less) to work the harvests.

Twenty-six land-grant colleges, designed to bring technological knowledge to budding farmers, were instituted in the mid-1850s, and university co-op extensions brought farms to the communities for the first time in 1914.

But as Karl Stauber, former head of the U.S. Department of Agriculture and now director of the Northwest Area Foundation (a rural development funding group in Minnesota), points out, only two American presidents ever attended a college of agriculture, and today the top five members of Congress are from the suburbs, not rural areas. This lack of connection to farmlands has created what he calls a "silent crisis" in which the drive to balance the budget, coupled with discretionary funding, has eroded public dollars for agriculture.

Enough Calories

Paradoxically, in 1995 production was up around the globe, but much of it was attributable to plants grown to feed livestock, the chief export of much of Latin America and Europe. More people were, and are, hungry: in 1995 the U.N. reported that 800 million people in the world suffered from undernourishment.

A report also issued in 1995 found that one-third of all Americans are "obese," or 20 percent over their normal weights; and 10 to 15 percent are overweight, not necessarily because they have better nutrition, but because they consume more sugar and fat products, which, combined with a sedentary life, contribute to weight gain. On average, Americans consume more than 3,000 calories a day, compared to an average African's 2,000.

But if Americans change their diet to the recommended fruits and vegetables, most of which come from California, Florida, and Texas, Ohio State agricultural economist Luther Tweeten notes that it could affect the whole economy. "The Midwest and the Southwest would be hard-hit because those regions produce most of the soybeans, corn, and other crops used to produce fats, oils, and livestock," he says.

People Must Eat

Malthus, who said populations will increase as long as they can eat, did not know about agricultural technology. Plant gene enhancement has been going on for a long time, but with the advent of biotechnology, in which geneticists can take specific genes from one species and implant them in another, it is now a big-time business. A bacterium that kills bollworms, for example, can be bred into cotton seeds, and—voilà!—better yields of cotton and no more bollworms, in one blow.

Already small companies and big companies, like Monsanto, have perfected drought-, insect-, and weed-resistant seeds. Farmers pay more for the seeds, but will save in the long run. The Delta & Pine Land Company, for instance, made $89 million in insect-resistant cotton seeds in 1996, a great profit compared with the $60 million it made in all seeds in 1995.

The Food Security Act of 1985 makes farmers prevent soil erosion by developing conservation strategies, and the Conservation Reserve Program pays landowners to let some fields lie idle for several years. Satellites now map croplands and read moisture levels of soil and identify the areas in need of fertilizer.

Keeping the soil rich and healthy, farmers plow the debris into the soil, then shoot seeds into it using no-till drillers. To keep the soil rich in nutrients, some farmers plant native grasses between crops, and plant crops among trees. Some crops planted together mutually benefit each other. Following an ancient Mayan practice, for example, some Midwest farmers plant squash as a ground cover under corn, around which beans, which give nitrogen to the soil, can entwine. In other cases, one crop naturally repels the insects of another.

In the rainforest, techniques keep the soil on slopes. Coffee farmer Pedro Herrera in northern Colombia, who grows his crops

Chapter 14: Soil Degradation

on a hillside, uses what he calls "live barriers" to keep the soil in place. "I plant sugarcane across the slope, so the soil doesn't slide down. I feed the cane to the cows; the cows provide milk for my family and the market. I give the manure to the earthworms, and what the earthworms produce, I give to the plants as fertilizer," he says. Herrera produced his own insecticide of liquified hot chili peppers (invented when he realized bugs never ate his chili).

Urban Agriculture

Population predictions indicate that as many as 80 percent of humans will live in cities within the next 50 years. Urban agriculture, according to Jac Smit of the Urban Agriculture Network in Washington, D.C., is therefore logical. "If that's where the stomachs are going, that's where the food will be," he says. This means not just a plot worked by squatters, but everything from crops grown in the suburbs and trucked into the city, to what the French call "potager gardening," which is growing enough baby sprouts for lunch in one small pot on the terrace. Some co-op extensions are already giving courses. Cornell University, for example, gives an adult education course called "New Farmers, New Markets" in New York City. Director John Ameroso also teaches high school kids how to work the land and keeps a few acres north of the city to grow extra food for the homeless.

In the future our food habits will probably change: more bison, less beef, because cattle require four times the amount of water to stay alive. Foods will be labeled with the type of pesticide used; more hybrid fruits and vegetables and genetically perfect edibles, such as tomatoes, will be sold; and many people will grow their own salad greens at home, hydroponically, to give the soil a rest.

❓ What You Can Do

Soil testing kits are available at many plant stores.

For a publication list, contact FDA, Center for Food Safety and Applied Nutrition, 200 C Street SW, HFS-555 (Room 5809), Washington, D.C. 20204; (800) FDA-4010; (202) 205-4314.

For a booklet on food additives, as well as other publications on food health, contact International Food Information

Council Foundation, 1100 Connecticut Avenue NW, Suite 430, Washington, D.C. 20036.

Biotechnology Information Center, National Agricultural Library, Beltsville, MD, 20705; (301) 504-5340; e-mail: biotech@nalusda.gov.

Famine Prevention Project, Rodale Institute, 222 Main Street, Emmaus, PA 18098; (215) 967-5171.

For information on urban agriculture, contact Urban Agriculture Network, 1711 Lamont Street NW, Washington, D.C. 20010; (202) 483-8130.

John Ameroso, Cornell University Co-op Extension Urban Agriculture Project, 16 East 34th Street, 8th floor, New York, NY 10016; (212) 340-2900.

To fight bugs with bugs, contact The Bug Store, 4472 Shaw Boulevard, St. Louis, MO 63110; (800) 455-BUGS; (314) 773-7374; e-mail: bugstore@mo.net; website: http://www.bugstore.com/program.html#m.

For information on carcinogens in food, contact the American Crop Protection Association; website: http://www.acpa.org/.

The U.S. Department of Agriculture Statistics Source website: http://www.usda.gov/nass/pubs/pubs.html.

15 Terrorism

Say It Isn't So

NOTHING IS SAFE. When the parked rental truck blew up in the parking lot on the morning of April 19, 1995, it left the Alfred P. Murrah Federal Building in Oklahoma City a pile of rubble. One hundred and sixty-seven people died; 460 were injured, many of them children at the daycare center. Photo credit: Lizz Dabrowski, "The Oklahoma Daily."

In the United States between 1970 and 1980, the FBI recorded 962 terrorist incidents. Some were personal vendettas, phony kidnappings staged to collect insurance; one was a TWA hijacking in New York to bring attention to Croats' desire for independence in Yugoslavia. But the 247 bombs that exploded in public places throughout the decade were placed by groups with political grievances to settle: Puerto Rican independence, Zionists, the New World Liberation Front, and numerous others. In 1977, when the Hanafi Muslims took 34 hostages at three sites in Washington, D.C., killed one guard, and caused another to have a heart attack, law enforcement authorities declared war against terrorism.

Twenty years later in 1996, three years after explosives in a truck parked in the basement garage damaged and disabled the World

Trade Center in New York City, and one year after explosives in a parked rental Ryder truck blew up the federal building in Oklahoma City, an explosive device tore off the wing of TWA Flight 800, plunging the plane in several pieces into the ocean off Long Island.

Counterterrorist groups quickly convened with President Clinton and recommended increased human intelligence gathering, better detection of explosives, and more vigilant security in public places.

Terrorism is never a comfortable issue for democratic governments. How can a democracy protect its citizens without becoming a police state?

Terrorist acts raise nettlesome questions: how much attention should government give to those who commit violent acts against civilians in order to gain attention? Should they be ignored or encouraged to take their grievances through other, more civilized channels? Or should they, and the group they represent, be considered flat-out criminals, as the FBI and others have suggested?

Because they are "theater," terrorist acts inexorably draw attention to individuals or groups the general society may or may not want to know anything about. Each act, as British weapons expert Richard Clutterbuck says, is a "lethal kind of intimidation" that forces private beliefs into the public arena. Some of those beliefs are politically motivated; others are personal. Some purposes are known; others elude.

The Unabomber, for example, an alleged hermit who inflicted terror for 18 years by mailing letter bombs to strangers who happened to represent parts of society he was philosophically opposed to, killed three, injured twenty-two, and successfully terrorized hundreds. Some anti-abortionists kill people who work in abortion clinics as a demonstration of their passionate belief in life, as in Brookline, Massachusetts, in 1995 when a terrorist gunned down workers at two clinics. Some terrorists hijack planes simply to get somewhere else, as the Lebanese in 1996 who, bound for Cuba, decided to go to Miami instead.

Not all terrorists, however, explain their motives. The purpose of a derailed Amtrak train in Arizona in 1995, claimed by an unknown group called the Sons of Gestapo, remains unclear. The meaning of the Pan Am Flight 103 explosion over Lockerbie, Scotland, in 1988 remains officially ambiguous because no one has claimed credit despite the fact that 270 people were killed. Part of terrorism's ability to disrupt society depends on the ambiguous meaning. Terrorism is "violence for effect," according to terrorist policeman John Richard Thrackrah; our inability to read the perpetrator's motives puts him centerstage, where he can be coercive, manipulative, and callous.

Who and Why

International Grievances

We've come a long way from the small explosive device that disrupted Wall Street in 1920. Anarchists who subsequently fled to Russia took credit for that. Terrorists today are schooled in high-tech engineering, the use of refined optics and lasers in assault weapons, and they have money, some of it from governments such as oil-rich Iran and Libya. "Terrorists with secure phones, satellite maps, accurate positioning, and a sophisticated understanding of modern communications systems," says Nicholas Wade of the *The New York Times*, "could bring down not just a few buildings but large sections of a modern economy."

The makers of the fertilizer-chemical truck bomb that went off in the World Trade Center in New York City in 1993 were Muslim extremists with connections to Sudan, Afghanistan, and parts of the Middle East. Their intention was to upset a world financial center to bring attention to their anger with the United States' support of Egypt. They caused $500 million in damage, killed six people, injured thousands, and unsettled untold millions who viewed the results on television, many learning for the first time that unhappy dissidents live in the Middle East.

Also opposed to the United States' support of Israel, Muslim extremists target Americans abroad: in Beirut in 1985 in a TWA hijacking, in Egypt in 1985 in the ambush of the cruise ship *Achille Lauro*, and in incidents in Saudi Arabia in 1996, one of which killed 19 Air Force personnel when a truck bomb tore into their barracks. Religious zeal fuels the Hezbollah, a Shi'ite Muslim extremist group formed in 1982 as the "Army of God," based principally in Iran and Sudan. It has targeted the United States, "the Great Satan," as the source of all evil.

Other extremist groups around the world are financed by illegal trade in drugs and weapons. Money is the driver for international crime and drug cartels. The Russian Mafia, for example, does business globally with shady groups and individuals. In Peru the Shining Path guerrillas, ideological Marxist revolutionaries who survive in the wilderness, do a booming business in cocaine, much of it sold on the streets in the United States. Heroin translates into dollars that finance ethnic and religious ideologues in Afghanistan, India, and Pakistan.

Other groups have ethnic or cultural differences, in the name of which a lot of innocent blood is spilled. The terrorist factions of the Irish Republican Army, seeking independence for Northern Ireland from Great Britain, kill on average 76 people a year, according to Scotland Yard. They chiefly use car bombs placed on city streets in England and Northern Ireland. Basque Separatists, tucked away in the Pyrenees between France and Spain, who want to be independent of Spain, periodically plant bombs in airports in Spain, most recently in 1996 when 35 tourists were injured.

Poverty and population problems escalate long simmering ethnic feuds. In Bosnia, Serbs practiced ethnic cleansing against Muslims on a scale not seen since World War II. Hutus fighting Tutsis in Rwanda and Burundi resorted to mass slaughter of everyone from babies to elders to terrorize Tutsis off their land. Altogether 8,700 terrorist acts were committed around the world between 1968 and 1995, according to figures compiled by the U.S. Department of State.

Domestic Groups

The number of groups opposed to the U.S. government doubled to 800 in 40 states after the Oklahoma bombing, according to a report issued in 1996 by the Southern Law Poverty Center. Domestic groups are as varied in their composition and intentions as international terrorist groups: they range from super-patriots who want to dissolve the Constitution or secede from the country and form their own, to skinheads who commit hate crimes of all kinds, to the Ku Klux Klan and Neo–Nazis who harass and terrorize African Americans and Jews, among others. All communicate on the internet, fueling their fears and bonding against common enemies.

Almost 450 paramilitary militia groups are scattered around the country with about 15,000 members, mostly in California, Montana, and Michigan, according to a report by the Anti-Defamation League. Most live on farm acres in compounds where they can safely stockpile weapons and perform their daily training exercises. United in a belief that the United Nations will send invading armies and that the U.S. government is spying on them from black helicopters, many of them give courses in such things as bomb making and armed resistance and raise cash by selling how-to books and videos.

Chapter 15: Terrorism

The FBI, the lead investigative agency against terrorists, makes pre-emptive raids against cells they identify as dangerous. In June 1996 FBI counterterrorism agents raided the Viper Militia in Phoenix, Arizona, where, in a house in a suburban subdivision, agents found a bomb, a machine gun, and 70 rifles and shotguns. Just before the 1996 Summer Olympics in Atlanta, Georgia, federal agents arrested several members of a Georgia paramilitary group, thought to be planning to plant 12 pipe bombs at strategic locations among the games as a show of their disrespect for the United States and their distrust of foreigners.

Other domestic right-wing groups, such as the Aryan Nations, whose members believe the Lost Tribes of Israel do not include Jews, mix their antigovernment political beliefs with religious beliefs that somehow justify their opposition to others. Opposed to gun control, they also refuse to register their automobiles and to get driver's licenses. They oppose the tax laws and usually school their children at home. Because they are survivalists, they stockpile food and water and, being self-sufficient, are able to wait out any attack from the government. For four months in 1996, the FBI surrounded the Montana Freemen compound waiting to arrest them for defrauding the government of more than $1 million in phony money orders, securities, and checks. Only a need for cigarettes sent some of the Freemen out of their fenced bastion.

Modus Operandi

Bombs

Kidnapping, hostage-taking, sabotaging food supplies, assassinations, kneecapping, and drive-by shootings are all terrorist techniques. But car bombs in cities or in front of important buildings get a lot of attention and cause a lot of disruption.

Bombs, unfortunately, are easy to make. A fertilizer bomb was used in the bombing of the federal building in Oklahoma City, in the suicide truck bombing on a Marine compound in Beirut in 1983, and in many IRA bombs in the United Kingdom. The hardest part of making a car or truck bomb out of ammonium nitrate, or common farm fertilizer, is that it takes about a week to assemble the ton of fertilizer necessary to do the damage they did.

"Kill one, frighten ten thousand," advised Sun Tsu in *The Art of War*, written two millennia ago. Instructions for making crude pipe bombs are available on the internet and in training manuals sold by extremist groups. Six-inch nails are inserted into a section of pipe along with fuses, potassium compound and aluminum powder, igniters, and timers and closed with two end caps; and the device can be smuggled into a crowd or a building inside a jacket. The pipe bomb that exploded in Olympic Park at the 1996 Summer Olympics killed one, injured a hundred, and could have frightened thousands (but the games went on). Bombs cause not only primary injuries from flying nails and secondary injuries from broken glass, but psychological disruption: victims wonder why they were chosen and are afraid of being targeted again.

Chemical and Biological Weapons

More insidious are chemical and biological weapons. The deadly sarin released in a Tokyo subway in March 1995 and attributed to a Japanese extremist religious group killed eight people who were close to the source. A nerve gas developed by the Nazis in World War II, sarin interrupts the nerve synapses that paralyze the diaphragm, preventing the victim from breathing. The thousands who were injured suffered from nausea, vomiting, headaches, and convulsions, but were saved by the antidote atropine.

Worse are the nerve gases tabun and soman, which are not dispersed in air, as sarin is, and for which there are no known antidotes. Napalm, a gel gasoline and aluminum combination developed for the Vietnam War, sucks the oxygen out of the air, killing all living things. White phosphorus sticks to the skin, does not rub off, and ignites spontaneously on contact with air, making people human torches. Mustard gas, used widely in World War I, burns the flesh and lasts on surfaces—of buildings, the ground, trees—for decades. The most lethal chemical known is rycin, derived from castor beans and delivered in pellets, used by the KGB during the Cold War. Rycin was the poison injected from the point of an umbrella poked into a Bulgarian as he waited on a train platform in London. He died several days later.

Under surveillance from United Nations observers, Iraq is believed to have ample supplies of botulism and anthrax, diseases deadly to people and animals. They also are believed to have stores of sarin, which they claim can be delivered in a missile. Members of the Southern Poverty Law Center report that freeze-dried bubonic plague bacteria, as well as the nerve toxin rycin, are among the chemical weapons stored in domestic militia stockpiles.

Legally, chemical and biological weapons are universally banned. The Geneva Protocol of 1925, established after World War I, prohibits "asphyixiating, poisonous, or other gases" or similar liquid materials. The Chemical Weapons Convention also bans any chemical that causes death or incapacitation to humans and animals, and the Biological Weapons Convention prohibits the use of microbes for destructive purposes, including the development of microbes that eat metal designed to destroy planes in the air.

Nuclear Weapons

International treaties also govern the use of nuclear weapons, but the so-called designer bombs that use micro amounts of plutonium could, even if they did not detonate as a usual nuclear device, release enough lethal radiation into the air to incapacitate hundreds of thousands if they were placed in a building the size of the World Trade Center, according to Theodore Taylor, former deputy director of the U.S. Defense Nuclear Agency. Close to the source, radioactive fallout causes death; in widening concentric circles, it causes radiation sickness, including violent nausea and vomiting, diarrhea, and flaming headaches. In the long run, it causes cancers, especially of the thyroid and lymph systems. CIA Director John Deutsch said in 1996 that our ability to protect ourselves against a nuclear, biological, or chemical weapons attack "is very, very small indeed."

To alleviate the mass destruction of nuclear weapons, the Department of Energy (DOE) has established Nuclear Emergency Salvage Teams, which can be assembled and on the road on very short notice. Once at the site, the DOE volunteers can defuse weapons, if necessary, and decontaminate the area.

Fingerprinting the Evidence

Keener x-ray devices and fast computers have contributed to better detection of the tools of terrorists. After the TWA 800 went down off Long Island, counterterrorist experts recommended to President Clinton the use of tags on explosives so the origin could be easily traced. Semtex, for example, a plastic explosive used in the Pan Am 103 crash over Lockerbie, Scotland, can be traced to Czechoslovakia where it is manufactured. Some airport security systems, which are a combination of X-ray and CT-scan that produce a three-dimensional image, can detect plastic explosives by their density. Mass spectrometers and chromographs can identify explosive chemicals in the lab. Even plutonium can be traced to the source.

Is It Safe to Go Out?

Can a democracy support a police state? Counterterrorism experts from eight European and North American countries and Japan met in Paris in July 1996 and suggested, instead, treading a tenuous middle ground with greater vigilance, including human and electronic intelligence; more rigorous punishment of terrorist crimes, including the death penalty for terrorists; easier extradition of suspects; and the monitoring of communications on the internet.

After the TWA 800 disaster, President Clinton quickly signed into effect increased and upgraded security in airports. Airlines winced because they must bear some of the burden of the extra cost, which is easily in the millions of dollars. Author Joseph Finder, in an opposing editorial in *The New York Times* July 24, 1996, calls increased airport security "band-aid measures." Terrorists strike anywhere and everywhere: trains, buses, public places, large gatherings. They can deliver what someone has called "weapons of mass disruption" via missiles. What we really need, according to Finder, is infiltrated agents into known terrorist groups and relaxed restrictions on so-called wiretapping. Congress approved the use of "roving taps" of communications from suspects on computers, cell phones, and public phones. Finder suggests that the National Security Agency and the British Government Communications Headquarters, who listen to conversations to or from foreign countries, look for "trigger words" that identify terrorism in communications on modems, faxes, and telephones.

Critics pointed out that suitcases and passengers could be subjected to closer scrutiny in airports, but ancillary personnel, the clean-up crews, catering service personnel, and baggage handlers should have security clearances before being hired.

But we risk becoming a Big Brother society—listened to, watched, guarded, and restricted. Excessive suspicion on the part of law enforcement officers caused an out-of-control raid on an Idaho compound of patriot Randy Weaver in 1992, in which Weaver's wife and young son were killed by zealous FBI and Bureau of Alcohol, Tobacco, and Firearms agents, one of whom was killed by a shooter from the compound.

A Future Not Like the Past

Predictions for terrorism in the United States in the future are grim. Targeted not only by religious and political terrorists from Iran and other parts of the Muslim world but by super-patriots and paranoid militia within the country and by hoaxers looking for 15 minutes of fame, Americans may become like Brits in London, subjected over the years to unpredictable IRA bombs. "You learn to live with it," said a man who works in London's financial district, "because you learn to be cautious. Always cautious."

Joseph Finder observes: "Ours is a culture of seatbelts and air bags. We believe we have a natural right to a risk-free environment, and we're appalled when the fallacy of that belief is brought home," he says. "We've been astonishingly lucky."

What You Can Do

Terrorism in the United States is produced by the FBI: U.S. Department of Justice, Federal Bureau of Investigation, Washington, D.C. 20535-0001.

False Patriots: The Threat of Antigovernment Extremists is a report issued by Southern Poverty Law Center, 400 Washington Street, Montgomery, AL 36104.

Fact Finding Reports on Militias: contact the Anti-Defamation League, 1100 Connecticut Avenue NW, Suite 1020, Washington, D.C. 20036; (202) 452-8320.

16 Guns

Wild America

OUR NATIONAL ICON. There are more guns in the United States than people. The number of people who own them legally and know how to use them is a small percentage. It looks easy on TV or in the movies, like this scene from the 1973 Peter Yates film, "The Friends of Eddie Coyle." Photo credit: Movie Still Achives.

The 1995 FBI report *United States Homicide Patterns* states, "The leading weapon used against those under age 5 from 1975 through 1994 was personal weapons (hands, fist, and feet). The gun category was the leading weapon type for all remaining age groups, especially the 15 to 19 age group. In 1975, 66 percent of the murders of persons in this group were attributable to guns, while in 1994 the figure rose to 87 percent."

But there's more. According to the Children's Defense Fund, guns are the leading cause of death for black males 14 to 25, and the second leading cause of death (after vehicular accidents) for all teenagers 10 to 19. In 1994, 15 American children or teenagers died every day in a gun-related murder, suicide, or accident. Overall, handguns in the United States killed 40,000 adults and children and injured 150,000 in 1995.

Guns depersonalize crime. Tools of power rendering instant gratification, guns in the hands of the "frustrated underclass" instill fear, rob, and kill any agents of anger and humiliation. On weekends, jails and emergency rooms are full of gun users slapped out of their drugged and drunken delirium by the consequences of their bullets.

So many 20-year-old former "drug lords" languish in city hospitals as hopeless quadraplegics, funded by Medicaid, that emergency room doctors actively lobby Congress for safer guns and for anything that will restrain the out-of-control street wars. Fast-shooting medium-caliber semiautomatics, many produced in this country, have largely replaced revolvers. New semiautomatic guns, according to physician Garen J. Wintemute, who did a study of gun type and wounds, will probably lead to an increased number of shootings. They are lightweight, trigger-quick, cheap, and have greater fire power. One jailed drug peddler observed that young gunmen just aim into a crowd and shoot until a bullet kills someone.

The FBI murder statistics found that for all murders a new trend has replaced the traditional crime of "passion and arguments among family members or acquaintances." In the bloodless prose of the FBI: "Every American now has a realistic chance of murder victimization in view of the random nature the crime has assumed." In other words, a stranger can pick anyone off.

Our Very Own Gun Culture

The problem is not just druggies killing druggies or young black males warring over territory. Guns have facilitated the brute expression of disgruntled postal workers (34 since 1986); clients displeased with their lawyers (8 killed, 6 wounded in San Francisco); radical anti-abortion supporters; psychiatric patients; family members, many of them teenagers who kill the whole family; children who kill their tiny siblings; and the clearly insane—snipers from towers, shooters in schoolyards and fast-food restaurants.

While surplus war weapons—AK-47s, Uzis, and the like—are smuggled in from Brazil, China, and Russia to join the 230 million or so guns and the 71 million handguns thought to be in the United States, petty salesmen set up shop in their garages. Caches of grenades, World War II weapons, bomb parts, fertilizer, and assault weapons are periodically raided by police in small towns across the country. Those arrested are usually unconnected to any of the serious stockpilers among the super patriotic and paramilitary groups in the country. They are just guys with a penchant for guns and profit. They sell to collectors and petty criminals, like the one in a small town in Massachusetts who recently held up a convenience store with a World War II machine gun.

Is that You, John Wayne?

A hundred years ago, President McKinley was shot "by an Anarchist" with a concealed pistol while he was visiting the Pan-American Exposition in Buffalo, New York. He died within a few days and was replaced by Vice President Theodore Roosevelt. Two years later, the first Hollywood film, using cuts and staged action, was produced. *The Great Train Robbery* was twelve minutes long and set the pattern for audience taste for several decades to come: a dramatic crime with good guys and bad guys, fist fights on a moving train, and lots of hand-tinted smoke from revolvers in fights in a forest, on horseback, shot at the feet of a reluctant dancer, and pointed directly at the camera.

If Hollywood is our collective memory, it helped us celebrate the conquering of the West after the Civil War when surplus rifles and Colt revolvers came on the open market. Keeping law and order among the hundreds of thousands of settlers who had crossed the country in Conestoga wagons in the middle 1800s required guns to defend property against wild animals, criminals, and Indian attacks.

By the time Hollywood became a film town, downsized ranches released a bunch of out-of-work cowboys who were keen marksmen and facile riders and able to do stunt work. Tom Mix was a famous rodeo rider. Dime novels created heroes out of heroes, such as Buffalo Bill, former sheriff, and provided scripts for Hollywood Westerns. Armed with a rifle for use against the bad guys, with a pistol slung sexily from his right hip, a cowboy cornered trembling bank robbers, saved quivering heroines, and rode into and out of town under a volley fired from his revolver. "Get your guns, men, and we'll ride over the ridge and take out those bandits," were words that, spoken in John Wayne's velvet voice, thrilled millions. Revived after World War II, Westerns flooded movie houses and television, where shows like "Maverick" fed a generation that played with toy guns.

Lee Kennet and James LaVerne Anderson in *The Gun in America* note that a uniquely American myth imagines individuals defending their country with guns. In the same way that the Lexington farmers, armed with guns stolen from the British and smuggled into farmhouses in Concord, Massachusetts, fired "the shot heard round the world" that began the American Revolution, so did Western pioneers defend their rights against Indians.

The Second Amendment, drawn up in 1788 after the Revolution, called for "a well-regulated militia" and for the "right of people to bear arms." Today, extremist groups use this as justification for stockpiling weapons to be used against enemies either from within the government or from those to whom the government is indifferent, such as the U.N. forces thought by some paramilitary groups to be amassing on the Canadian border.

Eastern Sharpshooters, Style Is All

In the East, guns had a place in hunting and duels—Alexander Hamilton was killed in one with Aaron Burr. Most schools had marksmanship clubs. Before he was president, Theodore Roosevelt, an avid big-game hunter, formed an association of marksmen, some of whom went on to join an Olympic team and win a gold medal. The National Rifle Association (NRA), formed in 1871 and today the most powerful lobby against gun control, sponsored shooting contests. In 1905 when Congress allowed surplus-arms sales to rifle clubs, the NRA served as the clearinghouse. During World War I, the National Defense Act encouraged rifle practice, which existed in many schools until recently.

City guns have always been different than western guns. Few American gentlemen were outfitted with custom guns, as members of the British upper class were, but New York City tailors offered suits with trousers with a discreet hip pocket for a revolver. Mass production of weapons flooded the market with pistols and rifles, many sold by mail order. One inventor offered a pistol/pocket watch that could be "fired at a highwayman while apparently merely obeying his command to 'Hand over your watch and be quick about it.'"

Bans

When immigrants crowded into cities on the East Coast in the mid-1800s, the so-called "Establishment" perceived them, or their

Chapter 16: Guns

impoverished situation, as threats. About the same time that New York City policemen began carrying guns, New York's Sullivan Law of 1911 (still in effect) required permits to carry guns. Lee and Anderson observe that the United States became an armed society. Guns were no longer used against common enemies or in hunting for food. Instead, "the enemy became internal. Society felt threatened by criminals, ethnic groups, racial groups, rioters, and malcontents."

"Get More with a Gun"

An advertisement in 1920, showing a cowboy on his front porch gunning down invading men and horses, extolled a new gun: "The Thompson Submachine Gun incorporates the simplicity and infallibility of a hand-loaded weapon with the effectiveness of a machine gun." Tommy guns, as they were called, did not wind up on many ranch porches, but they were the weapon of choice for some natty Mafia gangsters operating crime syndicates in Chicago. "You can get more with a smile and a gun than you can with a smile alone," said mobster Al Capone.

Because a miss was nearly impossible, many Tommy guns were used in drive-by killings of thugs who were too dangerous to fire after a job. When Tommy guns and sawed-off shotguns were used to slaughter one of Al Capone's rival gangs in the Valentine's Day Massacre, legislators were stirred into action. Then, as now, finding the antidote to criminal use of guns stymied lawmakers. The Federal Firearms Act of 1938 outlawed machine guns and restricted interstate commerce on guns by requiring tighter registration and forbidding permits to felons.

IF GUNS ARE OUTLAWED, ONLY OUTLAWS WILL HAVE GUNS (bumpersticker, 1990): After the Sullivan Law in 1911, criminals rented guns. After the Federal Firearms Act in 1938, they smuggled them.

In the 1960s and early 1970s President John Kennedy, Martin Luther King, and Robert Kennedy, among others, were assassinated by gunmen. The general public cried out for some common controls on guns. As Congress struggled to limit imports and mail-order "Saturday Night Specials," the NRA defended the guns of their 500,000 members, many of them from small-town America, descended from the line of individuals fiercely guarding their rights to hunt and to defend themselves and their families against "enemies."

157

The Gun Control Act of 1968 restricted imported arms (like the one thought to have killed President Kennedy) and imposed restrictions on federal licensed dealers to prevent sales of rifles to minors under 18, pistols to those under 21, criminals with records, and drug addicts.

In 1994 a total of 240 federal field inspectors checked up on 235,150 federally licensed arms dealers. By 1996 the Bureau of Alcohol, Tobacco, and Firearms had eliminated 100,000 of those for illegally selling guns. At the end of the Cold War in 1990, surplus Russian assault weapons flooded the world market. Among them were the AK-47, super in war, absurd on the street, and the .9mm semiautomatic Makarov, firing a rapid 6 to 8 shots from a single clip and small enough to slip into a pocket, which is what made it the preferred pistol of the KGB.

In 1990 Congress passed the Assault Weapons Ban, which forbids the manufacture of a long list of semiautomatics and their clips. The ban was repealed by the House in 1996. In 1993, several years after President Ronald Reagan was shot by a street assailant along with his press secretary, James Brady, who was rendered a paraplegic, Congress passed the Brady Bill. It forbids gun purchase by convicted felons and requires a five-day waiting period after purchase (to avoid crimes of passion).

States, however, have made stronger laws. New York requires a 60-day waiting period and forbids juveniles from owning guns. California, in addition to a 15-day waiting period, background checks bans on assault weapons and juvenile possession, and requires safety training for gun owners, including child-accident prevention rules.

In a 1995 Harris Poll of 2,000 teenagers, almost one-third of public, private, and parochial school students said they feared being hit in a drive-by shooting. In 1990 Congress approved the Gun Free School Zones Act, which forbade guns within 1,000 feet of any school. In 1995 the U.S. Supreme Court declared the act unconstitutional because courts can't regulate every aspect of schools. Many schools nevertheless continue to scan students with metal detectors at the entrance, and students remain fearful.

Do Guns Deter Crime?

Approximately 49 percent of American households claim they have a gun for protection. (This figure is thought to be low because respondents are reluctant to reveal they own a gun.) Another tack currently in vogue among states is issuing gun permits to all adults who have no criminal records and show no sign of insanity. So far, 28 states allow adults to carry concealed weapons for the purposes of protection. Whether or not it deters crime is uncertain, but gun owners feel safer.

But there is also a lot of argument as to whether guns act as a deterrent to crime. In 1993 physician Arthur Kellerman published a study done in three separate counties of 388 murder victims and their families. He found that unlocked and loaded guns were present in 50 percent of the victims' homes and that the mere presence of a gun in the home raised the risk of suicide five times, and of homicide by a family member as much as seven times. In 14 percent of the cases, a gun was not successful against forced entry. Kellerman's study, funded by the Centers for Disease Control and used by groups who wish to ban all guns, has been accused of being methodologically unsound.

Another study done by two criminologists, Gary Kleck and Marc Gertz, of Florida State University, found that, on the contrary, guns were good deterrents against crime. In a national telephone poll of 5,000 people, 213 claimed they had used a firearm against an attacker using knives, sticks, or something other than a firearm. Seventy-six percent did not fire the gun, 16 percent shot at the attacker, and the rest fired a warning shot. When the 18 percent of armed citizens met an attacker with a gun, they did not fire their weapon. On the basis of their polling, Kleck and Gertz projected that between 2.1 and 2.5 million U.S. citizens use guns for self-defense each year. The claim, criticized by some as a leap of faith, is applauded by the NRA.

Remember Bernie Goetz

But if everyone is armed, who is the good guy and who is the bad guy? If homeowners use an unregistered weapon to subdue an intruder in their home, they pay fines and go to jail. If they kill the intruder, they are tried as a murderer. In 1984 Bernie Goetz used a registered pistol to shoot at a gang of teenagers on a New York City subway train when they accosted him looking for his wallet. He shot four, leaving one irreparably paralyzed, who sued and won a $43 million dollar suit against Goetz.

In at least two instances, victims of gun shootings are suing the arms manufacturer. Relatives of the victims killed in the San Francisco law firm in 1993 received permission to sue Navagar, the manufacturer of the assault weapon used by the enraged ex-client. In two separate cases in New York, families are suing weapons producers of handguns sold illegally to minors who killed their victims.

Is It Guns or Is It Us?

Critics point out the weakness of the federal laws and recommend better inspection, more careful bookkeeping with registration, and circumspection with the registering of arms. Philip J. Cook and Thomas B. Cole, in an article in the *Journal of the American Medical Association* (June 1996), suggest attacking illegal arms in a double-pronged attack by reducing the supply, cracking down on scofflaw salesmen; and by reducing demand, making arms highly expensive and ownership undesirable. Police in Kansas City, for example, have been actively stopping cars and seizing illegal guns. Former New York City Police Commissioner William Bratton reduced gun homicides by 40 percent in two years by actively adding more policemen to work the same hours as "the competition" and going after known illegal gun salesmen.

But do these measures solve the problem? Others suggest imposing huge taxes on ammunition or selling harmless bullets. Communities periodically offer money for surrendered no-questions-asked guns. But guns, unless they are smelted down, do not deteriorate, and parts can be sold.

Other countries manage without killing each other: London and New York City have approximately the same rates of crime, except for murders, in which New York City exceeds by 50 percent.

The New York Times reporter Nicholas D. Kristof compared the enormous rates of gun crime in the United States with the low rates in Japan, where weapons are summarily banned, and Switzerland, where every able-bodied male is issued a machine gun to be used in the event of war. The major difference he found was that the United States has "an underclass that feels excluded from society."

Sociologist Geoffrey Canada, who works to salvage children in the South Bronx ghetto where he grew up in the 1950s and 1960s, notes a major difference that has occurred in the ghetto's adults: "There used to be neighborhood busybodies, women who watched

Chapter 16: Guns

out the windows and reported on neighborhood kids to their mothers. Now, you never see them. The adults are afraid of teenagers," he says.

At the daycare center that he runs, Canada notices that five and six year olds can still be saved. But the critical ages are eight or nine when kids start to assert their own independence. They prefer to walk alone to school where they enter the War Zone, Canada says. A nine year old was recently gunned down in the crossfire between two drug lords. In a couple of years the drug lords will give them new, polymer, lightweight semiautomatics for selling drugs to playmates.

Meanwhile, the older kids in the War Zone are on a treadmill going nowhere, he says. Nor will the problem end, because the numbers are up. There will be more teenagers in a couple of years than there have been since 1956. These kids now, Canada says, "the children of war, are just piling up, with no goals and no heroes."

❓ What You Can Do

Contact Handgun Control, Inc., 1225 Eye Street NW, Suite 1100, Washington, D.C. 20005; (202) 898-0792. (Public citizens' lobby for gun regulation.)

Coalition to Stop Gun Violence, 100 Maryland Avenue NE, Washington, D.C. 20002-5625; (202) 544-7190.

The National Rifle Association has a list of places that teach civilian marksmanship; 11250 Waples Mill Road, Fairfax, VA 22030; (703) 267-1000.

"Guidelines for Workplace Violence Prevention Programs for Health Care and Social Service Workers" is a free publication for a self-addressed label from: OSHA Publications, P.O. Box 37535, Washington, D.C. 20013-7535; website: http://www.osha.gov.

For a list of National Criminal Justice Reference Service documents by fax, call (301) 251-5518. They maintain a 24-hour fax service.

17 The Economy

Deconstructing the American Dream

KEEPING THE FAMILY TOGETHER. The gap between rich and poor in both the industrial nations and the third world reached an all-time high in the 1990s. Making ends meet for many, like this family, can mean stretching salaries and tips, playing a little Bingo and the lottery, and sharing clothes and toys. Photo credit: Roger Archibald.

After World War II, "the boys" came home from the Front. They married their high school sweethearts, got GI loans to go back to school and VA loans to buy little single-family homes and cars, rolling again off the assembly lines in Detroit. In time, they had 2.5 children and moved to a larger home next to a good school in a safe neighborhood. Mom was the homemaker, and Dad worked for steady wages with predictable annual raises. They saved—in the short run for Christmas, in the long run for college for their kids—while the government saved part of their salary for their retirement. War as a rite of passage had bought them the rights to comfort and security in a country retooling for a progressive peacetime.

That was then; this is now.

In January 1996 a Peter D. Hart poll on the economy found that 64 percent of Americans were satisfied with their personal finances, but only 43 percent were satisfied with the economy in general. Fifty-nine percent thought their personal finances would stay the same or worsen, and an astounding 73 percent thought the economy in general would not change or would get worse. In other words: I'm okay, but the country is not.

Why do people have such angst about the country? Mortgage foreclosures at 4 percent in 1994 were down a full point from 1980; delinquent mortgage payments (4 percent) were lower than they were in 1990 (4.7 percent). The national median price for a home was $112,200; and not only were interest rates low, but banks were giving $70,000 mortgages to those whose income was only $22,800.

Despite the fact unemployment was the lowest in 30 years, at 5.8 percent, inflation was only 2.5 percent; the Gross Domestic Product (GDP) had grown 2.6 percent since 1990; and mutual funds, called "the savings account of the 1940s," were nestled in a stock market in the 5,000s. Nevertheless, one-third of another group polled were worried they would lose their job, and fully one-half worried that their income would not be enough to meet future expenses.

Black Monday

"They told us it would be ten percent this week, ten percent next week, and ten percent the week after," said a former employee at Digital Equipment Corporation in Massachusetts. "We didn't know until we got to work on Monday morning if we would be chosen to get the ax. It was terrible." Companies call it downsizing; others have called it "profits without people." In 1995, 300,000 workers were fired in the telecommunications and banking industries, and 600,000 defense workers were let go from military bases closed after the end of the Cold War.

American manufacturing boomed after World War II until wartorn Europe and Japan produced competitive goods. By the 1980s German and Japanese cars and electronics forced the downsizing of American companies that responded by merging with other companies or doing other things. Many people shifted from manufacturing jobs to the service industry, working in banks, or selling insurance or real estate.

In the 1990s the high-tech industry began shaping itself to fit in a global market, and it became every man for himself, or what ecologist Garrett Hardin has called the Lifeboat Mentality: If you keep

Chapter 17: The Economy

everybody aboard, you'll sink; if you put too many out, you lose a safe balance. Many companies work better streamlined.

The Invisible Hand

The bottom line is the "invisible hand" of the market economy: when supply exceeds demand, prices fall; when demand exceeds supply, prices rise. The software engineers who were lured into new companies at high salaries suddenly find themselves on the street. "Somebody always gets hurt in a market economy" is the mantra of economists.

But not for long. Temporary, part-time, and per-diem workers, such as nurses, once a staple job in the American economy, work on contract and provide stiff competition for regular workers because they ask for and get no benefits. Neither can they expect raises or bonuses. Some of the so-called Slackers, Generation-X first-time workers, move from job to job in search of a career, live home with their parents so they can begin to pay off often humongous school loans and accumulate some capital before becoming fully emancipated.

Since 1990 more than 400 programs in entrepreneurship in graduate business schools have been developed to teach students how to start their own small companies. Professionals with skills have become consultants, working, according to *The Wall Street Journal*, "project to project." With all the job security of actors, they have taken big cuts in pay and kissed benefits good-bye. They finance their "valleys" with capital from credit cards and loans, which they pay down when they have "peaks."

No one saves much, but savings have not been popular for the past 10 years, as the real purchasing power of the dollar has weakened. On paper, the average per capita income of about $25,000 would seem adequate, but it buys less than it did 10 years ago. The price of a four-year college education is up 95 percent just from 1990. In 1996 a public four-year state university cost on average a little less than $30,000. Ivy League college room, board, and tuition was astronomical, more than $100,000.

To pay for four years of preparation for life in the real world, many students patch together loans from different sources, which they promise to pay back. In 1994 students were financed by $47 billion in financial aid, half from federal loans. Many new physicians take the highest paying jobs they can find to begin to alleviate some of their mountainous school debt. Forget altruism.

Nor is General Motors, once a staple of the American Dream, doing so well. In 1994 Detroit produced 15 million cars and trucks, down one million from 1986. The downward trend reflects a number of elements in the economy: high prices of new cars not easily affordable on shaky salaries and a saturated market filled with serviceable used cars.

No Credit? No Problem!

Most everyone with a mailing address gets "free" credit cards in the mail. For a low introductory interest rate, many offer credit lines of as much as $50,000. In very fine print, the offered "fixed" rates will soon evolve into a "percentage-plus-prime" rate, which often can be as high as 20 percent. The average person has between three and four credit cards, with a total debt of about $4,000, according to the Bank Card Holders of America. But a growing number have five- and six-digit debt—more than five times higher than their income—from having been downsized, from unexpected medical expenses, or accumulated expenses from having to buy medicine or to supplement slim alimony payments in a divorce. Others slipped into casino gambling debts.

Total credit-card debt in the United States rose to $366.4 billion in 1994, up from $236.4 billion in 1990, with a projected amount of $660.9 billion in 2000. In 1996 a record 1.1 million people filed for personal bankruptcy, a legal transaction in which everything but a home and a car is sold before banks grant amnesty for debts. In 1992, 900,000 claimed personal bankruptcy, most because they had lost their job.

Despite anxieties about the economy and the future, many downsized workers find they are developing brave new priorities. "I work for myself and my family now," said one engineer, "not for somebody else's company. And I'm concentrating on being happy." Another said he liked the challenge of not being protected by a company. "Nothing in life is ever guaranteed, anyway," he said. "You always have to do it on your own."

Chapter 17: The Economy

Move Over, Methuselah

When someone asked comedian Henny Youngman how old he was, he replied, "I'm so old, when I order a three-minute egg, they make me pay up front." Something like that might be ahead for aging Baby Boomers. By 2025, 20 percent of the population will be 65 or older, many will be solely dependent on Social Security payments, and there may not be any money left. Begun in 1935 as a safety net for the elderly, social security was intended to be a stipend paid back to workers who would use it to supplement their own savings and pension plans to live on in old age. Invested in a fund, the money was used in the budget and collected interest. In 1995, 140 million workers pay into a social security fund that is used to pay 40 million *current* retirees.

But within the next 20 years, the workforce will decline substantially as the number of retirees rises steadily. By 2029 economists predict that there will be no more full Social Security benefits to be paid. Sociologists see also a rising tension between retirees and those who work, or between the old and the young. Medical advances between now and then might prolong life beyond 100, putting a strain on economies everywhere. Norman Macrae, former editor of *The Economist,* predicts that euthanasia will replace abortion as the trick social issue of the day. "Euthanasia will be regarded as more moral," he says, "because otherwise poor countries will face the great-granny surplus one or two generations later."

Like an Elephant

Economists say the economy is like an elephant encountered by a blind man—he gropes and finds an ear and describes an elephant as being wrinkled and about the size of his hand. Composed of everything that anyone does that remotely affects profit and loss, the economy has indicators that let economists know how it is doing: interest rates, unemployment rates, retail prices, consumer prices, earnings from big companies like General Motors, wage growth, GDP growth, sales of existing homes, sales of new homes, and housing starts. Economists also add up tariffs from imports, profits from exports and foreign debts, and they keep an eye on banks and stock markets.

Doomsday Denied: A Survivor's Guide to the 21st Century

The Source of Anxiety

In the bickering 1990s Washington, D.C., has been fueled by Democratic and Republican talk about the National Debt, the Budget Deficit, and Entitlements. Anyone with credit card debt can take solace from knowing that our country has a national debt of $5 trillion. It's the biggest, but it's not the first nor the same debt we've had in the past. We started the country in 1795 with a national debt of $80 million. After the Civil War it was $2.7 billion, and after World War II it was $271 billion. The Debt is serviced: we pay the interest. In our more than 200 years as a country, we've enjoyed many surplus times, but only eight surplus periods since the Great Depression in 1931, and the last was in 1969. Economist John Steele Gordon notes that it took us 204 years of independence to take on a $1 trillion debt, but only five years to accumulate $4 trillion more.

The Budget is what it costs to run the country year to year; the Budget Deficit is the difference between what we make a year—the Gross National Product (GNP)—and what we pay. In 1996 the Deficit was 68 percent of the GNP. Because most of the Budget pays interest on the National Debt and provides money for entitlement (or welfare) programs, entitlement programs are the sore subject of political debate. Incorporated into the Constitution to serve the welfare of the people in times of bad health, sickness, or old age, entitlements were given no spending limits. Entitlement programs are funded in the House of Representatives in appropriations committees and watched over by the Congressional Budget Office and the Executive Office of Management and Budget. In 1995 a Republican Congress swore to balance the budget by 2002, and in 1996 a congressional welfare bill that eliminated aid to dependent children and forced people off welfare in 2 years was signed by Democratic President Bill Clinton.

Workfare, aimed at easing people off welfare and into jobs, is the problem of the states that must find unskilled jobs for the thousands expected to leave welfare in the near future. Observers of the labor market wonder where the new jobs will come from, and they worry that a combination of raised minimum wage and an influx of new workers will bounce out low-paid, unskilled workers (the "Working Poor") already there. Fast-food companies, like McDonald's, employ 2 to 3 million workers at minimum wage. Although the country could use real help like that provided in the Civilian Conservation

Corps and Works Progress Administration in the 1930s (rebuilding the crumbling bridges and roads), the talk is confined to theorists.

Mr. Rich, Meet Ms. Poor

At the turn of the last century, there were what could be called wage gaps. Railroad magnates like Cornelius Vanderbilt built empires on the backs of devoted employees who were proud to be a part of his organization and full of aspirations of someday becoming equally as rich and powerful. Charles Dickens summarized the chasm between the rich and poor in Victorian England, culminating in the pathetic Tiny Tim, crippled son of faithful company man Bob Cratchit, who was forced into cruel and unassuming poverty by the wretched Ebeneezer Scrooge.

These days, the characters are different. The average poor person in the United States is a single woman with a couple of kids. She struggles to make it on one or two minimum-wage jobs, keeping the family car together to carry the kids to and from school and her to her jobs. The father of her children has fled, and may turn up on the "Deadbeat" page of the local newspaper, having neglected to honor child support payments pledged in a divorce. Or he never committed to marriage in the first place, leaving his family forever in the shadowy realms of social welfare.

She worries about meeting the rent and spends what free time she can at the welfare office, getting food stamps, filling out forms for Aid to Families with Dependent Children, and joining the hundreds of thousands of others applying for better public housing. She makes less than $15,141 a year, which makes her, along with 38 million others (or 14.5 percent of the total population), officially "poor," according to the U.S. Census Bureau. She is also one of 22 million who are classified as the Working Poor, people, who despite their jobs, have no savings, no benefits, and barely make ends meet. In 1995, 39.7 million people had no health insurance. One crisis—an accident, a serious illness—can send them over the edge.

On the other end of the scale are the rich. Ten percent of the rich in America control 70 percent of the nation's wealth. Many are in the entertainment business, rock stars or movie idols, or baseball or football players sullenly holding out each season for more annual millions. Economist Lester Thurow explains the huge gap between the top and bottom salaries as a winner-take-all philosophy in which there is more competition for fewer spaces. Because there is so much data and so little time for major money-movers, like agents, name recognition is all, says Thurow. Madonna, for example, because she is a proven commodity, will never be out of work.

On a grander scale, the 1996 United Nations Human Development Report revealed that there are 358 billionaires in the world who "control assets greater than the combined annual incomes of countries with 45 percent of the world's people."

The same report found that Tanzania had the lowest per capita income among the poor of the world, at $70 a year. Per capita annual income for the U.S. poor was $5,814, lower than the Netherlands ($7,105) and Japan ($9,070).

Fast Money

Currency traders, who deal in "hot money," buy and sell daily, electronically moving mega sums of investment capital through international banking routes around the world to take advantage of the most profitable short-term interest rates. In other shady businesses, counterfeiters became desktop publishers sometime before early 1996 when "Superdollars," close to perfect copies of U.S. $100 bills, were found to be circulating in the Middle East. The CIA cautiously estimated that there were $1 billion in use, so much, in fact, that the U.S. Treasury issued a new $100-bill design, using techniques embedded in the paper that are thought to be unreproducible. But copies have become so easy to make with superb new technology, experts estimated that there were close to $380 billion in counterfeit U.S. currency in circulation in 1996.

In search of fast money, many people who never gambled before take weekend trips to one of the many gambling casinos in the United States, either on Indian reservations (where a percentage goes to the state), in private clubs, on ships parked offshore, and in the huge gambling halls of Atlantic City and Las Vegas. Bus companies run day trips for pensioners. While most are content with one-armed bandits (slot machines), others find themselves persuaded to hock their cars, their homes, and, in the sweat of moment, their firstborn. Gambling debt is one of the major causes of extreme credit card debt in the United States in the 1990s.

For those who win lottery or sweepstakes jackpots, the money is fast and big. On the other hand, the chances of winning millions of

Chapter 17: The Economy

dollars in the Publishers' Clearing House Sweepstakes, which are run throughout the year, are roughly one in 300 million. People do win, and many big-time winners experience big-time troubles. Strangers sue them, family members develop serious disputes, disgruntled ex-spouses haul them into court for increased alimony and childcare support; and their winnings, classified as income, are taxed by the IRS at the highest rate annually because the winnings are doled out as a trust. Many winners change their names and leave town.

New York changed its advertising campaign for its state lottery, emphasizing the more responsible uses of big winnings, such as paying for a college education or saving for the future, instead of buying two Jaguars and investing in a condo in Cancun.

Thirty-six states run lotteries, begun as a source of funds to aid ailing state education and welfare programs. A report by *Money* magazine in 1995 revealed that out of a collective $32 billion culled in state lotteries, the states paid out $21 billion in prizes and to pay the costs of running the show and kept only $11 billion. *Money* magazine also found that states with lotteries lowered annual allotments for education if education allotments were to be augmented with lottery funds.

Called a tax on the poor because poor people tend to spend more money than others on lottery tickets, state lotteries offer tiny odds of winning. Out of any lottery in which the bettor chooses the best six numbers out of 44, the odds are 1 in 7,059,052, according to James Walsh in an article in *Consumer Research* magazine (March 1996). Odds of winning a best six numbers out of 49 are one in 14 million.

Hold the Starch

At least three government agencies have full-time staffs primed to track down drug dealers and the amazing estimated $100 billion of untaxed money laundered in the United States every year. For a dealer, experts say, getting the drugs on the street is easier than getting the money to a bank. Most of it is cash collected in small bills, so it must be "laundered."

One operation in 1995, as explained by a report by the Royal Canadian Mounted Police, went like this: $500,000 in fives and tens were carried in a suitcase by a courier through Canada to England. There he deposited it in a bank. Then he flew to the Channel Islands and bought several "shelf" companies—they are corporations incorporated in exotic places like Liberia, that come with directors, off the shelf, as it were. Money from the London bank is sent to the shelf companies that then wire it into accounts of North American corporations that are fronts. These companies then loan money to drug traffickers, who use some of it to invest in real estate.

When the Oil's Gone

Environmentalists can't wait for the market forces to kick in on issues like clean air, water conservation, coastal construction, and alternative energy sources, like solar heating. According to the market economy, when something is scarce, like oil, the price goes up, and the market will adjust by finding a substitute, by conserving what's left, or by developing new technologies. Economists use the analogy of the Bronze Age: iron was around, but rarely used because copper and its alloys were available for bronze. It wasn't until copper sources dried up that iron became the premier metal.

Until recently, solar technology has been expensive and complicated. Now new technologies have made it far more accessible on the general market. Some geologists foresee the end of known oil reserves by the middle of the next century.

The Oracles at Delphi

Economy as a discipline grew out of the era of scientific wits like Newton and Copernicus, for whom the template of logic could be imposed on all human systems. As planets moved around the sun with predictability, the thinking went, so did humans engage in predictable formulas of profit and loss, individually or among great civilizations. According to economist Adam Smith, the country's economy should be run like a family, with income equaling current bills, with some set aside for saving, and no debt incurred that couldn't be paid back quickly. British economist Maynard Keynes, who died in 1928 and who was embraced by every American president except Reagan, believed that the economy was a global machine and people were its parts, contributing to their local market forces, which contributed to a major market force.

Economists, like climatologists, construct models. They gather together all of the indicators in the economy, like inflation; unemployment figures; interest rates; demographics that indicate where

Chapter 17: The Economy

women are working, how much they are making, and who is caring for the kids; how many people are getting divorced; the number of recent immigrants, alien and legal; how many teenagers will start working; and what's happening in Congress and the White House. Then economists try to figure out what might be a trend and if it might be exponential. They use results of public opinion polls, listen to what people are concerned about on talk radio shows, and chat it up over the office water cooler and neighborhood fence. And if they are hired to be oracles, as those are who sit on the President's Council of Economic Advisors, they try to come up with the best prediction for the next few weeks.

"Prognostications are impossible," says Frank Wyckoff, economist at the University of California–Davis. "We don't know where we are because of inherent changes in the system." Take unemployment, for example, he says; the numbers are all after the fact. "It's impossible to determine how many jobs there are. The number keeps changing as some appear while others disappear." One of the biggest drivers in economics is self-interest. "People don't *need* anything," he says. "They *want* things." And if all politics is local, so is economics, although economic seers look at the country as a whole. "It's a dynamic system; it's volatile; it's always fluctuating," says Wyckoff.

Remember the Renaissance

A millennium or so ago, a severe economic depression followed the outbreaks of Black Plague that began in Venice in 1326 and raged north throughout Europe. Countries' economies faltered: there were fewer to work the fields; trade ships sat idle in ports; social unrest and political disruption filled the cities. But historians and economists alike point out that the Plague was followed by the Renaissance.

People respond positively to perceived challenges. No less now. For factors that far outweigh all of the argumentative banter in Washington, the world economy is in a state of flux. Some countries and individuals will benefit; others will fail. Change is always the name of the game, but now it's global economic change that affects us. Nothing is really stable. If you want to teach your kids anything about the economy, one economist said, it should be a tolerance for ambiguity—certainly not an expectation of stability.

❓ What You Can Do

For expert help on debt-reduction and restoring credit, contact Bank Card Holders of America, 524 Branch Drive, Salem, Virginia 24153; (540) 389-5445. Their Debt-Zapper Program for $15 will help you organize your debt.

To find out your retirement benefits, call the Social Security Administration and ask for your Earnings and Benefit Estimate Statement: (800) 772-1213.

18 Privacy

Strangers in the Closet

PRIVACY BEGINS AT HOME. Posters like this one decorated post offices, train and bus stations, and other public places during World War II in the days of eavesdropping spies. They reminded the public that discretion and secrecy protected the whole country, and that privacy was a matter of personal control. Photo credit: U.S. National Archive, Still Picture Branch.

A hundred years ago, there were no phones to bug, and cameras were the size of breadbaskets. People peeped through keyholes, stood tiptoe on chairs to peer over transoms, and pressed ears against the wall, hoping for the critical word or action that would reveal a secret love or that the butler did it. Men covered their heads, ladies covered their ankles. Curtains shielded windows; doctors' lips were sealed; embarrassing family members were kept in upstairs rooms. Everyone had secrets; privacy was all.

But today people argue over exactly what privacy is. The media have given us access to details of private lives we may or may not want to know. "How did you feel?" became the mantra of the TV reporter at the scene of the catastrophe. The intimate self-revelations of guests on "Oprah" and other talk shows, watched from the privacy of our living rooms, have made us into voyeurs. The coziness of the Net, on which a visitor can be any sex or age he or she wants to be, helps create a false atmosphere of trust in which we, from the privacy of our desks, enter a very public cyberworld.

But as we grow comfortable with revealing our feelings and ideas in public, we feel more protective of the hard facts of who we are. And those details—our social security numbers, credit card numbers, telephone numbers, bank account numbers, street addresses—are fast becoming public data. A 1995 Louis Harris poll found that 80 percent felt they had lost "all control" over the personal information that can be collected by professional investigators and hackers.

Crooks with stolen social security numbers, for example, have collected tax refunds from the newly dead, opened accounts in strangers' names, even applied for mortgages. Can you protect yourself? If you live in one of the 30 states that use the social security number on a driver's license or go to a university that uses it as an ID, or if you receive mail from the IRS, which puts your number on your mailing label—no.

A social security number can call up your credit history too, if you are applying for a loan. If a clerk punched erroneous data into your credit record, you may find yourself turned down not only for credit, but for a job as well. It was estimated that half of all credit agency reports contained errors, not necessarily committed by malefactors, just simple typos.

Party Lines

Your home phone may or may not be bugged, but your cell phone is wide open. In 1995 the cell phone industry lost $650 million, or 4 percent of its overall income, paying for criminals' use of stolen numbers. Cell phone numbers are relatively easy to steal: they emit code numbers and PIN code signals to transmitting towers. In transit, thieves perched on overpasses or sitting in nearby cars collect the numbers with scanners stuck to their windshields. The numbers—your private numbers—are then cloned into another telephone. The Secret Service estimates that more than 60,000 numbers are stolen each month in the United States and Canada. True criminals rent the cloned phones cheap to anyone anxious to make a call—students, drug dealers—and you get a fantastic bill, and the phone company picks up the tab. What can you do? Keep a close watch on your phone bill and change your PIN frequently.

Long-distance calling cards are also vulnerable. Criminals in public places have been caught using binoculars to see the access codes a caller punches in at a public phone. And criminals are in the system. In 1994 an MCI employee was arrested and accused of having stolen 60,000 calling card numbers, with which he made $50 million in illegal calls.

Virtual Spies

In 1996 a 21-year-old Argentinean was caught breaking into a Harvard University computer system from his home several thousand miles away. Harvard was only one target: on his list were other universities, the Department of Defense, and NASA. He was caught because Harvard used a wiretap ordered by the Deptartment of Justice, which legally cannot bug university computers.

Hackers, or cyberpunks, use a little technological knowledge to take heady power trips. Convicted hacker John Lee boasted that he could commit "a crime in five keystrokes": change credit statements and bank balances; access free plane tickets, hotel rooms, and limos charged to no one; change utility and rent rates; send free software over the Net; and get insider trading information.

Cyber criminals have different motivations, but many are young and smart and have grown up with computers. Many "want the 'good life,' after growing up in poverty," said criminologist Gene Stephens. "They are proud of their skills of deception and arrogant enough to feel they won't be caught." In 1996 a Senate Permanent Investigations Subcommittee report revealed that banks and corporations lost $800 million in 1995 to hackers.

What hackers have proven is that, even if you change your password frequently, there is no privacy on computers—e-mail is public mail—and that, if they can cruise in cyberspace with the ease of a spaceship in a video game, they can go anywhere. In 1996 CIA Director John M. Deutsch declared cyberwar on hackers, recognizing the lack of gatekeepers in the war room, in air traffic control centers, at international financial transfers of money. Discovering the key that decodes the Escrowed Encryption Standard that federal law enforcement agencies use to transmit information, hackers flew deeper and deeper into government secrets. As a result, effective encryption has become a full-time concern; now the key is kept "in escrow" in a government agency. Deutsch equated the computer threat to national security with nuclear/biological/chemical weapons. "The electron," Deutsch said, "is the ultimate precision-guided weapon."

Balance of Power

The recurrent problem, as information thieves make out like bandits, and as terrorism raises its ugly head, is how much power a democratic government can give to its law enforcement agencies. Cries of "Big Brother" rang out when video cameras were placed in high-crime areas in Baltimore, Maryland, and Redwood City, California. James M. Fox, former chief of the FBI's New York office, said, "You just can't collect stuff like you used to. In some cases, the FBI can collect far less information than your local credit bureau."

The current Anti-Terrorism Bill allows for investigation of anyone in contact with "foreign powers or factions" (which presumably can include your aging cousin in Canada). Under current law, only the FBI and police can legally look at your telephone call record and your bank records if they suspect you of a crime.

In 1996 President Clinton signed the Communications Decency Act, designed to protect children from "indecent" speech on the Net, but it was overruled in a judgment by three federal judges in Philadelphia who supported the First Amendment's right of free speech, supported by the American Civil Liberties Union.

In the workplace, it is legal for employers to spy on employees for whatever reason, no matter how insulting it might be for the employees. Employers can listen in on telephone conversations and read computer screens remotely. Employers are suspected of listening to voicemail messages and reading e-mail. They can look in desks, files, and lockers. Cameras in bathrooms are used when employees are suspected of drug use, and cameras and listening devices can be installed where employees gather to smoke. Background checks look at every detail, from sexual practices to religious beliefs. And they

Chapter 18: Privacy

are not always accurate. The person your employer hires may not be the person you think you are.

Nor is your body protected. In 1996 a patient discovered that her psychiatric records were publicly displayed on a computer file at her HMO. With the Human Genome project coming to a close and the new capability of knowing not only your ancestors back a few million years, but your personal genetic faults, medical privacy is a prime concern in Congress, where no fewer than seven bills seek to set some uniform federal standard. The Bennett-Leahy Bill will make it illegal for companies to use your medical records for marketing purposes. As it stands, the police, health agencies, and medical researchers can access your medical records, as can any idle scoundrel employee on his coffee break.

James, May We Bond?

Spy shops almost went out of business in 1996 when 40 shops of the Spy Factory were raided by Customs Service personnel and indicted for smuggling. What had formerly been confined to international spies became big business a few years ago when customers combined curiosity with disposable income. For a few dollars, you can buy a teddy bear with camera eyes to spy on your toddlers or the babysitter, cameras hidden in vents to see if your roommate is raiding your room, cameras the size of a dime that can fit into a tie tack, bionic ears that amplify the conversations of your neighbors, listening devices placed on phone jacks or under tables to hear what your spouse says in your absence, lasers that pick up conversations on the other side of windows, scramblers to mix up your telephone conversations, audio jammers that protect your conversations within 150 feet, and night-vision goggles for who knows what.

But wait. Soon to appear at your airport security checkpoint, when they are perfected and legalized, are millimeter wave videos and radar skin scanners that see through your clothes. They pick up non-metallic items, such as carbon fiber knives, and detect powder, such as cocaine or heroin. But they get pretty personal, and there will probably be specific male or female scanners (and a refusal or two). Microwave imaging devices see inside your body, wherever drugs might be hidden, for example, eliminating body searches.

Digital cameras, used in public surveillance, store faces on fast computers, so terrorists can be tracked in crowds coming and going at an airport, for example. Spy satellites, with a resolution of 1 meter, will be able to provide continuous 24-hour coverage of a battlefield, and come equipped with a laser ID to tell friend from enemy. The future is an electronic wonderland. "There will always be some better form of security on a computer system," said Frank Steen, director of Harvard Arts and Sciences Computer Services, after their system was invaded by the Argentinean hacker. "And just as fast as they put one up, someone else will be out there trying to crack it."

What Is Privacy?

Ironically, neither the Constitution nor the Bill of Rights mentions the word "privacy." The closest mention is in the Fourth Amendment, which prohibits "unreasonable search and seizure" of personal property without a warrant. Over the years Congress has passed a number of laws—the Privacy, Freedom of Information, and Fair Credit Reporting Acts, for example, and federal agencies have issued rules that define, control, and restrict ways in which they may access people and their property. Altogether, they have created the illusion of a right to privacy, which, while not legal, is the bedrock of every cultural belief and probably one of the "certain inalienable rights" referred to by Thomas Jefferson in the Declaration of Independence.

What is privacy? It's however you define it. "Although we live in a world of noisy self-confession, privacy allows us to keep certain facts to ourselves if we so choose," wrote Caroline Kennedy and Ellen Alderman in *The Right to Privacy*. "The right to privacy, it seems, is what makes us civilized."

What You Can Do

To find out how to get your credit report, contact Equifax, (800) 685-1111; Trans Union, (800) 916-8800; TRW, (800) 682-7654.

To find out if the FBI has a file on you, call the FBI Freedom of Information/Privacy Acts Section: (202) 324-3000.

Also try the Freedom of Information Act Clearinghouse: (202) 588-1000.

For fact sheets on privacy in the workplace, contact The Privacy Rights Clearinghouse, Center for Public Interest Law, University of California, San Diego, 5998 Alcala Park, San Diego 92110; (619) 298-3396.

Privacy Times, P.O. Box 21501, Washington, D.C. 20009; (202) 829-3660. A biweekly newsletter on privacy topics.

19 Alien Abductions

No Postcards from the Edge

WE'RE NOT ALONE. The 140-foot-diameter National Radio Astronomy Organization radio telescope in Green Bank, West Virginia, is used by the Search for Extraterrestrial Intelligence (SETI). SETI's Project Phoenix searches the thousand nearest sunlike stars, looking for suns with planetary systems similar to Earth's. Photo credit: SETI League, used by permission.

In 1950, three years after the first "flying saucers" were reported in the press, a national poll found that 47 percent of Americans believed that UFOs were "real." Hundreds of thousands reported having seen one. In 1995, after three-and-a-half decades of official denial, the number of believers was up to 50 percent. More alarming, a 1991 Roper poll revealed that 4 million Americans believed they have been abducted by aliens.

The aliens who abduct humans and flying saucers, or UFOs, might be two separate, unrelated phenomena. A hundred years ago, the discovery of canals on Mars and H.G. Wells's popular novel *War of the Worlds* gave the public a handle on what they could not explain: Martians. They looked like us, the belief went, but they were smarter and meaner. In 1996 each week an average of 12 million viewers faithfully turned on *The X-Files*, a television series about a pair of FBI agents who investigate the government cover-up of UFOs. Moviegoers saw *Independence Day*, a modern-day version of *War of the Worlds*. And E.T., a short-legged, big-eyed, wrinkle-skinned alien from who knows where and the box-office success of the same name helps filter the unknown into the mainstream on T-shirts and souvenirs and posters in libraries exhorting people to read, while artists across the country draw pictures of the creatures and experiences they are unable to explain otherwise.

Officially—that is, in the lexicon of government, science, and academia, as well as among most "educated" people—UFOs do not exist, and alien abductees are lying, are mistaken, or are given to fantasy. The problem is, a culture bound by the scientific method, in which the unknown can be tested hypothetically, has little flexibility for dealing with anomalies. Where is the proof? we ask.

"There is not one physical shred of evidence of UFOs, "says Philip Klass, head of the Committee for the Scientific Investigation of Claims of the Paranormal (CSICOP), editor of the *Skeptical Inquirer* and a 20-year debunker of the phenomenon. Even believers in UFOs are frustrated by the absence of souvenirs, photos, recordings. "Why is it, with all the 35-mm auto-focus cameras and hand-held video cameras people now own, there are still no clear and convincing photographs of UFOs, much less alien beings?" asks Harvard psychiatrist John Mack, who has hypnotized alien abductees since 1990. Despite the fact that at least two presidents (Carter and Ford) have seen UFOs and numerous members of Congress have requested deeper investigation and more open files, government refusal prevails. In 1995 the Air Force issued a flat-out dismissal (and took a several-inches-thick document in which to do it).

A Different Reality

For abductees, pictures aren't necessary. Carol, for example, a sane and competent woman in her 40s, related this experience to writer C.D.B. Bryan. She is sitting on her porch, waiting for her friend to

Chapter 19: Alien Abductions

drive up from Washington, D.C., to join her at a cabin on a lake in a state park in West Virginia. It rains and stops, and a heavy bank of fog rolls down the hill toward her cabin. She watches it idly then sees a pair of gray legs in the fog. In terror, she leaps over the porch railing and runs to her car. It starts, but as she frantically backs it up, three small gray-skinned aliens appear in front of the car. One points at her engine and the car slips out of gear. There are, in fact, no gears left. The door opens, and she floats into the fog, and next becomes aware of being terribly cold and reclining, absolutely paralyzed, in a well-lit room. A tall creature with a large head, a small ridge of a nose, a slit for a mouth, and huge completely black eyes, plunges a short double needle into the joint on her thumb. Carol finds the pain excruciating, but she can't cry out. The alien puts its hand on her forehead, and the pain vanishes. Then the alien injects a gold liquid into her thumb, and instructs a much shorter gray alien to use a needle with a suction cup on the vein on her left arm. The short "assistant" drops the suction cup, and her blood runs down her arm. Carol notices that the tall alien apparently shoots the shorter one across the room. Then the shorter one returns and successfully takes a small amount of blood.

Methodically, they remove her clothes, and inject another liquid through a double needle into her abdomen below the navel. "You will eat only cow," the tall alien says to her telepathically. "Cow!" Carol thinks. "I'm a vegetarian!" The shorter alien then pulls her sweater over her head but has difficulty getting her Levis back on, so she is released from her paralysis, pulls on her pants, and is escorted out.

Back in her cabin, she has no memory of the event, and only wonders why it is a lot later than she thought it was. She prepares hot dogs for dinner, takes a bite, and throws up. When she goes back to the porch, she notices her car in the middle of the road and thinks it has rolled down from its parking place. She goes out to re-park it, and when she grips the handle, she instantly recalls everything that happened.

The Taken

The primary characteristic of abductees is what Mack calls their "ordinariness." Their ages range from two to 60-something, they live all over the world, they are not insane, and most are very reluctant to relate their experiences. Historian David Jacobs, who has written a history of UFOs and hypnotized 60 abductees, describes them like this: "They were Protestant, Catholic, Jewish, white, black, male, female, younger, older, professional, nonprofessional, married, single, divorced, employed, unemployed, articulate, and inarticulate." In some cases, several generations of one family have been abducted.

No one knows how long abductions have been occurring—some observers believe aliens have been doing this for several millennia, but hypnotic regression of abductees did not start until the 1960s, when New York City artist Budd Hopkins, who had seen a UFO, brought some abductees together with a psychologist. Since then, Jacobs and Harvard psychiatrist John Mack have used hypnotic regression after screening their genuine subjects for authenticity.

Mack, a 1977 Pulitzer Prize winner (for a biography of Lawrence of Arabia, *A Prince of Our Disorder*) and a founder of a Harvard psychiatric teaching hospital, is the director of the Program for Exrtraordinary Experience Research at Harvard's Center for Psychiatry and Social Research. In 1994 the "professionalism" of his alien abductee research was questioned by a Harvard board, who voted a year later not to censure him. The criticism was aimed at the validity of using hypnotism to recover trauma, without introducing suggestion.

Until recently, abduction experiences were not widely publicized, and researchers were astounded by the similarities of the reported experiences: most are taken from their bed, their car, or the outdoors. They see an intense light, are taken against their will by "floating" sometimes through walls, into what appears to be a spacecraft. There they are paralyzed, placed on their backs on a sterile, usually white table, where, usually nude, they undergo "medical" tests. In some cases, men are forced to ejaculate and their sperm, collected; and women receive fertilized eggs in their uterus. Sometimes abductees are cut, their skin scraped, and "implants" placed up their nose in the sinus. Often they have nosebleeds.

Part of the medical procedure is what Jacobs calls Mindscan: floating above the table, the tall alien puts its face inches away from the abductee's and gazes into his or her eyes. After the experience, all have a sense of "missing time": they cannot account for the passage of several hours.

Severe headaches, sleep disturbances, excessive inattention, and nervousness later drive many to therapy, but the post-traumatic stress symptoms do not make sense until they are hypnotized. In recalling the events, most remember terror, humiliation, and rage. Abductees also recall feelings of great love and compassion from the aliens. Most claim they are deeply changed by their experience; they have a sense of mission, although they do not always know what the mission is. Some claim they have an expanded sense of themselves as being part of the whole Earth, with an obligation to care for the planet.

Because much of society denies the existence of aliens and alien experiences, those who have had them are forced to go underground. In the breeding hole of denial, all sorts of fungi grow, from New Age wannabes' fantasies to government disinformation to tabloid headlines ("Woman Gives Birth to Alien Baby Which Kills Her!"). "If what these abductees are saying is happening to them isn't happening, what is?" asks John Mack.

The Abductors

Most abductees report two types of aliens. The first type is a tall, gray- or grayish-white skinned being with three or four long fingers, a large pear-shaped head with compelling black eyes, and otherwise minimal features; a long thin neck, slim body with no sexual characteristics, and no feet. Some describe the arms as "octopuslike," without bones. They communicate telepathically.

The shorter aliens, about $3\frac{1}{2}$ feet tall, have gray skin of a smoother texture, with large eyes in a large head that is sometimes hooded. Abductees believe these aliens act as assistants. That they might be sophisticated robots controlled by a superintelligence remains a possibility; some abductees sense that aliens' "engulfing" eyes might be dark glasses.

But longtime observers of the alien phenomenon believe that aliens might be superb shape-changers. Some abductees report seeing extremely tall (taller than tall humans) blonde "Nordic-types"; reptilian beings with webbed feet; and apparent hybrids, part human, part alien.

The Real X-Files

The term "flying saucers" was born in June 1947 when an air rescue pilot, looking for a downed Air Force plane near Mt. Ranier, Washington, radioed that he had spotted nine disk shapes skipping through the air at speeds between 1,000 and 2,000 miles per hour. Later, the pilot,

Kenneth Arnold, called them flying saucers because of their shape.

The military was in a cautious mood two years after the close of World War II and at the beginning of the Cold War: if flying saucers were not a clever invention of the enemy, officials believed, then the enemy shouldn't know anything about them. National security at the time also included averting national hysteria if, in fact, little green people from Mars had suddenly chosen to visit New Mexico.

Less than two weeks after flying saucers were sighted over Washington, something exploded in the air 75 miles north of Roswell Army Air Base, New Mexico. Pieces fell on private ranchland. The next morning the owner saw scattered debris over a wide area. The scattered material looked like, but was not, tinfoil, with strange markings on it. The army surrounded and cordoned off a vast area and issued a statement saying it was a weather balloon. But rumors spread that the wreckage was a flying saucer and that the bodies of four small aliens had been recovered by the army.

In 1966 the official Air Force investigation, Project Blue Book, claimed that there was no evidence that flying saucers were extraterrestrial. Top Secret documents, reportedly declassified from 1952 when they were shown to President Eisenhower, revealed, however, that the Roswell explosion was from two colliding flying saucers and that four alien bodies had been retrieved. Thirty years later, the Roswell mortician came forward and said he remembered getting a request from the army to make four small caskets that could be hermetically sealed. Other witnesses from the time saw and described the wreckage, and in 1995 a video of an 8-mm film was distributed spuriously, showing an autopsy of a supposed alien.

But Roswell was small potatoes. In 1952 there were 1,500 sightings of flying saucers. Around the world, fast cigar-shaped or disklike craft zoomed across the sky in formation singly or in groups—by day, by night, flashing bright white lights, or red, blue, and green lights. In China in 1987 an estimated one million people watched a UFO spiral through the sky. In empty fields, farmers came across small gray people carrying off calves. A deputy marshall chasing a speeder in Socorro, New Mexico, in 1964 startled two men in white coveralls who leapt into an egg-shaped craft with red insignia and took off in a roar of blue and orange flame straight up for 25 feet, before vanishing silently into the horizon.

In the 1970s cattle in Kansas and across the Plains were mutilated at night, apparently by superb surgeons using laser tools: whole

Chapter 19: Alien Abductions

organs were excised without blood being released. In the 1980s wheat fields in England were arranged into geometric patterns at night. Although two pranksters have claimed credit for crop circles, astronomer Gerald Hawkins analyzed their geometry and found new non-Euclidean theorems corresponding to a diatonic scale: in other words, if Hawkins is right, crop circles are the closest thing we have to the elaborate musical communications scheme devised in the film *Close Encounters of the Third Kind* (*Science News*, October 12, 1996, p. 239)

But flying saucers were seen before we started calling them "flying saucers." Between 1896 and 1897, hundreds of sightings of airships were reported throughout the United States: huge cigar-shaped craft with people visible aboard, speaking "jibberish," or other languages, or English. Newspapers reported several encounters that esteemed members of communities had had in empty fields where men in strange costumes asked to have their water buckets filled. In Texas a judge met up with a couple of young men who explained their ship was created by a "secret inventor," was financed by New York capitalists, and would soon take over the railroad as fast mass travel.

Does E.T. Reverse the Charges?

It takes 30,000 years for light to travel from our sun to the center of our galaxy, the Milky Way. How can these space visitors get around so speedily? Or do they go through black holes or manipulate gravity electromagnetically?

To answer the question, Does life exist elsewhere in the universe?, the Search for Extraterrestrial Intelligence (SETI) was begun in 1960, funded by government money. It set up radio telescopes to send out and to listen for ordered pulsed signals coming from the depths of the universe that would signify an intelligence wishing to communicate. When government funding ran out in 1993, SETI turned to private support. It now runs programs at the Harvard/Smithsonian-The Planetary Society radio telescope, which is governed by the BETA (Billion Channel Extraterrestrial Assay) project, which listens in the 1.4 to 1.7 GH microwave band; Project Phoenix, at the SETI Institute, Mountain View, California, which runs a targeted search for nearby suns with a computer program designed by its director D. Kent Cullers, who, blind from birth, is an exceptional listener; and the Arecibo Radio Telescope in Puerto Rico, described by astronomer Dan Wertheimer of the Berkeley SERENDIP listening program as big enough to hold "10 billion bowls of cornflakes." Arecibo scans 30 percent of the sky in the 424 to 436 MHz band.

So far the only outstanding signal was received by the Big Ear radio telescope at Ohio State University in 1977. Called "Wow!" (after the comment written in the margin of the printout sheet), the short burst of steady pulsed signals, never heard from before or since, might have been from a military satellite.

SETI President Paul Shuch emphasizes that SETI has nothing to do with alien abduction experiences. But within the scientific community, SETI must defend itself against charges that any search is futile.

Ernst Mayr, Professor Emeritus of Zoology at Harvard, joins many others who think the chances of actually connecting with a space life-form are virtually nil. Mayr points out in a debate sponsored by the *Harvard Gazette* with physics professor Paul Horowitz, director of the SETI BETA project at Harvard, that intelligent life might be rare: only one in 50 billion species on Earth reached a level at which it could invent the computer. What if, he asks, an alien civilization pulsed us steadily until, say 1900, when it gave up, making a dialogue impossible? Horowitz countered that dead civilizations are not new: the Ancient Greeks are gone from Earth, but their "one-way communications speak powerfully to us, now and in the future," he said. Mayr thought it would be improbable to find intelligent life "in the small part of the universe we can monitor with a radio telescope." Horowitz replied that we broadcast to a hundred trillion sunlike stars in the Milky Way alone. "Only an innumerate," he added, "would say, 'Don't hassle me with your numbers, we are alone.'" And if someone *is* out there, would they answer? Horowitz believes that if more advanced systems receive our signals, they will probably devise a response because they will be curious about Earthlings.

What Do Aliens Really Want?

Are aliens even *from* outer space? In 1996 NASA announced that microscopic life from Mars was found in a meteorite in Antarctica, deposited 13,000 years ago and thought to have originated three billion years ago. If we're lucky, a Martian welcoming committee will sit down with our TV cameras, due to arrive on a NASA project within the next few years, and explain the whole thing.

But meanwhile, if they—the aliens, the UFO pilots, the cattle surgeons, the field geometry specialists—want to communicate with

Chapter 19: Alien Abductions

us, how would they do it? And are they, already? "What are the criteria for evaluating information from the cosmos?" asks John Mack.

We struggle with cognitive dissonance. Why, when aliens can float through walls and think in hundreds of Earth languages, do they need needles and syringes? What do they inject? Why do they take abductees so many times? Do they have a long-range plan?

Theories range across the board. Perhaps, many psychologists suggest, they are symbolic of a collective mind change: We are in the midst of a major psychic paradigm shift that is creating a whole new dimension among humans. Some physicists are fascinated with the idea that aliens might be manifestations of a quantum wave function or part of a parallel universe.

Such is the belief of Jacques Vallee, a French computer scientist on whom Steven Spielberg based his main scientist in *Close Encounters of the Third Kind*. Doomed to find answers, and to expect a sequential revelation of a mystery, humans are caught in a learning curve, he suggests. Trying to make sense out of aliens' contradictions captures us whether we accept them or not. "We know from behavioral psychology that the best schedule of reinforcement is one that combines periodicity with unpredictability," he says. "I have been led to conclude that there is a spiritual control system for human consciousness, and that paranormal phenomena like UFOs are one of its manifestations." Vallee is quick to add that the whole process of change could be a natural human evolutionary movement. Or it could be artificial, and we could be some higher intelligence's experiment.

Other social observers, like Keith Thompson (in his book *Aliens and Angels*) believe that humans are suffering from an overdose of the scientific method: We've maxed out on provable facts and have encountered empty places where, for all of human history, gods and spirits and fairies and gremlins have dwelled, dealing out their tricks unpredictably.

Alien Encounters 101

How can we join all the loose ends of this phenomenon and live with it comfortably? If the manifestations are sporadic, and if major unknowns continue—are UFOs radioactive, for example—the best we can do is accept the possibility that something is out there. Use crime-scene forensic techniques, suggests UFO researcher Victoria

Alexander, who has developed a guide and an alien abductee kit that encourages the collection of hard observable data—where are the needles stored, for example. David Jacobs found that asking different questions got more interesting insights. When an abductee said an alien doctor asked her to memorize a list of names, Jacobs asked, "What was the alien doing while you memorized?" instead of, "What was the list?" (The alien doctor was observing her, Jacobs discovered.)

Thompson suggests that regular abductees adopt "proactive" strategies, to be more awake and aware when they are "taken." He suggests that they practice martial arts to develop their chi, do serious meditation, and learn lucid dreaming.

Aliens may be satisfied with the great unanswered, but we humans need our tangible souvenirs and our scrapbooks filled with photographs. Never leave home without your camera.

What You Can Do

Help scan the heavens with an amateur dish. The nonprofit organization SETI League runs Sky Survey, with 5,000 watchers scanning the so-called Water Hole in the Milky Way, at 1.4 to 1.7 GHz. For information, contact The SETI League, Inc., 433 Liberty Street, P.O. Box 555, Little Ferry, NJ 07643; (800) TAU-SETI; website: http:/seti1.setileague.org/homepg.html; e-mail: n6tx@setileague.org.

Connect with happenings at the Big Ear Radio Telescope at the University of Ohio website: http://everest.eng.ohio-state.edu/^klein/ro/.

If you are an abductee wishing to share your experience, contact The Program for Extraordinary Experience Research (PEER), P.O. Box 382427, Cambridge, MA 02238.

Dr. David M. Jacobs, Department of History, Temple University, Philadelphia, PA 19122.

The following organizations collect UFO data: J. Allen Hynek Center for UFO Studies, 2457 West Peterson Avenue, Chicago, IL 60659; (312) 271-3611; and The Fund for UFO Research, P.O. Box 277, Mt. Rainier, MD; (703) 684-6032.

20 Chemicals

Unmixing the Elixirs

LANDSCAPES FOR BETTER LIVING. When chemical plants go, do chemicals? Storage tanks must be removed through a wall in this former factory being made into an apartment building. Toxic chemical residues from smokestacks, products, and the factories themselves are a major problem of the 1990s. Photo credit: Roger Archibald.

A millennium ago chemists turned lead into gold. It never became a big industry, however, because alchemists weren't interested in making gold for everybody. It wasn't until the late nineteenth century that visionaries working in dim laboratories joined their unfettered imaginations with cheap labor, factories with behemoth machines, and simple chemical formulas that transformed something small into something big. Batteries stored invisible power, petroleum could be spun into plastics, and we could produce things like saccharin—sugar without fields and fieldhands—and mimic nature. Miracles were everywhere.

In the 1990s we find ourselves dealing with the contents of Pandora's Box, having released things with names like "polychlorinated biphenyls" and "2.3.4.-T." In this brave new world, we have landfills packed with corrosive sodium chloride, rivers with fish eating mercury, air dense with products of combustion engines. Plastics clog sewers; six-pack holders strangle seals. Lead is everywhere. Processed foods, like "cheese" made out of soybeans, are the mainstay of convenience stores.

But for the better part of a century we have been able to feed millions of people with grains grown without insects or weeds. Supermarkets selling food with preservatives and antioxidants have diminished decay in transport and storage. Chlorinated water has averted public epidemics of disease, like cholera. Pharmaceuticals have alleviated the pain of countless illnesses. Trains, planes, and cars carry us wherever we want to go.

The downside is, around the world, governments struggle with balancing the power of chemical pollution: some chemicals, like polychlorinated biphenyls (PCBs) are banned; others, like chlorofluorcarbons, are restricted. Some are replaced by substitutes: sterile moths, for example, do as good a job as some pesticides. Not all countries have the same bans, however, and clouds know no borders and carry acid rain around the world. Environmentalists call for summary bans on whole classes of chemicals while scientists wrestle with understanding the complexity of multiple factors and protection agencies weave a path through the smog of lobbyists. There are no easy solutions.

Air

Most people spend between 80 and 90 percent of each day indoors, in schools, offices, apartment buildings, homes. Many newer buildings are sealed drums with temperature-controlled air circulated through vents. They become breeding grounds for all kinds of problems. Those you should be aware of, according to the American Lung Association, are asbestos, a carcinogen that disintegrates and becomes airborne when it ages; formaldehyde, a gas released in plywood, particle board, some glues, and fabrics in carpets, drapes, and upholstery (it causes headaches and upper respiratory problems). Microorganisms, like viruses, bacteria, molds, and fungi, live in vents, air conditioning units, planters, and unclean washrooms. Copying machines give off ozone; felt-tip pens release benzene. Carbon monoxide can accumulate and filter up from indoor parking garages.

Chapter 20: Chemicals

For a full smog experience, Los Angeles is the poster city. That dense foglike yellow haze that makes eyes red and throats sore is full of ozone, particulates, carbon monoxide, sulfur dioxide, nitrogen dioxide, and lead. The Clean Air Act called for National Ambient Air Quality Standards, set up by the EPA, which are monitored through most urban areas.

But know the enemy: Ozone (O_3), ground or tropospheric ozone, is the same composition as the ozone that is being eaten by chlorine in the stratosphere. It is a product of combustion engines and is created by the effects of heat and sunlight on hydrocarbons and nitrogen oxides. It is an oxidant, irritates lung tissue, and damages white blood cells. It doesn't matter whether you smoke or not. A study done in Los Angeles found that breathing capacity was diminished in nonsmokers to the same level as pack-a-day smokers. Consume lots of vitamins C and E if you live near smog.

Particulate matter is a collection of dust, soot from smokestacks, natural things like pollen, and tiny bits of metal. The smallest particulates are easily breathed in, and in the lungs exacerbate asthma attacks and childhood bronchitis; they also heighten the risk of cardiopulmonary deaths.

Carbon monoxide (CO) is a product of fossil fuel combustion and is highly toxic. It is worse in stalled traffic that inches along, because CO is released when fuel is not completely burned. It's colorless, odorless, and tasteless and causes drowsiness, headache, and, in enclosed spaces, death because it combines with hemoglobin and prevents the body from absorbing oxygen. Catalytic converters on cars have diminished levels of CO, as have cleaner gasolines, but there are more combustion engines clogging city streets.

Sulfur and nitrogen are the major sources of acid rain. Power plants are the biggest offenders, as are metal smelting plants, refineries, and paper mills, as well as combustion engines. Sulfur dioxide is a gas released from burning oil and coal, as is nitrogen dioxide, and they are highest in cities with lots of traffic, and thought to be a major cause of chest colds and lung infections, especially in children.

The so-called dry reaction of these corrosive acids, which are the effects of industrial pollutants in the air, eat away at city buildings, and kill vegetation that, in turn, poisons the soil and mobilizes heavy metals, like lead and aluminum, which work into the groundwater. Water supplies become polluted, and the acid and metals infiltrate freshwater rivers and lakes and kill salmon and trout.

Acid Rain

Acid rain is rain with a pH level of about 5, not quite vinegar, but close. In the 1960s and 1970s many factories built their smokestacks higher to push the offending toxins, sulfur and nitrogen oxides, farther away from the Earth. The result was that they got closer to the jet stream and sailed over other countries, and they also got close to clouds from which they fell in rain or snow that, over time, killed leaves and needles on trees, especially in northern forests, and leached the nutrients into the soil and ultimately reached groundwater, a source of drinking water. In rivers and lakes acid rain contributes more sulfur and nitrogen that joins with metals to kill fish.

Lead

Lead is a heavy metal that is found in air, water, and soil, from which it turns up in food. It's been around ever since humans discovered smelting. Traces of lead from ancient Greek silver refineries, carried north by the wind, have been discovered in Finnish lakes. And it is slow to go: nonleaded gasoline has been used since 1984, but a major source of lead is currently found in soil by the side of the road and in city gardens, where it was deposited over the years from passing traffic fueled by leaded gasoline.

More than 100 years ago, physicians recognized the link between lead and "insanity"—it affects the central nervous system, slowly producing changes, and it is extremely dangerous to the nervous system of the developing fetus, in which it is fed through the placenta, and in the newborn, who drinks it in mother's milk. Airborne lead, which is breathed in as dust, comes from flaking lead paint and lead in the soil. A recent study at the University of Pittsburgh found that seven year olds exposed to low levels over prolonged periods were highly aggressive. Another study found that ingesting lead from lead-soldered food cans and water pipes and faucets over a 50-year lifetime was directly related to hypertension in adult men.

Workers in high-risk jobs involving lead—bridge and tunnel work, street construction, woodworking, truck and bus body manufacture, foundries producing railroad equipment, and battery production—have higher incidence not only of central nervous system problems but reproductive system defects.

Chapter 20: Chemicals

Small European villages have been plagued with lead problems for centuries. In a small village in Italy, for example, a study found lead poisoning came from homemade wine. Lead seeps into wine production in lead arsenate in mildew treatment on vines, in grape collection containers, in lead wine presses, in the tanks where wine is fermented, in pottery containers, and in metal caps on glass bottles, which contain lead that leaches out if the wine sits for a long period of time.

Lead is made into 129 compounds and used in everything from hair dyes to brake linings. It turns up in older copper water pipes soldered with lead. Many tap water faucets are brass, containing lead covered with chrome.

Heavy metals, such as lead, cadmium, and mercury seep into water supplies for drinking and fishing from carelessly dumped industrial wastes. In 1986 the Superfund Act required companies with nine or more employees to report all releases of toxic chemicals into the environment. Two thousand superfund sites are scattered over the country, cost a huge amount of money to clean up, and are often difficult to identify completely. In 1996 a NASA high-altitude research plane, able to take 7,000 measurements a second at a speed of about 500 miles per hour, 12 miles high, helped map the extent of the green and gold effluent from a Superfund site in Leadville, Colorado.

Food

Lead gets into food in insidious ways. Airborne, it falls into the soil as well as on the leaves of the leafy greens we are all exhorted to eat. Fruits have higher lead content in stems and skins, so peeling is advised. In soils with high lead content, it is absorbed by the roots. If this is fed to cows, it produces leaded meat. If the food is then processed and packed into cans containing lead-soldered seams or served on pottery plates with lead glazes, more lead gets into the system. Your doctor can do a blood test to check on your levels of lead, and if levels are high, chelation treatments are available.

Artificial Food

Chemists have had a love affair with artificial sweeteners for more than a century. The story of saccharin is the story of food safety.

Discovered in 1879, it was patented in this country around 1900. But France banned it in 1890, as did Germany in 1898, after it was suspected of causing illness. In 1912 it was banned from soft drinks and food in the United States but allowed in chewing tobacco. When sugar was rationed in World Wars I and II, the ban was relaxed, and saccharin again was on the market until the 1970s, when researchers found a direct link with bladder cancer. The importance of its use by diabetics, however, has restrained its being completely banned.

Cyclamates, another artificial sweetener, are banned in the United States, but aspartame, marketed as Nutrasweet®, is not. Composed of two amino acids, L-phenylalanine and L-aspartic acid, aspartame is suspected of causing brain cancer and possibly epileptic seizures and is banned in some European countries.

Isolating cause and effect in food products is very difficult. Junk food, for example, and antacids go together. Refined flour products, such as white bread, have few traces left of the grains that went into making the flour. Because processed food is refined, doctored, dressed up, and otherwise produced to be a skillful imitation, it lacks the chemical complexity of the real food that the human stomach has evolved to digest. Preservatives and additives, such as food colors, antioxidants, nitrosamines, PAH, which is released during grilling and smoking food, are suspected carcinogens. Fungi, such as ergot, often grown in grains during storage, can cause mass hysteria and have been suggested as a cause for the hysteria that induced witches and witchhunts in Salem, Massachusetts, in the 1660s.

Pesticides

"Pesticides" is a blanket term for all the "-cides" that kill weeds (herbicides); insects (insecticides); fungi and molds (fungicides); rats, squirrels, mice (rodenticides); worms (nematocides); and spiders (ascaricides). A 1996 study by the National Research Council discovered that one-third of the 1.35 million new cases of cancer can be traced to diet—ironically, not to chemicals in the diet, but to the fats, where the "-cides" reside. Studies done in the Corn Belt found connections between elevated levels of herbicides in drinking water and high cancer rates. In the 1960s national breast cancer rates in women were 1 in 20; in the 1990s, it is 1 in 9.

Risk assessment among herbicides is a ball tossed back and forth by manufacturers, the EPA, and physicians and scientists who try to

Chapter 20: Chemicals

isolate the effects of a particular chemical on humans. TCDD Dioxin, which is a contaminant of chlorine-based chemicals, was labeled "the most potent animal carcinogen" by the EPA in 1984. A byproduct of the herbicide 2.4.5.-T, also known as Agent Orange, it is also released by burning chlorine wastes in plastics, trash, trees and biomass, and electrical insulation. A problem in landfills near homes, such as Times Beach, Missouri (which was evacuated), and thought to be a current threat to drinking water in Niagara Falls, New York, dioxin is controversial. Critics say it causes cancer in humans; proponents claim low doses are low-risk in humans. A long-term study in Italy as a result of a chemical plant explosion that released tons of dioxin into the air in 1976 will reveal the extent to which it affected people who were exposed while in the womb.

Herbicides get into the food chain on the farm, but workers absorb them daily through the skin. The highly toxic paraquat, restricted to use only by weed-killer professionals around the world (except in the third world) has been linked to several human deaths. Other herbicides give an overdose of hormones to the plant, which causes it to grow too much and die.

Several studies link herbicides to prenatal deformities and disruption of human hormones with decreased fertility. The herbicide atrazine, for example, has been found to make females masculine in fish and bird species; and to feminize males in fish, bird, and mammal species. Recent studies of sperm counts in American and British men blamed insecticides for reductions of as much as 25 percent among those born in the 1970s.

Insecticides

With the increase in disease-carrying insects, humans are challenged to come up with effective controls that will not disrupt the whole food chain, killing birds and animals and causing sterility or fatal illnesses in themselves. Methyl bromide, a compound used in pesticides, is thought to cause cancer as well as fifty times more damage to statospheric ozone than CFCs. In 1995, 100 nations agreed to phase out its production by 2010. Used in crops in California and Florida, methyl bromide will be banned in the United States in 2001.

Chlorinated hydrocarbons have been used to make insecticides for many years. Ironically, insects, because they breed so quickly, develop immunities to insecticides. But humans suffer for a long time because the deadly chemicals are stored in animal fats and are slow to disintegrate in the environment.

Organophosphates are nerve toxins that enter the skin via a vapor. Malathion, an organophosphate, is a legal, political, and economic subject in California, where it is used, usually via aerial spraying, against the wishes of a worried public, to wipe out the California medfly (Mediterranean fruit fly). Citrus fruits are California's main export, and Japan refused to import the fruit that had *not* been sprayed against the insect. In 1983 aerial spraying apparently eradicated the fly, but when it reappeared the next year, politicians claimed it had been imported by a careless tourist from Mexico or Hawaii.

Exactly why the medfly continues to defy malathion is unclear. Agriculturalists with the U.S. Department of Agriculture maintain that the fly is periodically imported, then breeds and travels in concentric circles, away from its port of entry—for example, the Los Angeles airport. According to this theory, spraying eradicates it until it comes again. But University of California–Davis entomologist James K. Carey believes that medflies have been in residence in California for the last 100 years, but that they occasionally "disappear" because they spread around the state's citrus crops along watercourses and mountains. Recent mitochondrial DNA studies of the insect traced its original home to West Africa and its migration north to the Azores, where it was recorded in 1830. From there it went to the Caribbean and, at some point, to California.

Farmers are reluctant to use deadly insecticides except when necessary, because they kill beneficial insects too. In south Texas in 1995 malathion was sprayed on cotton crops to wipe out boll weevils, which eat cotton. But the malathion killed everything, including the natural enemies of beetworms and aphids, which also survived the malathion and, in turn, reduced the cotton crop yield to 55,000 bales—a drop of 250,000 bales from the previous year.

Alternatives to deadly chemicals are being found every day. Geneticists have successfully developed crop seeds that have weed and insect repellents built into their DNA (see chapter 14). Integrated Pest Management involves a holistic approach, with crop rotation, deep ploughing, the introduction of micro-organisms, and covering the soil with tarps to kill weeds with heat. Satellites give vegetative index data that points to exact areas where insects, such as malaria mosquitoes, are active, for target spraying in controlled areas. Locusts, for example, are impossible to control once they start

Chapter 20: Chemicals

swarming, but when they are gathered in a group of several thousands on the ground, identifiable by satellite, they can be zapped before they fly off.

To replace insecticides, scientists are experimenting with biochemical pesticides made from insect hormones like neuropeptides. Researchers have also isolated fungi that live on locusts, manufactured them into a liquid, and used them as a natural killer to the hosts. Some plants, like marigolds, produce natural insecticides. Other plants, like water hyacinths, absorb heavy metals. These hyperaccumulators are being bred to clean up soil that has been badly contaminated by DDT or nuclear waste.

What You Can Do

The following organizations provide information:

EPA—Toxic Hotline: (800) 424-0346
 Lead Hotline: (800) 532-3394
 Safe Drinking Water Hotline: (800) 426-4791
Indoor Air Quality Information Clearinghouse: (800) 438-4318
National Pesticides Telecommunications Network: (800) 858-PEST
CDC Lead Poisoning Prevention Branch: (800) 488-7330

West Coast—Western Regional Lead Training Consortium: (800) 572-5323
Lead and remodeling old homes: (800) 424-5323
National Institute for Environmental Health Sciences, Clearinghouse on Environmental Health Effects: (800) 643-4794
Chemical Manufacturers Association, Chemical Referral Library: (800) 262-8200
National Cancer Institute: (800) 4-CANCER
American Lung Association: (800) 586-4872
National Institute for Occupational Safety and Health (NIOSH): (800) 35-NIOSH
Ozone Action, 1621 Connecticut Avenue, Washington, D.C. 20009; (202) 265-6738
Superfund Hotline: (800) 424-9346; (703) 412-9810.
National Toxicology Program at the National Institute of Environmental Health Science website: http://www.niehs.gov/ntp/ntp.html

For information on beach cleanup and information on obtaining a copy of *A Citizen's Guide to Plastics in the Ocean*, write or call the Center for Marine Conservation, 1725 De Sales Street NW, Washington, D.C. 20036; (202) 429-5609.

For a soil test for heavy metals and pH level, send a sample of your soil, labeled with your name and address, and $10.00 to Agricultural Experiment Station, The University of the District of Columbia, 4200 Connecticut Avenue NW, Washington, D.C. 20008.

For the booklet, *Protect Your Family from Lead in Your Home*, send 50¢ to Consumer Information Center, Deptartment 338C, Pueblo, CO 81009.

For nonchemical-based alternatives to pesticides, contact Organic Plus, Inc., Albuquerque, NM; (505) 243-6430; e-mail: organic-plus@sciso.com; website: http://www/sciso.com/cgi-bin/svend. Or contact the National Integrated Pest Management Network National Server website: http://ipmwww.ncsu.edu/nipmn/states/National.html.

21 Psychics

Psi-Zing Up the Unknown

EXPLORING HUMAN POTENTIAL. In the last century, amazing Scottish psychic D.D. Home defied belief among everyone from his family to Czar Alexander with his abilities to levitate, as in this scene from 1863. He could also levitate objects, other people, and the chairs he sat on; plus handle hot coals, talk to dead spirits, and elongate his body by half a foot.

A hundred years ago groups regularly gathered in darkened rooms where they joined hands in a circle and concentrated, while a medium called up a member of the dead, who would materialize from behind a velvet drape, speaking in a remote voice. Some mediums, like Russian aristocrat Madame Blavatsky, the founder of the Theosophical Society, produced "ectoplasm," a substance that oozed out of her head or neck and sometimes took on a human visage.

Studying psi phenomena like this was serious business: Harvard psychologist William James believed in the intervention of the spirit world in daily life, and medical journals, like *The Lancet*, published articles exploring the possibility that the brain could send thoughts along lines like those used in newly discovered X rays, and claiming that "some of these unknown rays may supply the key to much that is obscure in psychical phenomena."

Today we seem less interested in calling up the dead than in figuring out what's going on. We are awash in a glut of information in the media, on the internet, but we distrust what we hear and see. Part of it is because we've been imbued with advertising for a century, tricked and cajoled into buying this or that. And now there are serious disconnects in the messages we receive: for example, to smoke Marlboros is to be truly masculine/to smoke cigarettes is to die. Government coverups are everywhere; political spin doctors are the whirling dervishes of deception. The Kennedy assassination investigation was closed 30 years ago, but books claiming Oswald was not the shooter persist. And we live with urban myths, unprovable rumors that gnaw at our rational understanding. Is it true, for example, that the polyester strips in $20 bills can be scanned from a distance, revealing how much money you have in your pocket or your purse?

Telephones and planes have replaced our need for mental telepathy: Tibetan monks who practice out-of-the-body visits from mountaintop to mountaintop do it to stay in touch. In our global media village, we can hear the wishes and feelings of people from around the world with the flick of a switch.

But we can't read the hidden present. And we can't read what others who are important to our lives really feel. Enter psychics.

In the 1990s psychics turned up everywhere—on television infomercials, in magazines with 900 numbers ($1.50 to $4 a minute), in New Age weeklies, free at the health food store. Across the country, psychic fairs are held regularly in hotel rooms, where rune readers, tarot card readers, palm readers sit at small round tables with flickering candles, offering their wares for about $1 a minute. No one knows how many operating psychics exist, much less how many people consult them. In France almost 50,000 people declared themselves

Chapter 21: Psychics

to be engaged in some kind of paranormal career on their tax forms in 1995—a sudden resurgence of astrologers, psychics, and people who practice witchcraft.

Forbes magazine reported in June 1996 that several big-time investors consult psychics across the country who specialize in stocks, bonds, commodities, and investments. Minnesota psychic Robert C. H. Parker claimed his advice is as good as any financial analyst. "I just don't do all the paperwork they do," he said.

Police, the FBI, and various other law enforcement agencies use psychics, although they are reluctant to talk about it. Psychic Dorothy Allison has been solving murders and finding bodies for frustrated detectives across the country for close to 30 years. Like any true psychic, Allison's psychic ability sometimes comes up dry. "I don't know where it came from. I don't know why it works. I don't know how it works," she told *The New York Times*. "I don't know why in some cases I go dead, completely dead, I do nothing, and in others, I'll give you the name of the killer in a second."

Maggy Blackman of the Rhine Research Center in Durham, North Carolina, says, "Stay away from 900 numbers. Nobody can be psychic for eight hours a day. It simply doesn't always work." Blackman is director of development and public relations at the laboratory that took up where famed doctor J. B. Rhine did his ESP investigations at Duke University. She calls herself a "bubble-burster. There are only about 300 parapsychologists in the world who have their work peer-reviewed before publishing it," she says. "We're the most widely known parapsychology lab in the world, and we try to provide accurate information about psi phenomena." The lab does research in ESP and psychokinesis, offers a summer education program for serious students, and has an ongoing project in remote viewing.

In New York City, the esteemed American Society for Psychical Research has been studying psychic phenomena since 1885, supports scientific investigations, and publishes research results in their newsletter and journal. "We get a lot of calls from people looking for psychics," said librarian Rosie Schapp. "We used to give referrals, but we don't now for fear of lawsuits. It's such a subjective field; it's like recommending a doctor."

Several consumer guides to psychics are said to be in the works. Some psychics work by telephone, others in their homes. Author Michael Crichton, in his book *Travels*, writes that he visited with a spirit from Ireland, channeled by a California medium who conducted the session with Crichton sitting on her unmade bed. Prices range from $1,500 a day to about $75 to $80 for a 45-minute reading. "People are looking for something," says Maggy Blackman, "and even if a seer sees something vague, people will twist it until it fits something they want to believe in. Let the buyer beware. Don't go back if a psychic tells you they see something bad; they will only charge you a lot more money."

A couple of years ago a New Jersey woman tried to sue a psychic to whom she had paid more than $9,000 to remove a curse from her dead husband. The whole issue came up in a $10 horoscope reading with the psychic who suddenly saw the curse, and, over a period of months, performed several rituals, incantations, and recitations of the Twenth-third Psalm, and buried a jar of water (holding the "curse") in a casket in a cemetery. When the woman had no more money to throw after the psychic, she complained to the Division of Consumer Affairs, got a lawyer, and discovered that the psychic had left town.

Frauds muddy the waters. Many New Age groups give courses in psychic ability, and with a certain amount of psychic exercise and meditation, many people are able to set up shop, riffle their Tarot decks, and give vaguely plausible readings. But the difference between honing your own ability and being a true psychic is like the difference between singing in the shower and being Pavarotti.

Psychic Terrie Brill, who specializes in reading stock numbers, says, "What happens is, my vibratory rate goes down—my blood pressure, my heart rate—everything slows. There's also a kind of veil in front of me, like everything is blurred. And then I will read the name of the stock and either hear or see what number the stock is going to be at."

In his book *Anatomy of Genius*, Psychiatrist Jan Ehrenwald says that the gifted psychic's first impression is like a flash, similar to an epileptic seizure in the right brain, that must be followed by left-brain cognitive input to give it shape.

"Everybody's psychic," says Therese Pendragon, a psychic who has been practicing for 30 years in Salem, Massachusetts. Recommended by members of the National Park Service in Salem, Therese and her husband, Michael, read Tarot cards and palms. "It's like music," she said. "We can all perform music, but only some of us are gifted. I have inherited my gift. The genes have memory."

Chapter 21: Psychics

Like all gifts, true psychic ability doesn't come free. Edgar Cayce, a healer who died in 1945 in Virginia Beach, was an amazing visionary who healed and prescribed herbal medicines while in deep and sudden trances. "I don't do anything you can't do," he often said, "if you are willing to pay the price." The price for him, according to his biographer Harmon Hartzell Bro, was that, while he saw all the ills of the current and future world, he could work only for the good of humankind, and alone.

Exactly what psychics can do was the topic of 20 years of secret military and CIA research at the Stanford Research Institute and Fort Meade, Maryland. From 1972 to 1990 researchers used a small group of psychics in remote viewing experiments to see if it was possible to see behind Cold War enemy lines, track nuclear submarines, and find out what the Russians, long adept at psychic phenomena, were up to. They closed Project Stargate, leaving a dispute over whether psi could be statistically charted. University of Oregon psychologist Ray Hyman claimed there was no evidence of clear psychic functioning; statistician Jessica Hutts of the University of California–Davis believed there was ample evidence that some people were psychically gifted.

Accuracy in understanding psi is the name of the game. In a lecture at the American Society for Psychical Research in 1993, psychologist Keith Harary said that "conservative scientists" who are "closet psychics," afraid to talk publicly about their experiences, only cultivate an environment in which "sideshow" psychics flourish. Harary said they have cheapened and "demeaned what may be the most profound and sacred part of us—our deep interconnectedness with one another and the rest of nature."

One of Project Stargate's remote viewers, Joseph McMoneagle, became psychic after a near-death experience while he was in the army in Vietnam. He spent many hours as a participant in the project, sitting in windowless lab rooms writing or recording his impressions from the person who was sending the mental picture or words from afar. McMoneagle was good. "I was the only subject to have five first place matches out of six," he said in an interview in *Magical Blend* magazine (October 1996).

In an amazing experiment at the Monroe Institute in Virginia, McMoneagle remote-viewed six target sites on Mars for NASA. Without knowing where he was looking, he worked with sets of coordinates provided by a representative from NASA and "saw" a pyramid. "But it didn't make sense to me, because I was describing corridors and rooms that I knew didn't exist in the Egyptian pyramids." NASA called five months later and told him they were targeting a mission to one of the coordinate sites McMoneagle had viewed.

Psychics might be specially gifted, but more of the general population is experiencing strange things. In Santa Cruz, volunteers run a Spiritual Emergence Network, a telephone referral system that provides "alternative" mental health care. Even the *Diagnostic and Statistical Manual of Mental Disorders* that psychological therapists use to identify disease for their own edification and for a label for health insurance, for the first time in 1994 included "Religious or Spiritual Problems." It reads: "Examples include distressing experiences that involve loss or questioning of faith, problems associated with conversion to a new faith, or questioning of spiritual values that may not necessarily be related to an organized church or religious institution." For the first time, spiritual problems were separated from schizophrenia.

Exceptional Human Experiences

Most everyone has had moments at some time in their lives when suddenly something extra kicked in: the marathon runner gets a burst to finish the race; the physicist dreams the answer to his problem. This is psi. Psychologist Stanley Krippner ticks off some of the amazing abilities the human race has: the human retina can see a single candle flame five miles away; we have 14 senses (sight, hearing, smell, taste, pressure, pain, heat, cold, nearness, discrimination, vibration, kinesthesia, the visceral sense, and the balance sense.) Plus, Krippner reminds us, we have four basic smells: "fragrant, acid, burnt, sweat," but the trained nose, a perfume sampler, for example, can detect 10,000 different odors.

Humans have an amazing ability to refine, hone, and train their skills, Krippner says. The blind, for example, can "see" the risen full moon, and can tell the difference between black and white fabric. A good Braille reader taps agile fingers across tiny bumps 2 to 3 micromillimeters apart and reads a hundred words a minute. People with Multiple Personality Disorder rarely get sick, and age more slowly than the general population, because they leave those things to their "alters." Their bodies physically change as their minds determine they are someone else.

Chapter 21: Psychics

Biofeedback lowers blood pressure; empty pills cure diseases in the placebo effect; hypnotism cures warts; each year athletes break old records. How do these things differ from "religions" in other cultures in which shamans transform themselves and others in trances? "We all have reservoirs of life to draw upon of which we do not dream," said William James in 1900. Or, as Krippner says, if we could analyze how these phenomena happen, "we would be finding out about a superintelligence that exists in each one of us."

We seem anxious to connect. Physician Deepak Chopra has created a multimillion dollar industry by pointing out that at the level of quarks, according to quantum physics, we don't exist. Our cells renew themselves every few months, so each of us is a different person every second. Armed with this attitude, we don't need to carry illness with us for long, and we have the ability to cure others.

For a few dollars, we can buy machines that balance the hemispheres of our brains to enhance learning and bioelectrical devices that distribute our chakra energy. We can drink specially charged water and consume vitamins that prevent aging, and we can meditate, breathing in the vapors of appropriate incense or candles or body lotions. In a mixture of Eastern and Western philosophies, we heal ourselves with acupuncture and Chi Gong exercises, and heal others with focused meditation.

It takes discipline to maximize the use of our hidden abilities. Keep two journals, advises Joseph McMoneagle, "one to carry around for recording important and pertinent observations, the second to keep by your bed for recording your dreams." He suggests meditating 30 to 45 minutes every day. "Clean up the attic and the basement first, and then move on to higher thoughts or higher meditative contemplation." Visualization, being in control of your own visualization, is crucial. McMoneagle says, "What we do, think, and say has a decisive effect on what our future is going to be. If we can conceptualize a pill that will cure all disease known to man, a hundred years from now we will probably have that pill."

❓ What You Can Do

To apply for the summer education program, which is open to anyone seriously interested in pursuing a research career in parapsychology, contact the Rhine Research Center, The

Institute for Parapsychology, 402 Buchanan Boulevard, Durham, NC 27701; (919) 688-8241. Past students include retirees, anthropologists, statisticians, historians, priests, young students; many are international. Space is limited to 12 to 15 people. Apply to Dr. John Palmer, Director of Education, at the above address.

To take part in a remote viewing project, contact Maggy Blackman, Director of Development and Public Relations, at the above phone number. All you need is a fax.

For an exceptional human experience, contact Rhea A. White, 414 Rockledge Road, New Bern, NC 28562; fax: (919) 636-8734; e-mail: ehenetwork@.coastalnet.com.; website: http://www4.coastalnet.com/ehenet. White is creating a database of exceptional human experiences—"any psychic, mystical, or strange encounter experiences" and publishes a journal and a newsletter. Ask for a flyer, or send your exceptional experience to her at the above fax number or at her e-mail or website.

American Society for Psychical Research, Inc., 5 West 73rd Street, New York, NY 10023; (212) 799-5050. A membership organization since 1885, interested in psi research, maintains a library, publishes a journal and a newsletter, and holds a one-day conference every year in New York City.

Institute of Noetic Sciences, 475 Gate Five Road, Suite 300, P.O. Box 909, Sausalito, CA 94966; (800) 383-1394 (for membership information); fax: (415) 331-5673. IONS does a variety of psi research and welcomes your experience by letter or fax.

Spiritual Emergence Network, Santa Cruz, CA (408) 426-0902. Volunteers maintain phone lines to give "alternatives to mental health." Leave your name and address, and they will send an information packet.

For information on visiting Edgar Cayce's Association for Research and Enlightenment, Inc. (A.R.E.), contact A.R.E., 67th Street and Atlantic Avenue, Virginia Beach, VA 23451-0595; (800) 333-4499; (804) 428-3588.

For Further Reading

Chapter 1: Ozone Depletion
Makhijani, Arjun, and Kevin R. Gurney. *Mending the Ozone Hole*. Cambridge, Mass.: MIT Press, 1995.

Chapter 2: Global Warming
Firor, John. *The Changing Atmosphere*. New Haven, Conn.: Yale University Press, 1990.

Fisher, David E. *Fire & Ice*. New York: Harper & Row, 1990.

Schneider, Stephen H. *Global Warming: Are We Entering the Greenhouse Century?* San Francisco: Sierra Club Books, 1989.

Chapter 3: Insects
Harrington, Richard, and Nigel E. Stork, eds. *Insects in a Changing Environment*. San Diego: Academic, 1995.

Holldobler, Bert, and Edward O. Wilson. *The Ants*. Cambridge, Mass.: Harvard University Press, 1990.

Lehane, Brendan. *The Compleat Flea*. New York: Viking Press, 1969.

McGavin, George C. *Bugs of the World*. New York: Facts on File, 1993.

Winston, Mark L. *Killer Bees*. Cambridge, Mass.: Harvard University Press, 1992.

Chapter 4: Deadly Viruses
Dixon, Bernard. *Power Unseen*. Oxford: W. H. Freeman, 1994.

Garrett, Laurie. *Coming Plague*. New York: Farrar, Strauss & Giroux, 1994.

Lederberg, Joshua, and Robert E. Shope. *Emerging Infections*. Washington, D.C.: National Academy Press, 1992.

Chapter 5: Electromagnetic Fields
Becker, Robert O. *Cross Currents*. Los Angeles: Tarcher, 1990.

Brodeur, Paul. *Currents of Death*. New York: Simon & Schuster, 1989.

"Electromagnetic Fields." *Consumer Reports*, May 1994, pp. 354–359.

Raloff, Janet: "Physicists Offer Reassurances on EMF." *Science News*, 20 May 1995, p. 308.

Wartenberg, Daniel. "EMFs: Cutting Through the Controversy." *Public Health Reports*, May/June 1996, pp. 204–217.

Chapter 6: Natural Disasters

Levy, Matthys, and Mario Salvadori. *Why the Earth Quakes*. New York: W.W. Norton, 1995.

Wagner, Ronald L., and Bill Adler Jr. *The Weather Sourcebook*. Old Saybrook, Conn.: Globe Pequot Press, 1994.

Chapter 7: Asteroids and Comets

Gehrels, Tom, ed. *Hazards Due to Comets and Asteroids*. Tucson: University of Arizona Press, 1994.

Morrison, David. "Target: Earth!" *Astronomy*, October 1994, pp. 35–41.

Steel, Duncan. *Rogue Asteroids and Doomsday Comets*. New York: John Wiley & Sons, 1995.

Chapter 8: Cars

Riley, Robert O. "Specialty Cars for the 21st Century." *The Futurist*, Nov./Dec. 1995, pp. 8–11.

Sperling, Daniel. *Future Drive*. Washington, D.C.: Island Press, 1995.

Chapter 9: The Homeless

Benedict, Giamo, and Jeffrey Grunberg. *Beyond Homelessness*. Iowa City: University of Iowa Press, 1992.

Jencks, Christopher. *The Homeless*. Cambridge, Mass.: Harvard University Press, 1994.

Lavelle, Robert, and the Staff of Blackside, eds. *America's New War on Poverty*. San Francisco: KQED Books, 1995.

The National Alliance to End Homelessness. *What You Can Do to End Homelessness*. New York: Simon & Schuster, 1991.

Chapter 10: Deteriorating Infrastructure

Lowe, Marcia D. *Shaping Cities*. (Worldwatch Paper 105). Washington, D.C.: Worldwatch Institute, October 1991.

Perry, David C., ed. *Building the Public City*. Thousand Oaks, Calif.: Sage Publications, 1995.

Rabinovitch, Jonas, and Josef Leitman. "Urban Planning in Curitiba." *Scientific American*, March 1996, pp. 46–53.

Chapter 11: Population
Brown, Lester R., and Hal Kane. *Full House*. New York: W.W. Norton, 1994.
Cohen, Joel H. *How Many People Can the Earth Support?* New York: W.W. Norton, 1995.
Erhlich, Paul R., and Anne H. Erhlich. *The Population Explosion*. New York: Simon & Schuster, 1990.
Karplus, Walter J. *The Heavens Are Falling*. New York: Plenum, 1992.

Chapter 12: Cloning
Kitcher, Philip. *The Lives to Come*. New York: Simon & Schuster 1996.
Sofer, William H. *Introduction to Genetic Engineering*. Boston: Butterworth-Heinemann, 1991.
Stephens Gene. "Crime and the Biotech Revolution." *The Futurist*, Nov./Dec. 1992, pp. 38–42.
Suzuki, David, and Peter Knudson. *Genethics*. Cambridge: Harvard University Press, 1990.
Varma, Jay K. "Eugenics and Immigration Restriction: Lessons for Tomorrow." *JAMA*, 6 March 1996, pp. 734–737.

Chapter 13: Plutonium
Fisher, David. *Fire & Ice*. New York: Harper & Row, 1990.
Kiselyov, Sergei. "Inside the Beast." *The Bulletin of the Atomic Scientists*, May/June 1996, pp. 43–51.
Kressley, Konrad M. "Why Can't We Ban the Bomb?" *The Futurist*, July/August 1995, pp. 26–30.
Nuckolls, John H. "Post–Cold War Nuclear Dangers: Proliferation and Terrorism." *Science*, 24 February 1995, pp. 1112–1114.
Rothstein, Linda. "Nothing Clean About Clean Up." *Bulletin of the Atomic Scientists*, May/June 1995, pp. 34–41.
von Hippel, Frank. "Bomb Away." *Discover*, April 1992, p. 32–34.

Chapter 14: Soil Degradation
Glanz, James. *Saving Our Soil*. Boulder, Colo.: Johnson Books, 1995.
Rhodes, Richard. *Farm*. New York: Simon & Schuster, 1989.
Rodale, Robert. *Save Three Lives*. San Francisco: Sierra Club Books, 1991.

Smit, Jac, Anna Ratta, and Joe Nasr. *Urban Agriculture: Food, Jobs, and Sustainable Cities.* New York: United Nations Development Programme, 1996.

Tompkins, Peter, and Christopher Bird. *Secrets of the Soil.* New York: Harper & Row, 1989.

Chapter 15: Terrorism

Clutterbuck, Richard. *Terrorism in an Unstable World.* London: Routledge, 1994.

Simon, Jeffrey D. *The Terrorist Trap.* Bloomington, Ind.: Indiana University Press, 1994.

Thackrah, John Richard. *Encyclopedia of Terrorism and Political Violence.* London: Routledge, 1987.

"What Is Terrorism?" *The Economist,* 2 March 1996, pp. 15–16; 23–25.

Chapter 16: Guns

Canada, Geoffrey. *Fist, Stick, Knife, Gun: A Personal History of Violence in America.* Boston: Beacon Press, 1995.

Journal of the American Medical Association, 12 June 1996: Special Issue on Firearms.

Kellerman, Arthur L. "Gun Ownership as a Risk Factor for Homocide in the Home." *New England Journal of Medicine,* 7 October 1993, pp. 1084–1091.

Kennett, Lee, and James LaVerne Anderson. *The Gun in America.* Westport, Conn.: Greenwood Press, 1975.

Kleck, Gary. *Point Blank: Guns and Violence in America.* New York: A. de Gruyter, 1991.

Tonso, William R. *Gun and Society.* Washington, D.C.: University Press of America, 1982.

Chapter 17: The Economy

Buchholz, Todd G. *New Ideas from Dead Economists.* New York: New American Library, 1989.

Maurice, Charles, and Charles W. Smithson. *The Doomsday Myth.* Stanford, Calif.: Hoover Institute Press, 1984.

Chapter 18: Privacy

Alderman, Ellen, and Caroline Kennedy. *The Right to Privacy.* New York: Knopf, 1995.

Knightmare. *Secrets of a Super Hacker*. Port Townsend, Wash.: Loompanics Unlimited, 1994.
The New Scientist, (special insert) 4 November 1995.
Stephens, Gene. "Crime in Cyberspace." *The Futurist,* Sept./Oct. 1995, pp. 24–28.
Stoll, Clifford. *The Cuckoo's Egg*. New York: Doubleday, 1989.

Chapter 19: Alien Abductions
Blum, Howard. *Out There*. New York: Simon & Schuster, 1990.
Bryan, C.D.B. *Close Encounters of the Fourth Kind: Alien Abduction, UFOs, and the Conference at M.I.T.* New York: Knopf, 1995.
Jacobs, David M. *Secret Life*. New York, Simon & Schuster, 1992.
_____ . *The UFO Controversy in America*. Bloomington, Ind.: Indiana University Press, 1975.
Mack, John. *Abduction: Human Encounters with Aliens*. New York: Charles Scribners' Sons, 1994.
Thompson, Keith. *Angels and Aliens*. New York: Fawcett Columbine, 1991.

Chapter 20: Chemicals
Castellino, Nicolo, et al. *Inorganic Lead Exposure*. Boca Raton: Lewis Publishers, 1994.
Stapleton, Richard M. *Lead Is a Silent Hazard*. New York: Walker and Company, 1994.

Chapter 21: Psychics
Becker, Robert O. *The Body Electric*. New York: William Morrow & Co., 1985.
Browne, Mary T. *Mary T. Browne Reflects on the Other Side*. New York: Fawcett Columbine, 1994.
Chopra, Deepak. *Quantum Healing*. New York: Bantam Books, 1990.
Crichton, Michael. *Travels*. New York: Ballantine, 1988.
Lyons, Arthur, and Marcello Truzzi. *The Blue Sense*. New York: Mysterious Press, 1991.
McMoneagle, Joseph W. *Mind Trek*. Charlottesville, Va.: Hampton Roads Publishing, 1993.

Glossary

AC: Alternating current, changes direction 60 Hz, or cycles, a second.

Arborvirus: Virus transmitted by an insect.

Atmosphere (in ascending order):
troposphere: where weather happens and jets fly.
stratosphere: where the ozone layer is.
mesosphere: the coldest -sphere, -90°C, about 50 miles up.
thermosphere: where least amount of gases occur.
ionosphere: where ions from radiation collect.
magnetosphere: the outermost -sphere, which traps magnetic matter from the sun that causes the Northern Lights.

Biological classification: Kingdom, phylum, class, order, family, genus, species.

Chromosome: Each human cell nucleus contains 46 chromosomes which carry genetic material.

Cloning: Replication of a living thing asexually. Bacteria always produce clones because they reproduce by splitting in half.

The Commons: Antarctica, the oceans, and outer space.

Cosmic rays: Radiation from outer space.

DC: Electric current that always flows in the same direction.

Demographic transition: Demographer Frank Notestein's theory (1945) that is used in understanding the development of a population.
Stage 1: birth and death rates are high and population grows slowly.
Stage 2: birth rates are high, death rates are low from improved food production and healthcare; population grows fast.
Stage 3: general economic and social gains reduce the desire for large families; population stabilizes.

Demographic trap: Many third world countries get stuck in Stage 2 because a large population overwhelms the environment, making economic and social gains impossible.

Developing countries (or the third world): Latin America and the Caribbean, Africa (except South Africa), Asia (except China), Oceania (except Australia and New Zealand), Cyprus, Malta, the former Yugoslavia.

Disconnect: A break in understanding between mind and intuition, or people, or of the Earth.

DNA (deoxyribonucleic acid): The chemical chain consisting of 23 pairs of chromosomes (one from each parent) that carry genetic data. Arranged in a double helix, a pair resides in each of the 100 trillion cells in the human body.

Ecosystem: The interplay of specific water/soil/air/terrain/insect/bird/mammal groups.

ELF: Extreme Low Frequency, or 0 to 1 kHz (kiloHertz).

EMF: Electromagnetic field, a force field that radiates from any moving electrical current.

Endemic: Confined to a certain region or area, as a disease.

Epidemic: The spread of a contagious disease within a community.

Epidemiology: The study of the origin and spread of a disease.

Fujita Scale (tornado measurement):
   F0 (weak): less than 73 mph
   F1: 73–112 mph
   F2 (strong): 113–157 mph
   F3: 158–206 mph
   F4 (violent): 207–260 mph
   F5: 261–318 mph

Gene: The single unit of hereditary material, part of the strand of DNA. From its chemical bases come protein molecules. Humans have more than 100,000 genes in the each cell. "Gene pairs" mean chemical pairs, which is where genetic information can become damaged.

Hemorraghic fevers: Those that involve bleeding.

Human genome: All the genes that make up a human being.

Hybrids: Cars that are powered by a combination of fuel cells and liquid fuel.

Hz: Hertz, or cycle.

Microwave: 500 MHz (megaHertz).

Nanometer: One-billionth of a meter.

Pandemic: A widespread epidemic affecting people over a huge area, such as a country.

Pathogen: Any organism that causes disease.

Recombinant DNA: Genetic engineering: splicing bits of DNA strands from different organisms to form a new whole.

Revolver: A pistol in which the bullets are inserted individually in a revolving cartridge.

Glossary

Richter Scale: Earthquake measurement (0 to 8.6). (The difference between numbers is 10 times the size of ground vibration, 31 times the energy release.) Great = 8.0; major = 7.0–7.9. Anything above 6.0 can create damage in a high-population area. Earthquakes are also measured by the Modified Mercalli Intensity Scale: I to XII.)

Saffir-Simpson Scale (hurricane measurement):
Category 1: 74–95 mph; surge: 4–5 feet
Category 2: 96–110 mph; surge: 6–8 feet
Category 3: 111–130 mph; surge: 9–12 feet
Category 4: 131–155 mph; surge: 13–18 feet
Category 5: 155+; surge: 18 feet+

Second Amendment: Added to the U.S. Constitution in 1788: "A well- regulated militia being necessary to the security of a free state, the right of the people to keep and bear arms shall not be infringed."

Semiautomatic: A pistol in which the bullets are inserted in a clip in the handle.

Soil: The result of weathering of rock and crystal and the movement of organisms; divided into silt, clay, and sand.

UVA: Ultraviolet A rays: 320–400 nanometers; generally not harmful; allows body to absorb vitamin D.

UVB: Ultraviolet B rays: 290–320 nanometers; dangerous to living tissue.

UVC: Ultraviolet C rays: 40–290 nanometers; severely dangerous to living tissue.

Vector: Insect or small animal that carries a pathogen.

Zoonose: A pathogen that jumps from one species to another, as from an animal to a human.

Index

abortion, 110, 144, 157, 167
acupuncture, 50
AIDS, 32, 34, 42
airport detection systems, 150, 179
aliens, 185, 188
American Society for Psychical Research, 203, 205, 208
Antarctic, 1, 2, 4, 11, 69, 135
aquifers, 14
Arjunas, 66
asbestos, 192
aspartame, 196
Assault Weapons Ban, 158
atrazine, 197

Banana Kelly Project, 103
bankruptcy, 166
Basque Separatists, 146
Bermuda, 12, 56
Bill of Rights, 180
Black Market, 6, 125
boll weevils/worms, 27, 140
bombs, 124, 125, 143, 145, 147, 148, 149
Brady Bill, 158
bridges, 94, 97, 98
Brown, Lester R., 109
buckyballs, 72
Budget, 168
Budget Deficit, 168

Canada, Geoffrey, 160, 161
cancer, 2, 7, 34, 46–49, 123, 124, 126, 196, 199
Capone, Al, 157
carbon monoxide, 77, 192, 193
carbon dioxide, 11, 12, 13, 15, 17, 136, 137
carrying capacity, 108
cattle, 3, 42, 136

Cayce, Edgar, 205, 208
cellular phones, 52, 176–177
Chernobyl, 23–24, 126, 127, 128
Chicxulub, 65
chlorine, 2, 5, 6, 197
chlorofluorocarbons (CFCs), 1, 2, 5, 6
cholera, 33, 36, 42
cities, 38, 39, 102, 103, 107, 108
Civilian Conservation Corps (CCC), 89, 168–169
coasts, 14, 36, 107
cockroaches, 26–27
Cohen, Joel, 106, 112, 113
Comet Chiron, 68, 73
   Hyakutake, 69
   Shoemaker-Levy 9, 65, 69
   Swift-Tuttle, 69
consumerism, 112
credit cards, 166, 170
crop circles, 186
cryptosporidium, 33, 42, 94, 99

DDT, 22, 138
dengue fever, 34, 42
desertification, 135
dioxin, 197
DNA, 41, 117, 121, 122, 216
downsizing, 84, 164
drought, 12, 14, 60, 108, 111, 134
Dust Bowl, 133, 135

E.T., 182
earthquakes, 59, 61, 62, 63, 95
Ebola virus, 33, 40, 42
ecotourism, 111
electric cars, 80, 82
El Nino, 15
entitlements, 168
epidemiology, 33, 40
eugenics, 119
euthanasia, 167

Index

"Fat Man," 124
Federal Emergency Response Plan, 61
Federal Emergency Management Agency (FEMA), 56, 57, 60, 61, 63
fleas, 27, 36, 37
floods, 60, 62
flying saucers, 181, 185
food-borne diseases, 33, 39
Fresh Kills Landfill Site, 100
fuel cells, 80

gambling, 170
Goetz, Bernie, 159
The Great Train Robbery, 155
Gun Control Act of 1968, 158
Gun Free School Zones Act, 158

Habitat for Humanity, 88, 91
hackers, 177, 178
hantavirus, 35, 42
Hawkins, Gerald, 187
heat waves, 15, 60, 61
herbicides, 197
Hezbollah, 145
HIV, 32, 86
hobos, 89
home, 90, 91
Human Genome Project, 118, 179
hurricanes, 55, 56, 58, 59, 61, 62, 63
hybrid vehicles, 80
hyperaccumulators, 120, 199
hypercanes, 66
hypercars, 81, 82

Ice Age, 16
insecticides, 197, 199
insurance, 56, 57
integrated pest management, 138, 198, 199
internal combustion engine, 75, 78
Intergovernmental Panel on Climate Change (IPCC), 11–12
irrigation, 137

Jacobs, David, 183–184, 190
James, William, 202, 207
Jupiter, 65, 66

Karl, Thomas, 10, 135
Kesterton (California) Wildlife Preserve, 137
killer bees, 20, 24–25
Kuiper Belt, 68

landfills, 100, 101
landslides, 55, 64
La Nina, 15
lead, 77, 193, 194–195
Leggatt, Jeremy, 12
"Li'l Boy," 124
Lifeboat Mentality, 164–165
lottery, 170, 171
Lyme disease, 3, 37, 38, 42

Mack, John, 182, 184, 189
maglev trains, 101
malaria, 15, 21, 26, 42, 198
malathion, 198
Malthus, T.R., 109, 140
Mars/Martians, 41, 69, 182, 188, 205
mass transit, 78, 79, 101
medfly, 198
Meteor Crater, 67–68
methyl bromide, 5, 197
microtunneling, 99
migration, 38, 107, 108, 111
money laundering, 171, 172
Montana Freeman, 147
Monteal Protocol, 5, 6
Morse, Stephen, 32, 34, 40
mosquitoes, 19, 23, 26, 28, 34, 35, 38, 120
Mount Haleakala, 71
mustard gas, 148

Index

NASA, 1, 4, 11, 40, 66, 67, 70, 71, 72, 195
National Debt, 168
National Rifle Association (NRA), 156, 157, 161
National Center for Atmospheric Research (NCAR), 58
Near-Earth asteroids, 67, 68
necrotizing fascitis, 41
neo-traditional communities, 81
Nuclear Emergency Salvage Teams (NESTs), 149
nitrous oxides, 3, 11
National Oceanic and Atmospheric Administration (NOAA), 4, 59, 60, 133

oceans, 15
Oklahoma City bombing, 143, 144, 146, 147
overpopulation, 38–39, 108
ozone, ground or surface, 3, 192, 193
    stratospheric, 1, 3, 4, 35, 36, 135

Pan Am Flight 103, 144, 150
Pantex, 128
paramilitary groups, 146, 147, 155
Partnership for a New Generation of Vehicles, 80
pesticides, 138, 196
plague, Black and bubonic, 15, 26, 34, 36, 37, 149, 173
Project Blue Book, 186
Project Stargate, 205
psi, 205, 206

rabies, 39, 42
radon, 48, 52, 54
rats, 34, 39, 40
red tides, 36
remote viewing, 205–206
Rhine Reearch Center, Institute for Parapsychology, 203, 207
Rifkin, Jeremy, 119
Rocky Flats, 128
Rocky Mountain Institute, 80, 81, 82, 88
Roswell Army Air Base, NM, 186
Russian Mafia, 145
rycin, 148

saccharin, 191, 195–196
Sahara Desert, 66, 135
Sarin, 148
satellites, 4, 40, 58, 198
Seaborg, Glenn, 126
Second Amendment, 156, 217
semiautomatics, 154, 161, 217
Semtex, 150
Search for Extraterrestrial Intelligence (SETI), 73, 181, 187, 190
sewage, 99–100
Shining Path Guerrillas, 146
skid row, 89
Social Security, 167
  numbers, 176
solar energy, 12, 13, 17, 172
Southern Poverty Law Center, 146, 149
Spacewatch, 72
Spy Factory, 179
START I & II, 124
sulfate aerosols, 15
sulfur dioxide, 193, 194
Sullivan Law, 157
Superdollars, 170

thunderstorms, 58
Thurow, Lester, 169–70
ticks, 20, 25, 37, 38
Tommy guns, 157
tornadoes, 55, 58
tourism, 17, 76, 111
tsunami, 64
tuberculosis, 38, 42, 86
TULIP, 79
Tunguska, 68
TWA Flight 800, 144, 149, 150

Index

UFOs, 181, 183, 189
ultraviolet rays, 2, 3, 4, 217
Unabomber, 144
uranium, 124, 126, 127
urban agriculture, 141, 142
urban wildlife, 103
U.S. Constitution, 168, 180

Vallee, Jacques, 189
volcanoes, 6, 59, 60, 64

waste recycling, 100, 104
water, 14, 94, 95, 98–99
Wayne, John, 155
Wells, H.G., 9, 41, 182
wind energy, 9, 13, 17
Waste Isolation Pilot Plant (WIPP), 129
Workfare, 168
the Working Poor, 169
World Trade Center bombing, 144, 145
Works Progress Administration (WPA), 89, 169

The X-Files, 182
X-rays, 46, 52
xenotransplants, 117

About the Author

Stephanie Ocko is a journalist who writes on specialty travel subjects, including ecotourism and environmental issues. She has lived in Zaire with the Foreign Service and worked on scientific projects in Nigeria and the Kingdom of Tonga. Her book, *Environmental Vacations*, a guide for volunteers helping scientists in their fieldwork, won the Benjamin Franklin Best Travel Book Award in 1991 and 1992. She lives in Boston, Massachusetts.